TRAIN YOUR BRAIN:

How to Maximize Memory Ability in Older Adulthood

Robert G. Winningham
Western Oregon University

Baywood Publishing Company, Inc.
AMITYVILLE, NEW YORK

Baywood Publishing Company, Inc.
26 Austin Avenue
P.O. Box 337
Amityville, NY 11701
(800) 638-7819
E-mail: baywood@baywood.com
Web site: baywood.com

Library of Congress Catalog Number: 2009014066
ISBN: 978-0-89503-349-9 (cloth)

Library of Congress Cataloging-in-Publication Data

Winningham, Robert G., 1969-
    Train your brain : how to maximize memory ability in older adulthood / Robert G. Winningham.
        p. cm.
    Includes bibliographical references and index.
    ISBN 978-0-89503-349-9 (cloth : alk. paper)
  1. Memory in old age. 2. Memory--Age factors. 3. Cognition--Age factors. I. Title.

BF724.85.M45W56 2009
155.67'1312--dc22

                                        2009014066

Table of Contents

CHAPTER 10

CHAPTER 11

CHAPTER 12

CHAPTER 13

CHAPTER 14

Acknowledgments

I wish to thank the people who helped support me during the writing of this book. I wish to thank my wife, Camila Gabaldon-Winningham for being a tireless sounding board, editor, and motivator. I would also like to thank Nicole Perry, the copy editor, and the many people who helped along the way, including Linda Kunze, Jerry Braza, Eric Cooley, Mike Studer, and especially all the students and who have helped with research, activity development, and asking difficult questions.

Disclaimer

The information is this book is not a substitute for professional medical advice, examination, diagnosis, or treatment. Always seek the advice of a physician or other qualified health care provider with any questions you may have regarding a medical condition. Never disregard professional medical advice or delay seeking it because of something you read in this book.

CHAPTER 1

Introduction:
Can Memory Ability be Improved?

And in the end, it's not the years in your life that count. It's the life in your years. Abraham Lincoln (1809–1865)

You can't open the newspaper or watch the news without hearing a story about memory and ways to improve it. Approximately 10% of older adults have dementia and an additional 10% have mild cognitive impairment. People are concerned about declining memory ability, and many are motivated to do something about it. The good news is that there are things we all can do to improve our memory ability and reduce the chance of developing dementia.

This book contains information from recent scientific studies regarding ways that people can maintain or even improve their ability to make new memories. In addition, this book provides valuable information about how to create a cognitive enhancement program for yourself, loved ones, people living in facility-based settings, or anyone else who wants to maximize their brain health and memory ability.

A HOLISTIC AND MULTIFACTORIAL APPROACH

Throughout this book, I will assert that maintaining good memory and cognitive abilities requires a holistic approach that doesn't rely only on one factor or on one type of intervention. Memory and cognitive abilities are determined, in part, by factors that we cannot control, such as our genetic make-up, age, and previous life history. There are, however, many factors that affect people's memory ability and their likelihood to develop dementia that are very much in their control. For example, cognitive (thinking) exercise, physical exercise, body weight, nutrition, quality of sleep, exposure to stress, pharmaceutical intake, social support, and mood have all been linked to memory ability and the likelihood of developing dementia. In this book, we will look at the latest research to find and understand the factors that affect memory ability and the likelihood of

1

developing dementia. Then we will discuss how to modify one's behaviors, lifestyle, or environment to take advantage of what we are learning in neuroscience, medicine, and psychology. I have included extensive citations within most chapters, and full references are located at the end of the book, so those who are interested in learning more can find the research that this book is largely based upon.

Taking a holistic medical and psychological approach certainly isn't a new strategy. For example, psychologists often recommend talk therapy in conjunction with pharmaceutical interventions to treat depression. Likewise, diabetes researchers have found that the best treatment outcomes occur when a holistic approach is taken (e.g., see Knowler et al., 2002). We also know that cardiac patients benefit from a multifaceted approach that focuses on diet, physical exercise, and stress reduction in addition to pharmaceuticals.

CAN OLDER ADULTS REALLY INCREASE THEIR MEMORY ABILITY?

Many current memory programs rely on memory tricks or mnemonics, which, in my opinion, are not appropriate for many older adults who are already struggling from an impaired ability to concentrate and a reduced ability to make new memories. While these strategies do have their place (and they will be briefly discussed in Chapter 10), this book is going to focus more on keeping the brain and body working at their optimal levels. Mnemonics (and the books and memory programs that rely on them) don't appear to lead to long-term and meaningful changes in most older adults' memory ability (e.g., O'Hara, Brooks, Friedman, Schröder, Morgan, & Kraemer, 2007), making them somewhat outside the primary focus of this book.

With that said, there is an ever-growing body of knowledge that shows it is possible for older adults to maintain or improve their memory ability. Throughout this book, we will focus on the factors and interventions that appear to make a significant impact on cognitive functioning. It is important, however, to note from the onset that the most effective and powerful interventions usually require significant work and effort on the part of the individual. Scientists are discovering many factors that seem to affect our memory ability and the likelihood of developing dementia. I think you will be amazed when you start reading about all the factors that affect our memory ability.

One of the most important findings in brain and memory research is that it may be possible to prevent a decrease in memory ability by staying mentally active. However, many people are not anywhere close to getting the level of cognitive stimulation that they could. Many independent older adults don't challenge themselves to learn new things nor do they seek out new experiences; such inactivity can lead to brain atrophy, a decline in memory ability, and eventually a further withdrawal from cognitively stimulating activities. When independent older adults' memory deteriorates, they may be forced to move out of their home to someplace that provides more care, such as an assisted living facility (ALF). Once in an ALF, as more than one million Americans are, their memory ability is likely to further deteriorate because they will probably receive even less cognitive stimulation than they had while living on their own. Assisted living facilities provide a valuable service by helping people with cooking, cleaning, shopping, transportation, making appointments, and sometimes even reminding residents when to take their medication. However, once older adults decrease their engagement in the above activities, they usually get even less cognitive stimulation and are therefore at even greater risk for developing memory problems that could further decrease their independence and quality of life. Three chapters in this book were written to help people take advantage of the plethora of research findings that have shown us that staying mentally active can lead to better memory ability. In Chapter 4 we will discuss the research that supports the *Use It or Lose It* theory of memory and aging. Then in Chapter 12 I will describe many different cognitively stimulating activities that can be used to create a group-based cognitive enhancement class for older adults. In addition, people who are concerned about their own memory, loved ones who are concerned, or caregivers of older adults can also use these activities to create an individualized program of cognitive stimulation. The activities in this book were designed or chosen because they target and strengthen key areas of the brains (e.g., frontal lobes). The activities will also help people improve certain abilities (e.g., attention and word finding) that are vulnerable to the aging process. In Chapter 13 I will present information about how to implement a cognitive enhancement program and share insights and strategies that will maximize success.

LIFESTYLE APPROACH

About half of how "good" your memory and thinking skills are is determined by genetics, the other half is determined by our environment, lifestyle, and behavioral choices. This book is inherently optimistic because it focuses on the half we can control rather than on our genetics. When necessary, I will mention genetic influences, but this book will focus on the lifestyle factors that are under our control.

For a long time, the only risk factor for dementia that was widely replicated by researchers was age. Not surprisingly, increased age does indeed lead to an increased risk of developing Alzheimer's and other types of dementia. There isn't, however, anything we can do about our chronological age. Fortunately, many researchers interested in helping older adults maintain their cognitive abilities and quality of life have looked for and found risk factors associated with memory decline and dementia, and they have particularly searched for risk factors that are under our control (e.g., see Haimov, 2006). Here is a partial list of risk factors associated with an increased chance of developing memory problems or dementia:

- Smoking
- Sedentary lifestyle
- Obesity
- Poor diet
- High blood pressure
- Chronic alcoholism
- Anemia or low iron levels
- Poor diet
- Atherosclerosis (hardening of arteries)
- Pre-diabetes or insulin resistance
- Diabetes
- Visual and auditory impairments
- Depression
- Poor social support networks

FINDING A NONPHARMACOLOGICAL CURE

There is another way to view memory maintenance and dementia prevention. Given that Alzheimer's disease and other forms of dementia usually affect people very late in their lives, delaying symptoms could be as good as finding a cure for many people. In other words, if they never get the disease, or never develop significant symptoms of dementia, their lives won't be negatively affected by memory impairment. For example, it is now widely accepted that if we can delay the onset of dementia by just five years, the incidence could be cut in half (Pasinetti et al., 2007). All we need to do is figure out how we can delay dementia-related symptoms. Fortunately, a plethora of research has been done in the past 10 years, which is informing us how to do just that.

Small, Silverman, Siddarth, Ercoli, Miller, Lavretsky, et al. (2006) conducted a study to assess whether a short-term lifestyle intervention could cause an improvement in memory ability and lead to changes in how the brain functions during cognitive tasks. The researchers randomly assigned participants to either a control group that didn't do anything different or they were assigned to a 14-day lifestyle intervention that included a brain-healthy diet, relaxation exercises, cognitive exercises, and cardiovascular conditioning. The lifestyle-intervention group experienced improved efficiency in the frontal lobes of their brains. The frontal lobe is probably the most important of the four lobes of the brain in helping us pay attention and make new memories. The lifestyle-intervention group also improved their verbal test scores, even though the intervention only lasted 14 days. I am advocating a similar albeit more long-term approach to memory maintenance.

THE APPROACH USED THROUGHOUT THE BOOK

Like the book itself, most chapters will start with the scientific evidence that suggests that some factor or behavior is affecting adults' memory ability and their likelihood of developing dementia. For example, there are entire chapters on the effects of nutrition, physical exercise, cognitive stimulation, sleep, mood, and stress on memory ability and the likelihood of developing dementia. After reviewing how the above factors affect memory ability, each chapter will discuss possible interventions that can be implemented in an attempt to maximize memory ability.

This book was written for people who have normal memory abilities and want to maintain them. It was also written for people who want to help older adults who are just beginning to have mild memory impairment from developing full-blown dementia. However, it is important to note that this book is *not* intended to be used to help people who already have severe memory difficulties. The prognosis becomes much less optimistic as people develop more severe memory problems, especially for those who have been gradually worsening for many years. It is probably the case that there has been too much damage to the brain's cells and circuitry once people have developed mid- to late-stage dementia. With that said, I have seen quite a few people with mild cognitive impairment and even some with early-stage Alzheimer's disease improve their ability to make new memories by using some of the techniques and strategies suggested in this book. However, I have never seen someone with mid- to late-stage dementia improve their ability to make new memories by using the activities and behavioral recommendations in this book.[1] Even so, this book does contain valuable information for people who care for loved ones or patients with full-blown dementia.

Each year I have the opportunity to speak with thousands of older adults and their family members who are concerned about memory loss. There are some common questions and concerns that many people seem to have. Throughout the

---

[1] Although there are set diagnostic criteria for dementia, I see a fair amount of variability in how people use the terms early-, mid-, and late-stage dementia. Another thing that should be noted is that although I don't know how to improve memory ability in late-stage dementia patients, there is a lot we can do to help them maintain their dignity and quality of life. A lot has been written on how to work with more severe dementia patients. The interested reader will find a plethora of resources. I recommend contacting the Alzheimer's Association or visiting their Website at http://www.alz.org if you are interested in learning more about helping someone who already has dementia.

book there will be "Ask the Memory Doctor" boxes, which will include frequently asked questions about memory and aging. For example, many older adults and adult children of aging parents ask

1. My mom had Alzheimer's disease. Should I be worried that I will get it?
2. I know someone who is beginning to have memory problems, but they are unmotivated to do anything about it. Is there anything I can do to help them?
3. Should I be taking ginkgo biloba for my memory?
4. I want to take advantage of adding more fish into my family's diet, but I am concerned about mercury and other pollutants. Won't the pollutants in fish cancel out any positive effects from the omega-3 fatty acids?
5. If the "use it or lose it" theory is true, then why did Ronald Reagan get Alzheimer's? He must have led a very stimulating life.

The "Ask the Memory Doctor" boxes provide concise and useful information to anyone who has had questions about memory and aging.

There is a major hurdle that geriatric professionals and loved ones must overcome in order to help older adults benefit from the knowledge we have about preventing memory problems. We have to convince people to actually do the behaviors that can improve their memory ability and quality of life. People who work with older adults frequently claim that they have a difficult time getting unmotivated people to do the things that could improve their well-being. If you go to an exercise class at a residential care facility that has 100 residents, you are lucky to see 10 people who regularly participate in the exercise class. If you go to an average activity program at the same facility, you will probably see even fewer people in the class. If you start a high-quality memory enhancement class at an ALF, about half of the people who could greatly benefit from the program will be unwilling to go to a single class. In Chapter 14 we will discuss how to motivate people to do the activities prescribed throughout this book. There is no magic thing that we can say or do, but I will present some of the best information that the field of psychology has regarding ways to increase people's motivation. One of the ways that we can help people become more motivated to do the things that can improve their memory ability is to share with them the benefits associated with doing those behaviors. Many people will simply say things like "You should eat fruits and vegetables in order to maintain your health." I believe you will get a very different effect when you tell people, "Eating fruits and vegetables that are high in antioxidants can prevent your cells from dying or being damaged to the point that they won't work. Here is a list of fruits and vegetables that are very high in antioxidants. . . ." Similarly, it is one thing to say, "You need to reduce your stress level." I believe it is much more motivating to say, "Research has shown that people who are stressed out have brain cells that have aged much faster. And stress will impair your ability to make new memories. Here are some things that researchers have found can reduce older adults' stress levels and thereby help their memory ability. . . ." In other words, if we want to help motivate people to do the right things, we need to tell them exactly what the benefits of doing the behaviors will be. I have written this entire book with that principle in mind. Personally, I have found learning more about the potential benefits of living a certain lifestyle to be very motivating. It is often very difficult to begin a physical exercise program, reduce consumption of saturated fats, lose weight, or do mental activities that one finds very challenging. But regardless of age, almost all of us could benefit from being a little more motivated to do the activities that promote health, longevity, and quality of life.

I have striven to present an honest and holistic message, using a multifaceted and scientifically based approach. The bottom line is that it *is* possible to improve one's memory ability, but it takes work and a concerted effort. The rewards for such work, however, are invaluable—increased memory ability and a better quality of life.

IT IS (ALMOST) NEVER TOO LATE (OR EARLY) TO START ENHANCING MEMORY

Many older adults or their adult children don't seek help until dementia has firmly set in. Unfortunately, if people wait until severe memory problems develop, there is less we can do to help them improve their memory ability or even slow it down. It is common for adult children of older adults to be unaware of the signs of developing dementia, often because they mistake the fact that their parent can recall details from the past as a sign that their parent's memory ability is intact. Another common reason that loved ones have difficulty identifying dementia is that the signs are not always obvious if the affected person is living in a very familiar environment. For example, if someone who is developing dementia has lived in the same home for 30 years, they will often be able to skillfully navigate through their home and almost unconsciously know where things are and how to do things such as prepare food or wash clothes. The full level of impairment is often not noticed until the affected person is required to move to a facility that can provide more care. Once at their new home, the actual level of impairment and confusion becomes much clearer. Such failures to notice the cognitive decline are common and are certainly not the fault of adult children. I believe it is the responsibility of psychologists, medical professionals, and others who work with older adults to educate people and help them be able to identify memory problems. This is easier said than done, as it is normal to experience some loss of memory ability and the ability to concentrate as we age. In addition, I believe we also must educate the public about the risk factors associated with memory problems and dementia, especially since many of them are reversible. For example, I don't think that when the average person sees an older adult eating a diet high in red meat and low in fish, the first thing that comes to their mind is that this diet may be contributing to the older adult's memory problems. More-over, I don't think people are the least bit concerned to see that an 80-year-old who is very capable of walking a mile at a time doesn't ever do so. I hope that increased awareness of dementia-related risk factors will decrease the prevalence of memory problems in our society.

Aside from being aware of lifestyle factors that may be contributing to memory problems, we also need to be aware of memory problems before they become too severe. Once someone is diagnosed with dementia, they have, almost by definition, already experienced significant brain damage. And much of the damaged tissue cannot be regenerated. People need to become engaged in pro-moting good brain and memory health much earlier.

Most people who have mild cognitive impairment can improve their memory ability if they make some changes in their lifestyle. It is important to note, though, that the changes associated with memory and cognitive problems often begin during middle age. For example, some researchers have found the telltale signs of Alzheimer's in autopsied brains of people in their 40s. Important regions of the brain associated with memory (i.e., hippocampus) often begin to slowly atrophy in people's 40s. And the density of gray matter in the frontal lobe begins to decrease even earlier! So although it is almost never too late to begin making changes to maximize brain and memory functioning, middle-aged adults should be aware that it is not too early to begin benefitting from the information in this book.

Many middle-aged adults are not aware that they can improve their memory and delay memory impairment by changing behaviors while they are still relatively young. Although many baby boomers are already complaining about occasional forgetfulness, most are many years from being the age when they are at the greatest risk of developing significant and irreversible cognitive problems. However, I believe that people in their 50s or 60s, and even younger people, can greatly benefit from the research that is discussed in this book. Research has shown that even people in their 80s who increase the level of cognitive stimulation experience an increase in cognitive ability (e.g., see Winningham, Anunsen, Hanson, Laux, Kaus, & Reifers, 2003); imagine if they had started getting that stimulation 30 years earlier. We also know that older adults who get more physical exercise have better cognitive abilities. However, if people start doing those types of activities in the 50s and 60s (or even earlier), presumably the long-term benefits would be even greater. Therefore, I believe the research reviewed in this book can also be viewed as a wake-up call for many younger people who want to maintain an active and healthy life for many decades to come.

CHAPTER 2

How Memory Works

The stream of thought flows on; but most of its segments fall into the bottomless abyss of oblivion. Of some, no memory survives the instant of their passage. Of others, it is confined to a few moments, hours or days. Others, again, leave vestiges which are indestructible, and by means of which they may be recalled as long as life endures. William James (1842–1910)

This chapter introduces basic ideas, theories, and vocabulary related to memory in order to give readers a basic understanding of memory so they can better understand how age affects memory. In addition, someone who has a good understanding of memory can certainly develop cognitive enhancement interventions that are more effective. I will present the Modal Model of Memory, which is a relatively simple but powerful model of memory that explains how we make memories and why our memory fails us sometimes. The chapter will include a discussion about how there are really three very different kinds of memory and how those different memory systems seem to be affected differently by age. In fact, one of the memory systems (procedural memories) is very resistant to age-related changes and even brain damage. The important role attention plays in making new memories will be highlighted, as this factor is crucial in understanding why older adults begin to develop memory problems. Moreover, many of the proposed cognitive enhancement activities are actually designed to increase attention and thus the ability to make new memories. I will also present the idea that any memory failure can be attributed to either a failure to encode (i.e., make a memory in the first place), a failure to adequately store the memory over time, or a failure to retrieve the memory. Such a discussion will help clear up some common and counterproductive misconceptions about memory.

THREE STAGES

What happens when we try to learn something? First the information hits our sensory systems, such as our eyes, ears, or skin. Then, if we pay attention to that information, we can put it into our short-term memory. Then we may be able to ultimately transfer that information into long-term memory, which is easier

9

said than done. Much of this book is really about how we can maintain or even improve our ability to transfer information from short-term memory, or what is currently occupying our minds, into long-term memory.

Sensory Memory

The sensory memory store holds information that impinges upon our sensory systems for a very brief period of time. This store isn't particularly important for our purposes here, except for the fact that we must pay attention to that information in order to have it transferred into short-term memory. There are a lot of things in the environment that are being picked up by our senses that we never put into short-term memory. For example, if you are holding this book in your hands, then the tactile receptors in your hands are being activated and sending signals to your brain. If you are wearing shoes or socks, then that information is being picked up by your tactile receptors. There are probably some audible sounds in your environment that are being picked up by your auditory system. You probably were not aware of any of those environmental stimuli before reading the last few sentences, even though your sensory systems were responding to them. Sensory information stays in your sensory memory store for a very brief period of time, usually less than two seconds. The sensory memory phenomenon can cause some interesting perceptions. Have you ever seen a child twirl a sparkler in a circle? The light from the sparkler appears to form a complete circle, even though the light is traveling away from the child at the speed of light (670,616,629.2 miles per hour). The reason you perceive the light as forming a complete circle is that the information is still in your visual sensory store.

Short-Term Memory

If you pay attention to something in your sensory store, then you can put it into your short-term memory store. However, the capacity of our short-term memory store is fairly limited. In 1956 George Miller estimated that the average person can hold approximately seven digits or numbers (plus or minus two) in their short-term memory, which is known as "Miller's Magic Number." The capacity of people's short-term memory increases throughout childhood, peaks in their 20s, and then slowly decreases. The above developmental process is probably mediated by the thickness of the myelin sheath, which surrounds and insulates neurons (see Chapter 3 for a discussion of neurons and myelin sheath).

I have heard many people make statements such as, "My dad has very poor short-term memory." They may be making a true statement, but I don't think that is what people mean. They usually are trying to convey that their family member has a difficult time making new memories. Short-term memory is what is on your mind at any given moment. It holds only a small amount of information for a very short period of time. With all that said, it is true that someone who has an impaired ability to make new memories also often has a reduced short-term memory capacity. Moreover, regardless of age, one's short-term memory capacity is an important predictor of how well they can comprehend new situations, solve problems, and remember events or what they read. See Table 1 to view a short-term memory capacity test.

You can keep something in your short-term memory by rehearsing it over and over again. An example of keeping information in short-term memory through rehearsal is when someone looks up a phone number in the phone book

Table 1. Measure Your Short-Term Memory Capacity

If you are interested in measuring your short-term memory capacity (i.e., digit span), ask someone to administer the following test. Don't look at the numbers below. You can randomly change the numbers and retest yourself or others.

Instructions: Start with four digits, read aloud one digit per second, then wait 15 seconds before having the participant write the digits on a sheet of paper, in the correct order. The participant should concentrate on keeping the numbers on their mind. Continue until an error is made and then record the greatest digit span correctly recalled. Do both lists and average the results.

List 1

5	8	6	0						
7	3	1	5	4					
8	6	5	4	9	3				
2	9	2	0	1	4	9	Greatest Digit Span _____		
7	5	6	3	8	1	9	2		
5	4	6	9	3	7	2	8	3	
8	5	2	1	4	6	3	5	7	2

List 2

4	9	5	1						
8	2	9	4	6					
7	5	9	1	8	2				
3	0	4	7	2	5	6	Greatest Digit Span _____		
8	2	5	2	7	0	7.	3		
7	6	8	1	5	9	4	0	5	
6	3	0	9	2	4	1	3	5	4

and repeats it over and over in their mind until they dial the number. Fortunately, our short-term memory capacity is about the length of a phone number (and that might not be a coincidence).

Peterson and Peterson (1959) wanted to estimate how long people could keep information in their short-term memory without rehearsing it. They gave people three letters, which they wanted them to remember, but after giving them the letters, the research participants were required to count backwards by threes from some number that the experimenters also provided. Then, after 3, 6, 9, 12, 15, or 18 seconds of doing mental arithmetic, the participants would try to recall the original letters. They found that after 15 seconds, only about 10% of the participants could recall the letters (see Figure 1 to view Peterson & Peterson's results).

Many memory errors are related to people overwhelming their short-term memory. Some of the most frustrating and common memory errors occur when things that were in our short-term memory are pushed out. For example, all of us have experienced walking into a room and wondering what we had so deliberately

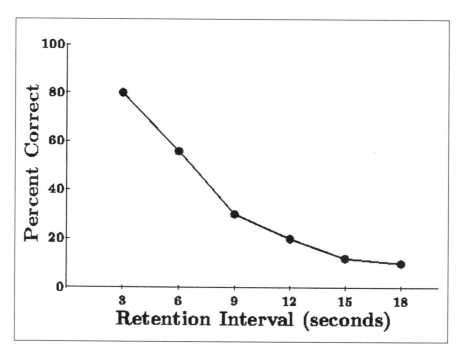

Figure 1. The effects of time on retention (Peterson & Peterson, 1959). Published by the American Psychological Association (APA). Adapted with permission from the APA.

come for. Another example would be when you just had an object in your hand, and then you lose it and can't find it anywhere in the house. Both of those memory problems are almost always related to overwhelming the capacity of our short-term memories. It works like this: you decide that you want to go into the kitchen to get a pair of scissors to open a package. At that point, the idea of scissors occupies your short-term memory. Then, as you walk down the hallway, you think about how you need to call the pharmacy before it closes. You wonder if your spouse could pick up the prescription on their way home. Then you see your cat and stop to pet her. That reminds you that you need to check her water dish, as it has been a while since you filled it. You ultimately arrive in the kitchen, clueless as to what you came for. The idea of scissors has been pushed out of your short-term memory by thinking about 1) the fact it is almost 5 p.m., 2) that you need to call the pharmacy, 3) wondering if your spouse could stop by the pharmacy for you, 4) seeing your cat, 5) thinking about the water dish, 6) remembering it has been a while since last filling it, and so on. Displacing information from short-term memory is analogous to adding books to a bookshelf that is full (see Figure 2 to view a graphic representation of the bookshelf analogy).

Figure 2. Short-term memory is like a bookshelf: You put a new book on one side and that pushes the oldest book off the other side. Your short-term memory is like that, you put a new idea in and that pushes the oldest idea out. Unfortunately, our bookshelves are fairly small, probably holding fewer than seven books (depending on their size).

In order to prevent memory errors caused by information being pushed out of our minds, we need to rehearse the information enough so it stays in our short-term memory. You have probably done this after meeting someone and learning their name. You repeat it in your mind while listening to them talk, then you are able to remember it at the end of the conversation and say, "Goodbye, _____, it was nice to meet you." Another way to decrease the likelihood of having information displaced or pushed out of your short-term memory is to reduce distracters in the environment while you are trying to do something. For example, at this moment I am writing this book in my home office, rather than my university office where I usually write. Before I started writing today, I removed all of the clutter from the desk (e.g. random business cards, electronic cables, old dog tags, scraps of paper, used checkbooks, paper clips, safety pins, junk mail, ear phones), so the objects wouldn't distract me, and they wouldn't take space in my short-term memory. I recognized that not everyone would be distracted by such objects in their field of vision (e.g., my wife), but I knew I would. Other examples of people's short-term memory being negatively affected by distracters (and possibly less pathological ones) would be reading while the television is on. The words from the television would get access to your short-term memory, thereby using up some of the space that would normally be used to comprehend and remember the reading material. Another example of distractions negatively affecting short-term memory capacity, and thus one's ability to remember something, is when you are having a conversation with someone in a noisy environment. If you lose your concentration for a moment, then words from other people's conversation may get access to your short-term memory and impair your ability to remember what the person you are talking with is saying. Unfortunately, such instances become more common when we get older because our ability to concentrate or pay attention diminishes somewhat with age. However, many of the activities presented later in this book were designed to enhance our ability to pay attention, even in the face of distracters.

A REVISED SHORT-TERM MEMORY CAPACITY

Miller's estimate that we can hold "seven plus or minus two" items in our short-term memory is a classic finding in psychology, but it is somewhat misleading. First of all, the estimate usually refers to our ability to hold numbers in our short-term. And the English words for numbers are all only one syllable, with the exception of seven. It turns out that longer words take up more space in our short-term memory. If someone with a normal short-term memory capacity tried to hold a list of three and four syllable words in their short-term memory, they would be lucky to remember four or five. This is why the Chinese, who have very short words for their numbers, usually can remember more numbers than English-speaking people. Conversely, Welsh-speaking people have much longer words for their numbers, and consequently they can't remember as many.

Some researchers are even beginning to reevaluate how they assess short-term memory capacity. Rather than assessing how many digits people can remember, they have been asking people to hold information in their short-term memory while simultaneously doing something else. This has been referred to as an active memory span. For example, we can give people a mathematical equation to look at and determine whether it is true or false, while they simultaneously try to remember a list of words. Here is an example:

$(8 \times 7) + 2 = 58$ (true/false?); ladder
$(10 / 2) + 1 = 5$ (true/false?); draw
$(3 \times 4) + 3 = 12$ (true/false?); shirt
$(5 \times 7) - 10 = 25$ (true/false?); piano

Afterwards people would be asked to report the words. The task seems peculiar, but notice what the task involves: storing some materials (words) for later use, while simultaneously working on other information (the equations), which is what we are often required to do in the real world. The number of words people can remember is probably a better predictor of how well they will remember everyday events, conversations, or what they went into the kitchen to get.

It is possible to increase the number of things you hold in short-term memory by chunking them into meaningful units. For example, if you wanted to remember an account number such as 588471945, you could chunk it into 588, 47, 1945. How could you hold the following 15 letters in your short-term memory, given that 15 letters far exceeds almost everyone's short term memory capacity: CN NTLCB LTAS APFY I? (See the end of the chapter for the answer.)

A MORE REFINED MODEL OF SHORT-TERM MEMORY

Short-term memory was originally envisioned as a place where we store a limited amount of information for a very limited amount of time. In addition, it was thought that the code was sound-based or auditory. For example, if you read a word, you "hear it" in your mind, right? Alan Baddeley proposed a model of memory that is more complex and is referred to as "working memory." For the purpose of this book, I will usually use the phrases "short-term memory" and "working memory" as if they are synonymous, but it is worth reviewing the modifications that have been made to our understanding of short-term memory because they are useful in understanding how we think, remember, and why we sometimes have memory failures.

Currently, there are four components to working memory. One is a phono-logical loop, which is generally what the original idea of short-term memory was, such that information is stored phonologically (or auditorily) and could be kept active by rehearsing it over and over (e.g., saying a phone number over and over in one's mind). The second component is the visuo-spatial sketchpad, which refers to the idea that, in addition to holding sound-based information in our minds, we can also think about visual and spatial informa-tion. For example, if you imagine walking into your bedroom, closing the door, and turning and facing the closed door, on which side of the door is the doorknob? That type of thinking would require a visuo-spatial sketchpad. Next, we have the episodic buffer, which is the newest addition to the model. The episodic buffer allows us to link visual, spatial, and verbal memory in a chronological order. The episodic buffer also provides a way for us to link new information with what we already know. Finally, the central executive component is involved with controlling and regulating the other systems. It allows us to pay attention to the important aspects of the environment, inhibiting our attention from irrelevant stimuli. It is probably the case that the central executive system is most vul-nerable to the aging process. For example, much of normal age-related memory impairment can be traced back to an impaired ability to concentrate and pay attention. See Figure 3 to view a graphic representation of the central executive and its subsystems.

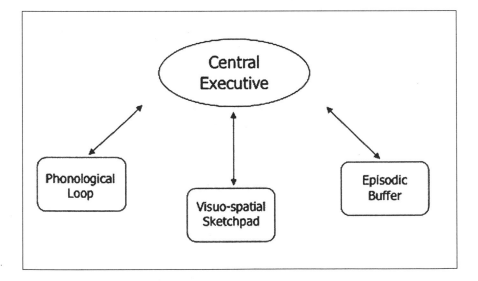

Figure 3. The central executive and its subsystems.

SHORT-TERM MEMORY PRIMARILY USES AN AUDITORY CODE

In the above description of working memory, it was noted that we have a phonological loop for sound-based information and a visual-spatial sketchpad for thinking about the world in a more spatial manner. However, we primarily think and remember using an auditory or sound-based code. If you are interested in demonstrating this phenomenon to participants in a memory class, consider using the following demonstration.

Read letters in the following lists to the participants, have them rehearse them for 15 seconds, then ask them to write all the letters down, in order. After both lists have been recalled, find out how many people got all seven letters in the correct order from each list. We would predict that many more people could correctly recall all seven letters from List A because they are acoustically different. People will have a much more difficult time correctly recalling all the letters from List B in order because all the letters sound similar and are easily confused with one another. This effect occurs because we use an auditory code to keep information in short-term memory and letters (or words) that sound alike can get confused.

List A (acoustically dissimilar)	List B (acoustically similar)
Q	D
M	G
X	T
R	Z
Z	C
A	E
O	B

Note: If you want to use the above demonstration with people who are experiencing some memory problems, consider using lists of five or six letters, rather than seven.

Given that our short-term or working memory store primarily uses an auditory code, the longer it takes to say a word in our mind, the more space it takes up. This is another reason that the short-term memory capacity estimate of "seven plus or minus two" is an overestimate of the number of everyday types of items that we can hold in our minds. Consider doing the following demonstration with your memory class.

Ask people to listen to List 1 while you read the words at the rate of about one per second. Then ask participants to hold them in their minds for 15 seconds, then instruct them to write the words down in any order. After people have written down the words from the first list, have them do the same procedure for the second list. You will find that people recall significantly fewer words from List 2 because they take up more space in their short-term or working memories. Using the bookshelf analogy, the words from List 2 are much larger books and take up more space.

List 1	List 2
hymn	gladiator
go	hypothetical
fun	fraternal
edge	electoral
soup	dissident
door	unfortunate
dry	particular
tap	driftwood

LONG-TERM MEMORY

How do you get information from short-term memory into long-term memory? That is the question that everyone wants to know. If we concentrate, we can almost always put at least some information into our short-term memory, but we can't always transfer it into our long-term memory. In order to help explain how memory works, we are going to review a classic psychology experiment that is discussed in almost every introductory psychology textbook.

Atkinson and Shiffrin (1968) and other researchers have used an ingenious experiment to demonstrate the existence and properties of both short-term and long-term memory. If we ask people to listen to a list of 15 words, then, immediately after the 15th word is read, the participants are asked to recall the words in any order, we would see a very predictable pattern. When we graph the results out, such that the probability that someone would recall a word is on the y-axis and the order in which the words were originally read is on the x-axis, we almost always find a U-shaped pattern, in which people recall more of the first words and more of the last few words (see Figure 4). We refer to the observation that the first words are recalled well as the "primacy effect" and the bump at the end of the word list as the "recency effect." The primacy effect occurs because people get to rehearse the first words longer and without as many competing words. For example, if the researcher presented the word *bicycle*, then the participant would repeat that word over and over in their mind (*bicycle, bicycle, bicycle, bicycle*), then the next word would be presented: *chair*, and the participant would repeat both words in their mind (*bicycle, chair, bicycle, chair*), then the next word would be presented: *plant* and the person would repeat all three words (*bicycle, chair, plant, bicycle, chair*), and then the next word would be presented: *magazine* and the person would repeat the words in their mind (*bicycle, chair, plant, magazine*). Words at the beginning of the list don't have as much competition for space and are rehearsed more. Notice in the above example that the person would have been able to rehearse the first word,

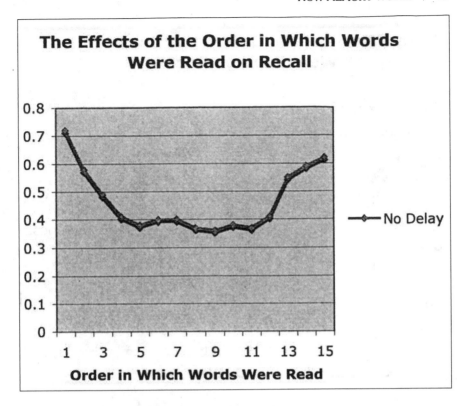

The Effects of the Order in Which Words Were Read on Recall

—◆— No Delay

Order in Which Words Were Read

Figure 4. Hypothetical data for a serial position curve study, without a delay.

bicycle, nine times, the second word, *chair,* would have been rehearsed five times, the third word, *plant,* would only be rehearsed twice, and the fourth word, *magazine,* would be rehearsed only once. The above difference in the number of rehearsals explains why people remember words at the beginning of the list better than words presented in the middle. But why do we find a recency effect. Or in other words, why do people recall the words at the end of the list so well?

One observation I have made while doing the above experiment with over 100 different classes is that most people first write the last words that were presented, as if they are still in their short-term memory (or on their bookshelf). What would happen if we had people do another cognitive task for 30 to 45 seconds after all 15 words were presented? If there is a delay between the time the last words are presented and when the participants attempt to recall the words, then the recency effect or bump in recall at the end of the list goes away. See Figure 5 to view what the data looks like when graphed out for both the delay and the no-delay conditions.

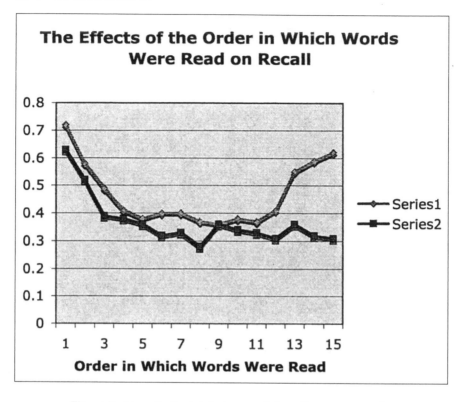

Figure 5. Hypothetical data for a serial position curve study, with and without a delay.

When there is a delay, the last few words are pushed out of short-term memory or pushed off of the bookshelf. This illustrates how our short-term memory holds only a small amount of information for a short period of time. Moreover, the information in our short-term memory is easily disrupted.

What did the above experiments teach us about making new long-term memories? We learned that rehearsal is important if you want to take something in short-term memory and put it into long-term memory. So the take-home message at this point is to rehearse, rehearse, rehearse! See Table 2 to view instructions for a serial position curve experiment.

The words at the end of the list were only remembered well with the no-delay condition because the M-word task pushed the last few words from the list out of short-term or working memory. This latter finding provides a great opportunity to explain short-term memory. Consider sharing the bookshelf analogy with the participants and how the M-words pushed the last words read off of their bookshelves.

Table 2. Instructions for a Serial Position Curve Experiment

Consider trying the following demonstration with a group of friends or a memory class.

1. Get at least six people together and read them a list of 15 words aloud at a rate of about one word per second. Here is a list: bicycle, chair, plant, magazine, coffee, calendar, wall, stove, light, phone, spoon, curtain, sunglasses, mouse, sink

2. After you read the 15th , ask them to write down as many of the words as they can remember. The words can be written down in any order.

3. Graph the results, such that the number of people who recalled each word would go on the y-axis and the order in which the word was read would go on the x-axis.

4. Then read the participants another word list, such as rug, fan, apple, picture, microwave, brush, mirror, sunglasses, telephone, flower, tire, window, calendar, flashlight, newspaper. However, after you read the 15th word ask the participants to think of as many words that begin with the letter "m" and write those words down. Be sure to inform the participants that the M-words don't have to be related in any way to the list of words that were read. Give the participants 45 seconds to list as many of the M-words as they can. Then, after 45 seconds, ask them to write down as many of the words you read as they can. Be sure the participants are aware of the instructions before you read the list.

5. Graph the results from the second list. As you read earlier in the chapter, people usually remember the first words from both lists reasonably well because they were rehearsed more and with fewer competing distracters. The relative increase in recall rates for words at the beginning of the list is known as the *primacy effect*. This effect is a good reminder that if we want to remember something, we should rehearse it a lot and do so with fewer distractions.

Ask the participants which words they wrote down first in the no delay condition. You will probably find that the last words read were often the first words written down, which is an excellent strategy (i.e., dump the contents of short-term memory before going back to the information that was actually stored in long-term memory).

Long-Term Memory and Rehearsal

How many pennies have you seen in your lifetime? Maybe you have seen five pennies a day, which would be 1,825 pennies in a year, which would be

18,250 for each decade you have been alive. There is no doubt that you have adequately rehearsed pennies and know what they look like. Right? OK, then please try to find the correct penny from 15 options in Figure 6.

Most people are unable to identify the correct penny, even though they have seen thousands of pennies. This happens because we don't really pay very close attention to pennies. We notice the color but not what is on them. It turns out that not all rehearsal is equal in its effectiveness. We can rehearse something at a very superficial level, maybe just long enough to keep it in our short-term memory (e.g., when looking up a phone number or seeing whether a coin is a penny or not), which probably won't get the information from our short-term memory into our long-term memory. Alternatively, we can rehearse something at a much deeper level by relating it to other things we know, using imagery, or trying to identify a mnemonic that will help us remember it. The above dichotomy explains why some things are quickly forgotten, while others are retained. In Chapter 10 we will discuss numerous strategies to improve memory, and many of them are designed to help improve the depth at which we rehearse the information.

Long-term memory is what we have stored in memory for longer than a minute. Once stored, it may stay there for a very long time. But there are several different types of long-term memories, which we will discuss next.

Figure 6. Choose the correct penny (Nickerson & Adams, 1979).
Permission to reprint granted by Elsevier Limited.

PROCEDURAL MEMORIES

People often think of memory as a unitary idea, but there are actually many different types of memory. The three most basic types of memory are procedural memories, semantic memories, and episodic memories. Of these types, the simplest type of memories are procedural memories.

When people think or talk about memory, they probably are not referring to procedural memories, which are best considered memories of how to do things. For example, riding a bicycle is a procedural memory for most people. Many of the features of procedural memories can be illustrated with the bicycle-riding example. For example, procedural memories seem to last for a very long time, which is consistent with the cliché, "It is like riding a bicycle, you never forget." Imagine what you would say to someone if you had to verbally tell them how to ride a bicycle. You would probably have a difficult time clearly articulating how to do that behavior. Procedural memories are notoriously difficult to verbalize, largely because they are not well-connected to the language centers of the brain.

Examples of Procedural Memories

Riding a bicycle
Walking
Putting on a shirt
Tying shoes
Cutting food
Driving an automobile
Typing
Typing a password
Brushing your teeth
Turning on your shower
Crossing your legs when you sit down
Scooting a chair forward when you sit at a dining table
Buttoning a shirt
Adding and subtracting
Signing your signature
Reading
Playing a musical instrument
Singing a well-rehearsed song
Reciting a well-rehearsed poem or story

Procedural memories are also difficult to change. For example, have you ever had to change a password (e.g., e-mail password) that you had typed many times? If so, you very likely made a mistake and kept typing your old password for a while. Related to that, procedural memories don't require a lot of conscious awareness and thought. For example, have you ever started driving a frequently traveled route (e.g., between work and your home) and all of the sudden you ended up in your driveway and thought, "I don't remember driving here, I don't remember making any turns, but I must have because I am here?" If so, then you have experienced how little conscious awareness is necessary to use procedural memories. Moreover, thinking about procedural memories can often degrade the behavior. For example, if you think too hard about a well-rehearsed golf swing or typing, you might make a mistake.

In order to make a procedural memory, one has to practice some behavior many times. During the learning phase, people usually devote a significant amount of cognitive resources (i.e., short-term or working memory) to the task. But once the procedural memory has been made, it is relatively permanent and requires very few cognitive resources. For example, when you first learned to drive, you had to devote all of your attention to the task, but after a while, you were able to drive almost without thinking about it. After a procedural memory has been made, the behavior is fairly automatic, or what we often refer to as being automatized. Actually, it may be hard to inhibit the procedural behavior if you need to ever change it. For example, it is common for people who are driving or walking on a frequently traveled route to miss their turn if they need to deviate for any reason (e.g., need to go to the store rather than directly home after work).

Procedural memories usually remain intact even when people experience traumatic brain injury, amnesia, or the development of dementia. We can take advantage of this phenomenon by exposing people with serious memory problems to a task many times. For example, people with dementia can learn where their room is, where the dining room is, how to set a brake on a wheelchair, how to use a long shoe horn, or button hook for buttons on clothing. The person may not remember learning the task, but they can learn to perform the task with enough practice (e.g., after practicing the behavior 100+ times).

MULTITASKING AND PROCEDURAL MEMORIES

Today it seems like many people are trying to do more and more with less and less time. I frequently hear people talk about how they need to multitask, which frankly concerns me. Humans are not very good at doing two cognitive tasks simultaneously. You can't effectively follow a conversation and effectively read a book at the same time. You can't completely listen to two conversations simultaneously. Similarly, you can't see the duck *and* the rabbit, in Figure 7, at the same time.

If people want to multitask, I would suggest doing one task that is procedural or automatized and thus doesn't require many cognitive resources or space in one's working memory. For example, you can brush your teeth (procedural task)

Figure 7. Rabbit-duck illusion. The viewer either sees a rabbit (with ears pointing to the left) or a duck (with its beak pointing to the left), but not all three at the same time. Jastrow (1899). The image was obtained from *Wikimedia Commons* and is in the public domain.

while listening to a talk-radio program (cognitive task). Or you can eat a bowl of cereal (procedural task) while reading the newspaper (cognitive task). Or you can hold the telephone while on hold (procedural task), while reading the newspaper (cognitive task). But you can't effectively listen to your spouse talk (cognitive task) while playing a game of Sudoku (cognitive task). Nor can someone in a business meeting read their e-mail while simultaneously tracking a presentation being given by a colleague. But someone could knit using a well-rehearsed method (procedural task) while listening to the same presentation given by a colleague (cognitive task), assuming they are not doing a pattern that requires a lot of counting, as that would take away cognitive resources.

SEMANTIC MEMORIES

Semantic memories are the second of three main types of memory, and they are our memories of facts and knowledge. Semantic memory is the sum of all our knowledge, vocabulary, and facts we know about our world. Semantic memory does not include autobiographical experiences (e.g., remembering your wedding day or where you were when you first learned of the attack on the World Trade Centers). As we get older, the amount of information in our semantic memory usually increases. In the 1990s I conducted a study in which I found that older adults living in assisted living facilities, and who were on average having mild memory problems, had a much larger vocabulary than college students at a fairly prestigious university. This finding is an important reminder that even people who are experiencing memory problems often have a lot of knowledge and wisdom to share. It is also worth noting that, other factors being equal, the more semantic memories one has, the easier it is to learn new things—the rich become richer.

EPISODIC MEMORIES

Episodic memories refer to personal experiences that we remember taking place. For example, remembering the birth of a child, a retirement party, or a vacation would probably be examples of episodic memories. If we were to use a book analogy, we would refer to our episodic memories as being autobiographies, whereas semantic memories would be encyclopedias. One could argue that semantic memories are simpler than episodic because semantic memories include only the factual information, whereas episodic memories usually include information related to time, place, and emotion. Episodic memories are made with one exposure to the event, whereas semantic memories often require a number of rehearsal trials. For example, you would probably remember meeting a new neighbor with just one interaction (episodic memory). However, you might need to rehearse their phone number, place of birth, or how many children they have a number of times before remembering that information (semantic memories).

DEVELOPMENT IS PREDICTABLE

First, children develop procedural memories. For example, we have seen in the laboratory that by six months of age infants can learn to kick their feet if that causes a mobile to move. Then, a little after they turn 1-year-old, they begin using words that they know stand for certain objects and actions, which are probably best considered semantic memories. But it isn't until about the age of three that they begin to have long-lasting episodic memories. The lack of long-lasting episodic memories from the first few years of life is referred to as *childhood amnesia*. Common first episodic memories are the birth of another sibling or a trip to the hospital. We often see predictable developmental changes early and late in life, such that the first abilities we acquire are the last to be lost, and vice versa. For example, the ability to make new episodic memories is one of the first memory encoding abilities to diminish in older adulthood, and it was the last to develop in childhood. However, the ability to make new procedural memories is rarely lost in older adulthood or with neurodegenerative diseases, and it is the first to develop during infancy.

PRESERVED PROCEDURAL MEMORY

In the past few years, a lot of research has been published that shows people with Alzheimer's disease, multiple sclerosis, Parkinson's-related dementia, and other amnesic disorders can in fact make new procedural memories. One of the first reports that showed how resilient our procedural memory system is came from Brenda Milner, who worked with a patient known by the pseudonym H. M., who had both of his hippocampi removed in a neurosurgery to treat his severe epilepsy. H. M. developed anterograde amnesia, which means he was unable to make new declarative memories. Or in other words, he was unable to make new semantic or episodic memories. However, H. M. could make new procedural memories and motor skills, even though he never remembered practicing the tasks. In one experiment, Milner trained H. M. to trace around the perimeter of a star by looking only at the pencil, star, and hand in a mirror (see Figure 8). This task is quite difficult at first, but H. M. learned to do it after practicing many times. In fact, his learning curve was quite normal. If you asked H. M. if he had ever seen or practiced the mirror drawing task, he would say "no"; however, he retained the skill. Physical and occupational therapists are beginning to take advantage of preserved procedural memories and teaching brain injured and amnesic patients new skills. Although procedural memories require a tremendous amount of practice, once made, they are very resistant to decay. One interesting use of the fact that procedural memories can be made by people with amnesia, dementia, or other types of brain injury is known as constraint-induced movement therapy. People who have lost the ability to use part of the body can exercise it more by not using the unaffected body part. For example, if someone has partial paralysis or paresis of the right arm, they can have their left arm put in a sling for 90% of their nonsleeping time. If people do this for two weeks, they often regain a significant amount of use in the affected body part, even if they have significant memory problems. They are essentially making new procedural memories for the affected arm and probably rewiring the central nervous system. Moreover, the regained abilities appear to last long after the treatment, which is characteristic of procedural memories (e.g., see Wolf, Winstein, Miller, Taub, Uswatte, Morris, et al., 2006).

THREE MEMORY PROCESSES

There are three things we do with our memories. First, we encode or make new memories. Second, we store memories. Third, we retrieve previously stored memories. It is important to be aware of the three above memory processes because any memory failure can be attributed to a failure of one the memory processes. Moreover, any attempt at explaining memory failures or preventing them from occurring must consider these processes. We can understand memory processes by using the computer as an analogy. Encoding memories is like saving a file on your computer. Once a file has been saved, you hope it will be stored. However, if another file is saved with the same name or there is damage to the hard drive, then the file might be lost. The same is true with human memory. Once a

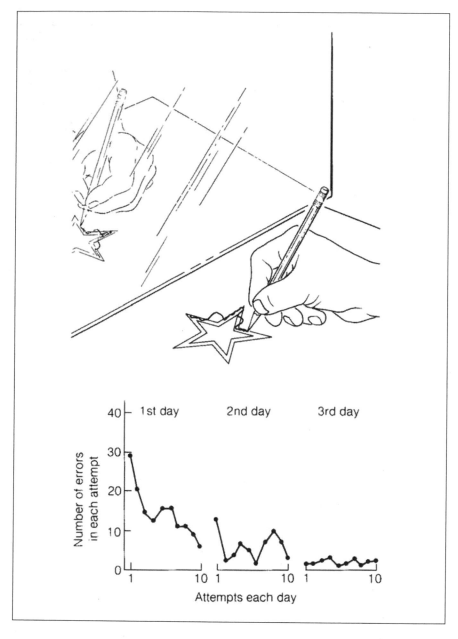

Figure 8. H. M.'s Mirror Drawing Performance. H. M.'s ability to do the mirror-drawing task improved, even though he had no conscious recollection of doing the task previously (Kolb & Whishaw, 1995). Permission to reprint granted from W. H. Freeman and Company.

memory has been encoded, it could be lost through decay, brain injury, or interference from another experience. Finally, we need to be able to retrieve our computer files. If you know where the file is stored on your computer, you can open the correct directory or folder and find the file. Or you can do a "find file" search, if you know the file name. However, it is possible that the computer file was adequately stored (encoded), but you nevertheless are unable to find it; that would be analogous to a retrieval error in human memory.

ENCODING

Most memory failures are probably a failure to encode (or make) a memory in the first place. Encoding memories is difficult and requires attention and a change to the neuronal structures and connections in the brain. When people say they are terrible at remembering names and jokes, they usually mean they are not effectively encoding memories and jokes. Let's use the book shelf analogy to better understand what happens when we fail to encode a name or a joke. Let's say you are at a social function and your friend introduces you to four people. Your friend first introduces you to Phil. You say nice to meet you, how do you know my friend? He states that they are business associates and that he sells him office supplies. Then you meet his wife, Theresa, and you comment on her pretty hat. Then you meet Diane, who your friend states owns the shoe store downtown, and finally you meet Diane's husband, Jon, who launches into a short story about a recent rafting trip. During the whole process of meeting these people and listening to what they have to say you are very attentive. Then, just a few minutes after learning these people's names, you are shamefully embarrassed that you can't remember any of their names. Why does this happen to most of us? The answer is simple: our short-term memory bookshelves are too small. Let's say your bookshelf holds six items. You heard Phil's name and that occupied the first space, but then you put another proposition on the bookshelf (business associate), and another (office supplies), and another (wondering if you can get cheap office supplies), and another (Theresa), and another (pretty hat), and another (Diane), and another (shoe store), and another (downtown), and several more propositions (about a rafting trip). The name Phil has long since been pushed off of the bookshelf, and unless you were rehearsing it or processing it at a deep level immediately after you first heard it, you would very probably be unable to recall his name. Even if you were presented several alternatives to choose from, you might not recognize the correct name.

The above scenario would be similar if you had heard a funny joke earlier in the week and then tried to recall it after a few days or even a few hours. Immediately after you heard the funny joke about a psychologist with amnesia, you would probably have most of it on your bookshelf, but shortly after the punch line was told, new information or thoughts would quickly displace the joke from your memory (e.g., I heard a joke recently. What was it? Let's see something about a . . . Oh, I am terrible at remembering jokes.) and the contents of the joke about a psychologist would be displaced from your bookshelf. Once again, making or encoding memories is hard work and requires attention and time devoted to the task. If you want to remember names or jokes better, you need to keep them in your short-term memory longer by rehearsing them and processing them at a deeper level. For example, if you are trying to remember someone's name, repeat it every so often in your mind and try to use it while speaking. Then even after the initial introduction, try to rehearse it a few times, and then do so again the next day and then a few days after that. Writing in a daily diary or journal can help facilitate rehearsal of names (or jokes) days after they were initially learned. Yes, it will take some effort, but unfortunately improving one's memory always does.

STORAGE

Over time, many of our semantic and episodic memories fade, especially if they haven't been used very often. For example, only about half of middle-aged adults remember the name of their first- or second-grade teacher, even though it was well-rehearsed and encoded in the past. We often forget phone numbers that were rehearsed hundreds of times and well-remembered in the past. Over time, unrehearsed memories simply decay.

Hermann Ebbinghaus published a seminal paper in 1885, in which he described the forgetting curve. He would learn lists of consonant-vowel-consonant (CVC) nonsense syllables such as WIJ, PAQ, HAJ. After he could go through a number of them perfectly (e.g., 16 CVC syllables), he would set them aside and come back to them after a certain period of time. The results of his work produced the first forgetting curve. The typical forgetting curve shows very rapid drop off in accuracy after Ebbinghaus first learned the list of CVC syllables, such that only 20 minutes later he had forgotten over 40% of them, 9 hours after learning them he had forgotten 60% of them. Afterwards, the forgetting leveled off and he would remember almost 25% of them after one month.

The forgetting curve is the steepest for nonsensical information like the CVC syllables Ebbinghaus used. It is less steep if the information is related to things the learner already knows. Another interesting concept that emerged from Ebbinghaus' work is *savings*, which refers to the finding that when we forget something that had previously been encoded, we can relearn it more rapidly. Another useful finding that has emerged in the area of forgetting is that we can limit forgetting by having increasingly longer intervals between rehearsal trials. For example, if you learn something at noon, you might want to rehearse it again at 8:00 p.m. (8 hour interval), again the next day at noon (16 hour interval), again the next day at 6:00 p.m. (30 hour interval), and so on. If you do so, the forgetting curve will become much flatter than what Ebbinghaus found.

RETRIEVAL

The final memory process is retrieval, which is the act of calling up a previously encoded memory. Many times we have a memory error even though we have encoded and stored a memory. This can occur if the memory cues are inadequate to activate the stored memory. Or we can have a memory retrieval problem if we slip into a Tip of the Tongue state, which is characterized by an inability to recall a specific word. Usually the word is a proper noun or commonly used noun. Tip of the Tongue states can be quite frustrating and have been compared to being on the verge of sneezing. See Chapter 12 for more information about Tip of the Tongue states and exercises that were designed to decrease word generation difficulties. Just as often experienced in Tip of the Tongue states, we will eventually retrieve the information. Another technique to aid a retrieval failure in which the material has been adequately encoded and stored, is to think of similar and related ideas. For example, if you are trying to remember a city that you went to while on a vacation, try to remember other places you visited while on that vacation and the names of other people present on the vacation, as they may serve as additional cues that may help retrieve the target memory.

WHY DO WE FORGET?

I have already presented the idea that any memory error can be attributed to problems with one of the three types of memory processing (i.e., encoding, storage, or retrieval). But there are other, more specific sources of memory errors, and it may be helpful in preventing such errors if we can identify and understand them.

Source Confusion

One of the most common types of memory errors is known as source confusion, which is when we misattribute the source of some information, thought, idea, or event. For example, have you ever been talking with someone and you thought of something you want to share with them, but decide to wait until the other person is done talking? Then later, you can't remember whether you simply thought about sharing the information or actually told the other person. This type of memory error is common and becomes more common through middle age and older adulthood. Another example of source confusion is when you are unsure whether you told a certain person a specific story before. Another example of source confusion is when you are unable to remember if you read something, heard about it from a friend, or just heard about it on television. The above source confusion errors are examples of knowing something, just not remembering specific instances with the information, which is a lot like the difference between semantic memories and episodic memories.

Inattention

One of the most common contributing factors to an inability to remember something is inattention. We often do not pay close enough attention to what we are being exposed to, and then we don't rehearse it or encode it at a deep enough level to make a long-lasting memory. Inattention is particularly problematic when people begin to develop more serious memory problems (e.g., mild cognitive impairment or early-stage dementia). To increase attention, try to reduce distractions in the environment. Also, try to exercise attention abilities by doing some of the exercises described in Chapter 12.

Decay

Sometimes memories simply decay and atrophy because of disuse, which is a clear example of a storage failure. Many times such decay is welcomed, as we don't need to remember every detail of our lives. Going to a high school reunion often reminds us how much we have forgotten: if we don't think about people we knew in high school or college, we shouldn't be surprised that decades of not rehearsing someone's name has led to complete decay of the memory for what someone's name is. If you have a memory of something you don't want to decay, then I would suggest trying to think about it every so often. The better you remember something, the less often you need to rehearse it.

Prior Knowledge

One interesting aspect of memory is the more you know about a topic, the easier it is to learn something new about that topic—the rich get richer. But the reverse is also true; if you don't know much about a particular topic, then it will be more difficult to create long-lasting memories regarding it.

Interference

Many times we make a new memory, then experience something that interferes with the veracity of the original memory. Moreover, it could just be the sum of intervening experiences that interfere with our memories. The longer it has been since the original event, the less likely we are to remember it, possibly because we have experienced more interfering events in the intervening time period. One interesting study that shows the influence of interferences was published by Baddeley and Hitch (1977). They asked rugby players to recall the names of opposing teams. The researchers were able to control for the effects of time passage and the effects of the number of games, because not all players were able to be at and play in all games because of injuries and illness. So, the researchers could compare the memory of someone who hadn't played in any games for three weeks with someone who had played in three games since the original game they both played in. Baddeley and Hitch reported that as the number of intervening games increased, players' ability to recall previous opponents' names decreased. Moreover, elapsed time was much less important than the number of previous games in predicting recall. It is difficult to limit the effect of interference, but it is a common contributing factor in memory errors.

AMNESIAS

The topic of dementia is extensively covered in Chapter 11, but it may be helpful to also discuss amnesia, including broad categories of amnesia, and some of the causes. In general, there are two broad categories of amnesia: *retrograde amnesia* and *anterograde amnesia*.

Retrograde Amnesia

Retrograde amnesia is characterized by an inability to remember events that occurred *before* some brain injury or traumatic event, which affected the central nervous system. Retrograde amnesia, in which the person is unable to remember events that occurred just before the injury, is most often caused by blows to the head. For example, it is common for people to be unable to remember the few minutes just before a serious bicycle or motor vehicle accident. It is as if the blow to the head disrupts the transfer of information from short-term to long-term memory. The person who cannot remember the three or four minutes that preceded an accident is unlikely to ever do so. Using our bookshelf analogy from earlier in the chapter, it is as if all the books were knocked off the bookshelf at the time of the accident. The length of time before the accident that was forgotten is somewhat predictive of the person's ultimate prognosis and the severity of the trauma.

Anterograde Amnesia

Earlier we discussed H. M. who could not make new memories after a neurosurgical operation to remove his hippocampi in an effort to treat his severe epilepsy. After his hippocampi were removed, he was unable to make new memories beyond a few minutes. This case taught us that the hippocampi are important in making new and long-lasting memories. But it would be false to assume that the hippocampi are the seat of memory, because H. M. still retained memories before the operation. Many forms of anterograde amnesia involve damage to the hippocampi and related structures. For example, Korsakoff's syndrome, which is caused by chronic alcoholism and a Vitamin B1 deficiency, is associated with anterograde amnesia or an inability to make new memories.

Moreover, Korsakoff's syndrome is associated with the atrophy of small structures just adjacent to the hippocampi called mammillary bodies. It is as if a circuit is broken when the mammillary bodies atrophy, which prevents the formation of new memories. We sometimes see similar effects after a stroke, although that may also be due to damaged frontal lobes and an inability to effectively pay attention. Other causes of anterograde amnesia include drug effects (usually sedatives or tranquilizers), infections (e.g., encephalitis), and strokes.

Psychogenic Amnesia

One class of amnesia is referred to as psychogenic amnesia (meaning having its origins in the mind). It is also known as dissociative amnesia. Psychogenic amnesia often has both a retrograde component, in which the person is unable to recall autobiographical or episodic memories, and an anterograde component, in which they have difficulty making new memories. There may be two types of psychogenic amnesia: one that affects memory in a more global fashion, and another type that seems to only affect memories for a specific event, which is usually very traumatic and distressing to the individual. Psychogenic amnesia is by definition not associated with any organic brain damage. People who have had a lot of traumatic experiences, such as soldiers or survivors of childhood abuse, are more likely to develop psychogenic amnesia.

Transient Global Amnesia

Transient global amnesia is a sudden and temporary form of amnesia that lasts for a matter of hours and usually resolves itself within 24 hours. During the episode, people don't remember events just before the episode, however they usually know who they are and recognize family members. Afterwards, people don't have much memory for events that took place during the episode. Transient global amnesia occurs in only 3–10 people out of 100,000, however it is quite distressing to the individual and their loved ones. After an exhaustive review of case studies, Quinette et al. (2006) reported that women are more likely to have an emotional event precipitate an episode, men are more likely to have some sort of physical exertion precipitate an episode, and younger people are more likely to have a history of headaches. We are not sure what causes transient global amnesia, but it may be a disruption of blood supply to the brain. The good news for people who experiences this type of amnesia and their loved ones is that most people don't ever have another episode, and it doesn't appear to be related to mortality.

PROSPECTIVE MEMORY

Prospective memory refers to our ability to remember to do something in the future. Or in other words, prospective memory is remembering to remember.

In most cases, memory is triggered by an external cue: if someone asks you a question, the content of the question is a cue. For example, if someone asked you what you did last weekend, the question would serve as a cue to recall your weekend. However, prospective memory often requires an internal cue.

In day-to-day life, our prospective memory is very important. However, we are likely to have greater difficulties with prospective memory as we enter older adulthood, experience stress, or have a lot of things to do and remember. The best way to prevent prospective memory failures is to create external memory cues. For example, you can write things you need to do on calendars. If you need to send a package to someone by July 1st, write on your calendar for June 24th to send the package. Be sure to check the calendar daily. Then there are those things that you need to remember when you are not able to write on the calendar. Consider carrying around a small notepad that you can write down things that need to be dealt with in the future. If you find yourself in a situation in which you can't write a note on a calendar or notepad, consider calling yourself and leaving a message or sending yourself an e-mail. Also, consider using Post-it notes and putting them in a prominent place (e.g., by the front door). Groot, Wilson, Evans, and Watson (2002) found that people who had memory problems because of a nonprogressive brain injury and non-brain injured people were both better able to remember to do future tasks if they took notes. Groot et al. also reported that there was a relationship between executive functioning ability (e.g., paying attention) and the likelihood that people would successfully remember their prospective memory task, such that people with worse executive functioning were more likely to not remember the prospective task.

The other commonly suggested strategy is to make lists of things that need to be done. A similar strategy is recommended for people who struggle with insomnia, especially those who think about things they need to do while they are trying to fall asleep. People with that particular symptom of insomnia may benefit (sleepwise and prospective memorywise) from keeping a notepad by their bed and jotting down things that come to their mind while they are trying to fall asleep. When people recognize that they should make a note about something they need to do in the future, then actually write a note, they will be more likely to remember the information, regardless of whether they use the note. The act of recognizing that something is important, and then writing a note will very probably be enough memory processing to help people encode a memory.

If you are trying to help someone else with their prospective memory, consider giving them a calendar with a pen attached. Or give them a notepad with a miniature pen or some Post-it notes. There are many new assistive technologies being developed for people with memory impairment and other limitations. For example, personal digital assistants (PDAs) have been developed to help people with memory and prospective tasks such a taking medicines at a particular time. Consider doing an Internet search if you know someone who could benefit from these new technologies.

AGE AFFECTS VARIOUS COGNITIVE ABILITIES DIFFERENTLY

People generally assume that all of our cognitive abilities decrease with advancing age. Many abilities do decrease during adulthood, but many do not. Here are lists of cognitive abilities that do and don't change with age.

Common Cognitive Changes with Aging
- Slower speed of processing and reaction times
- Less able to concentrate, especially in distracting situations
- Reduced short-term memory capacity
- More effort needed to encode new memories

Cognitive Abilities that Don't Change Much with Aging
- The ability to make new procedural memories
- The ability to recognize the correct answer among a list of alternatives

Cognitive Abilities that May Increase with Age
- The total number of semantic memories (i.e., knowledge)
- Vocabulary
- Wisdom

Answer regarding the chunking question: CNN TLC BLT ASAP FYI

Answer to the penny question: The penny in row two, second from the left is correct. It has the date on the right, Lincoln faces the right, the words "In God We Trust" are centered above Lincoln, and the word Liberty is on the left above Lincoln's shoulder.

CHAPTER 3

How the Brain Works

If the brain were so simple we could understand it, we would be so simple we couldn't. Lyall Watson (1939–)

This chapter will provide the reader with a basic understanding of how the brain works, in particular the reader will learn how it makes, stores, and retrieves memories. This information will allow the reader to understand memory from a biological standpoint. More importantly, this chapter will allow the reader to understand what happens to the brain (and memory) as we age, which will enable them to understand *why* we need to do certain types of cognitive and memory enhancement activities. In addition, a basic understanding of the brain will allow the reader to understand subsequent chapters at a deeper level. For example, after developing a basic understanding of the brain, the reader will be able to understand why researchers are suggesting that people eat a diet high in omega-3 fatty acids and antioxidants. The chapters on physical exercise, stress, nutrition, and dementia will also refer back to the neuroscientific information found in the brain chapter.

I believe it is important for people to understand why scientists are recommending certain lifestyle changes (e.g., improving nutrition, increasing physical exercise, and reducing stress). For the older adult, such knowledge can be motivating, as it provides a reason why they are being instructed to make difficult changes in their lives. For the professional who works with older adults, such knowledge will allow them to motivate the people they work with, and it will guide their development of wellness programs.

NEUROANATOMY

In order to understand memory, and various neurodegenerative diseases, it is helpful to understand the brain. There are four lobes or major sections of the brain: the frontal, parietal, temporal, and occipital lobes (see Figure 1). There are specific functions associated with each of the lobes and often to specific hemispheres (or sides of the brain). The brain and memory exercises that are

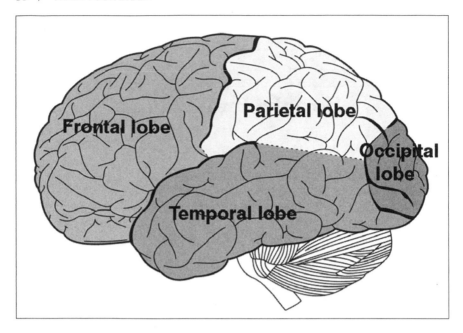

Figure 1. A brain with its four lobes highlighted. Public domain image
from *Wikipedia* http://en.wikipedia.org/wiki/Frontal_lobe

recommended in this book are designed to exercise specific parts of the brain
and thus certain cognitive abilities. Let's quickly review hemispheric brain differences (i.e., left versus right), the lobes of the brain, and their functions.

Contralateral Actions and Neuropsychology

The left side of the brain controls the right side of the body, and the right side of
the brain controls the left side of the body. Hemispheric differences are important
to consider when evaluating the potential effects of strokes or other types of brain
damage. If you see motor or muscle impairment on the right side of the body,
you can assume that the left side of the brain has been damaged (probably the
posterior or back part of the frontal lobe). If the left hemisphere of the brain has
been damaged, then it is possible that the left temporal lobe was also affected.
Given that the left temporal lobe is largely responsible for controlling language
for 99% of people, you might look for language deficits if you notice that the
right side of the body was affected by the brain injury.

It also appears that depressive symptoms are more likely in people who have
recently experienced damage to certain parts of the left hemisphere. It is as if
they are acutely aware and deeply bothered by their brain injury and possible loss

of function. The opposite may occur in people who have had damage to their right parietal lobe, such that they are often unaware of anything on their left side, and they are usually unaware that there is a problem. This is called unilateral neglect, because people neglect one side of their world.

You can remember some of the above facts with a mnemonic or memory trick. *Left hemisphere* begins with an L and so does language and laughter. If the left hemisphere is damaged, there might also be impairment of language ability and the ability to laugh (i.e., develop depression).

Frontal Lobes

The frontal lobes are probably the most important part of the brain when it comes to thinking, attention, and general cognitive ability. The frontal lobes are largely responsible for planning, problem solving, and what cognitive psychologists call *executive functioning*. Executive functioning includes a whole host of mental functions, all of which affect our ability to make new memories and handle novel situations that are outside of our normal routine. For example, if you are talking with a friend in a crowded and noisy room and they tell you that there is an important meeting that you need to attend in two weeks, then your executive functioning will need to be turned on and fully engaged. The first task for your executive functioning system is to inhibit or not pay attention to the interesting conversation taking place within earshot as you attend to what the person you are talking to is saying. Then, when you hear that you need to attend a meeting, you need to decide whether or not this is true. If you decide that you do indeed need to attend the meeting, then you are going to need to determine whether you will remember it later. If you decide that this will be a difficult thing to remember because it is late, you are tired, and you have a lot of things on your mind, then your executive functioning system might help you realize that you need to write it down. If you are unable to find something to write with, you might ask your friend if you can borrow their cell phone so you can call yourself and leave a message with the meeting information. Having those types of thoughts and coming up with effective strategies is what executive functioning allows us to do. Unfortunately, it appears that our executive functioning abilities slowly decrease as we age. And at some point, this can become problematic and lead to memory problems. We can try to improve older adults' executive functioning (see Chapter 12 for activities) and also provide them with strategies to compensate for brain changes (see Chapter 10 for more information about effective strategies).

Frontal Lobes, Attention, and Inhibition

One of the most important aspects of executive functioning is the ability to pay attention. However, the ability to have sustained attention, unfortunately, tends to slowly decrease during middle and late adulthood, which is probably the largest contributor to normal age-related memory impairment. If people are not able to have sustained attention directed toward something, then they are unlikely to make a new memory for that information. For example, we have all probably experienced the situation in which we are reading a book and we start thinking about something else while we simultaneously continue reading each word in front of us. When we snap out of our daydream, we may have absolutely no recollection of the material we just read; this is because we were not fully attending to what we were reading. A similar situation is common among older adults, even those without serious memory problems, such that they have a difficult time giving full and sustained attention to a situation. Many older adults describe the phenomenon as "not being about to focus" like they once could.

The ability to pay attention to something is actually driven by an ability to *inhibit* paying attention to other things. That may sound abstract, but it is at the heart of age-related memory problems. For example, if you are trying to pay attention to what you are reading right now, then you need to *inhibit* paying attention to what is outside your window, or what you are going to do tomorrow, or a conversation you had earlier today. If you are able to inhibit paying attention to those other things, then you are much more likely to understand and remember what you are reading. It is common for older adults to lose some of their inhibitory abilities. When someone's frontal lobes and inhibitory abilities deteriorate, we usually see behavior that would not previously be characteristic of them. For example, people who work in nursing homes often describe how some of the residents say and do very inappropriate things. For example, they may swear, assault people, or say racially or sexually insensitive things, even though they don't have a history of doing any of these things. The inappropriate behaviors occur because the frontal lobes, which normally inhibit inappropriate behaviors, are not working as efficiently as they used to. These types of behavioral problems go hand in hand with memory problems because they are both related to the frontal lobes' ability to inhibit.

Here is a list of other behaviors that are indicative of inhibitory deficits and often seen in people who enroll in memory enhancement classes:

Saying answers before the right time
Getting started before all the instructions have been given
Inability to stop working on the previous task
Emotional perseveration (i.e., they have a difficult time letting go of an emotion or feeling)
Repeating the wrong answer each time a certain question is asked
Socially inappropriate behavior
Off-target verbosity (see Chapter 13 for a detailed description)
Bossing people around
Inappropriate laughter

Here is a list of behaviors commonly seen in medical settings, such as skilled nursing facilities, which are indicative of frontal lobe impairment and inhibitory deficits:

Difficulty not crossing legs after a total hip replacement

Not waiting for all the instructions in a physical or occupational therapy session before doing some behavior

Shoveling food after having a stroke that impairs swallowing ability

Not cutting up food in small enough pieces after having a stroke that impairs swallowing ability

Getting up with no one around or without device, even though they are at great risk of falling

Bending over to pick something up even though they don't have the strength to get back up

Hurrying to the bathroom

Inappropriate sexual behavior

Many of the cognitive-enhancement activities described in Chapter 12 were specifically designed to exercise people's ability to inhibit and thus pay attention and make new memories. Enhancing older adults' inhibitory abilities should also mitigate some of the above behavioral problems. In addition, research has shown that when people process information at a deeper level by thinking about the meaning of a word, they activate more of their frontal lobes, which is associated with a greater likelihood of remembering the information in the future. A similar effect probably takes place whenever people think about information they want to remember at a deeper level or use a mnemonic technique. It appears that this may be a skill that older adults can learn.

Logan et al. (2002) asked young and older adults to remember a list of words while their brains were being imaged with a functional magnetic resonance imaging machine (fMRI). Some people were simply asked to use whatever strategy they wanted to help them remember the words. Others were required to determine whether each word was concrete (e.g., table or tree) or abstract (e.g., love or faith). When people used whatever strategy they wanted, the researchers reported that the younger adults remembered more words than the older adults. However, when people had to make a judgment about the word, there was not a statistically significant difference between the younger and older adults. Moreover, the researchers found that the older adults activated more of their frontal lobes when they made the judgments about the words. This is an exciting finding because it shows that older adults possess a great deal of neuroplasticity (e.g., the capacity to reorganize their brain circuitry). In addition, this finding shows us that older adults can recruit more frontal lobe activation and thereby improve cognitive performance.

TEMPORAL LOBE FUNCTIONS

The temporal lobes are important in auditory perceptions. As previously mentioned, the left hemisphere is involved in language perception for most people. The left temporal lobe handles functions such as understanding what people are saying and producing speech. The right temporal lobe is more involved in perceiving emotion in speech, music, and auditory pitch. The temporal lobe also handles functions such as knowing what objects are called and perceiving and remembering faces. Structures deep within the temporal lobe process new memories (i.e., the hippocampus) and emotions (i.e., the amygdala).

PARIETAL LOBE FUNCTIONS

The parietal lobes were once known as the *association cortex,* because they are where senses such as vision, touch, balance, and sound meet and combine, which allows us to perceive the world as a unitary experience, even though different areas of the brain initially receive and process the sensory inputs. The parietal lobe also contains the part of the brain that is responsible for processing tactile sensory inputs and pain.

OCCIPITAL LOBE FUNCTIONS

The occipital lobe is in the back of the brain and it primarily handles visual inputs. I remember discussing the occipital lobe in a graduate school class and a wisecracking student asked, "If the lobe in the front of the brain is called the frontal lobe, why didn't they name the lobe at the back of the brain the *backal lobe*?" I agree with that student, it would be easier to remember if they had called it the backal lobe.

The occipital lobe receives most of the inputs coming from our eyes. After the signals reach the back of the occipital lobe, they go to different areas of that lobe to undergo further processing. Part of the occipital lobe handles color processing. Another part of the occipital lobe processes motion. And a different area helps us remember what objects are (that part overlaps with the temporal lobe). It is interesting to note that if someone damages one of the above parts of the occipital lobe, they may lose the ability to perceive a part of their world. For example, people who have damaged the part of the occipital lobe that processes color may develop cerebral achromatopsia, which is an inability to see any color. If they damage the part of the occipital lobe that processes motion in our visual world, then they may stop seeing motion and instead see the world in a series of still images. Both of these conditions are rare, but they highlight two important principles of the brain. First, we need all of our brain. It is not true that we only use a small percentage of our brain. If part of the brain is damaged, we will usually see some behavioral or cognitive loss. Second, different parts of the brain have different roles; if a certain part is damaged, then the specific loss of function will be predictable.

ASK THE MEMORY DOCTOR

I hear people talk about left brain and right brain tasks. Are the two sides of the brain really that different?

The idea that some people are left-brained, while others are right-brained, has in my opinion, been dramatically overstated. There are actually over one million fibers connecting the left and right hemispheres and allowing them to rapidly communicate. However, the left and right sides of your brain are responsible for different tasks. With the exception of about 1% of the population, most of us process language in the left hemisphere, whereas the right hemisphere processes spatial ability. This is important knowledge if you are working with someone who has recently had a stroke or other type of brain injury. Given that the left side of the body is controlled by the right side of the brain, and vice versa, you can gain insight into which hemisphere was damaged by looking at which side of the body is most affected by the brain injury. For example, if you see that someone has right-side motor deficits, you can conclude that the left side of the brain was damaged. And, depending on the severity and location of the damage, you might also expect to see language problems. Another interesting trend is that people who have damage to their left hemisphere are more likely to become depressed, whereas damage to the right hemisphere is not associated with depression and is sometimes associated with a complete lack of awareness that anything is wrong. There is a useful mnemonic or memory trick that can help you remember this information. Left begins with L and so does language and laughter. If the left side of the brain is damaged, then the ability to use language and laugh may also be impaired.

HIPPOCAMPUS

There probably isn't a single area of the brain that is involved in making new memories, but there is now almost universal consensus among neuroscientists that the hippocampus is heavily involved in allowing us to encode or make new memories. We have two hippocampi: one on the left side of the brain and the other on the right side. They reside fairly deep within our temporal lobes.

We became aware of the importance of hippocampi in forming new memories after a patient (known by the pseudonym H. M.; see Chapter 2) had most of his hippocampal regions removed to control his intractable and worsening epilepsy, which had been attributed to a bicycle accident at age 9. H. M.'s hippocampi were removed in a neurosurgical operation in 1953, when he was in his late 20s. Fortunately, the surgery improved his epilepsy to a manageable degree;

unfortunately, it prevented H. M. from forming new declarative (i.e., knowledge-based or autobiographical) memories. It appears that the hippocampi are needed to make new memories, but they are less involved in older memories. Although H. M. experienced some loss of memory before the surgery (as retrograde amnesia), he generally retained the information and autobiographical memories he had before the surgery. It is as if the hippocampi become less important in keeping memories around after they have been consolidated or cemented into place.

We also learned from H. M. and other people who have experienced damaged to their hippocampi that the hippocampi are involved with some spatial memory tasks. An intriguing example of the importance of the hippocampi in helping us remember our spatial environment comes from a well-publicized study of London taxi cab drivers. Maguire, Gadian, Johnsrude, Good, Ashburner, Frackowiak, et al. (2000) reported that part of London taxi cab drivers' hippocampi were larger. The posterior or back part of the hippocampi were larger in the cabbies as compared with a control group; this area of the hippocampus appears to be involved in spatial learning. Apparently, learning the intricate maze of streets in London, which can take up to three years of studying at a local taxi school (with a 75% dropout rate), requires encoding an incredible number of spatial memories. Apparently, all this spatial learning is associated with the increased size of their posterior hippocampi. It turns out that our brains, and especially our hippocampi, are quite malleable and change based on experience. In other words, our brains possess a great degree of *neuroplasticity*, which means that the structure of our brains changes as a consequence of thinking and experience. Moreover, it appears that we retain this neuroplasticity well into older adulthood.

A powerful example of the neuroplasticity of older adult brains is the fact that they can grow new neurons in some parts of the brain. Eriksson et al. (1998) rocked the field of neuroscience when they reported that they had conclusively shown that older adults grow new neurons. Although the creation of new neurons, known as neurogenesis, doesn't occur everywhere in the brain, it does occur in the hippocampi! This is exciting news and demonstrates that older adults can rewire their brains, make new connections, and even grow new neurons.

It appears that the health and size of the hippocampal regions are important in predicting the likelihood of developing Alzheimer's disease. Heijer, Geerlings, Hoebeck, Hofman, Koudstaal, and Breteler (2006) looked at the brains of over 500 older adults, who were free of dementia, using brain-imaging equipment. They measured the size of people's hippocampi and tracked the participants for approximately six years, in order to see who developed dementia. They reported that the size of people's hippocampi at the beginning of the study was a very good predictor of who ultimately developed dementia. People with smaller hippocampi were significantly more likely to develop dementia.

Wouldn't it be nice if we could make our hippocampi larger? Wait, we *can* grow new neurons in that part of the brain. This is exciting news; the size of the hippocampal regions predicts dementia and older (and middle-aged) adults can grow new neurons there. Presumably, many of the activities described in this book would facilitate that process.

Ask the Memory Doctor:
   My dad experiences hearing loss and he won't get a hearing aid. Could his hearing problems be associated with his memory difficulties?

Hearing problems are common among older adults, even relatively young older adults. Thirty percent of people between the ages of 65 and 75 have significant hearing impairment. Not surprisingly, as we get older, we are more likely to experience hearing problems (see Figure 2).

   We know that there is a strong association between hearing impairment and cognitive functioning (e.g., see Baltes & Lindenberger, 1997). As hearing impairment worsens, so does cognitive ability. That could be due to general atrophy of the central nervous system or it could also be due to other mechanisms, such as a lack of cognitive stimulation. Certainly hearing impairment prevents people from following conversations or information that is only presented auditorily. If people are not able to hear what is being said, then we can't expect them to

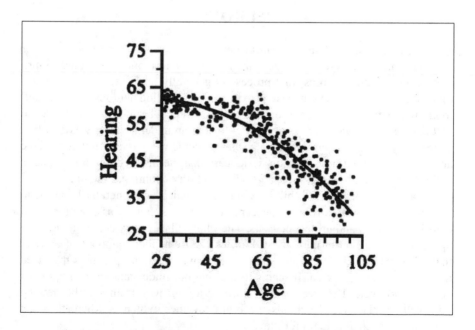

Figure 2. Baltes and Lindenberger (1997). Published by American Psychological Association (APA). Reprinted with permission from the APA.

remember that information. But the next question is Can hearing impairment negatively affect overall cognitive ability? Although the research is somewhat mixed and difficult to conduct, it is reasonable to assume that many people with significant hearing impairment are going to get less cognitive stimulation because they are going to be less engaged in conversations and less likely to seek out certain types of social situations that are conversation-dependent or occur in environments that have a lot of background noise. In addition, recent research has shown that older adults with hearing impairments may use more of their cognitive resources to figure out what others are saying, given that they might not hear everything that is being said. The reduction in available cognitive resources (i.e., working-memory capacity) might further impair their ability to attend to and remember information. Would a hearing aid help people improve their memory ability? People's ability to remember auditory information and perform well on cognitive tests increases if their hearing is improved with a hearing aid, and I would strongly encourage people with hearing impairment to consider getting (and using) a hearing aid, especially if they are noticing worsening memory ability. Moreover, I would encourage them to get a hearing aid sooner rather than later, as it will become more difficult to improve cognitive ability if it worsens too much.

NEURONS

Neurons are the cells in the central nervous system that are responsible for communicating. They release neurotransmitters and hormones, which are in turn picked up by other neurons; that process is generally how information is communicated in the brain. We have approximately 100 billion neurons. It is difficult to know exactly how many neurons the average human brain has. I think I recall that the correct answer on my psychology test as an undergraduate was 1 billion neurons, by the time I was in graduate school people were asserting that we have about 10 billion neurons, and now it appears that the most common estimate is 100 billion neurons—I guess it is a growing industry counting these things.

We also have at least 100 billion glial cells, which are generally believed to play a more supportive role in the central nervous system. For example, glial cells help nourish and protect neurons. The glial cells are very active in cleaning up debris in the central nervous system, as the tremendous amount of activity that takes place in the brain and spinal cord leaves many by-products that need to be removed or recycled. It seems to me that our understanding of glial cells is still incomplete. However, we have come a long way from simply viewing glial cells as the glue that holds the brain together, which is where they get their names, as glial is Latin for glue.

There are many different types of neurons, and their shape and function are different in different parts of the brain. For example, neurons in the outer layer of the brain, known as the cortex, can branch and communicate with up to 20,000 other neurons. However, neurons in the spinal cord need significantly fewer connections to other cells. In Figure 3, you can see the major parts of the neuron.

Neurons receive most of their input and information from other cells on or near their dendrites. Neurotransmitters such as dopamine, serotonin, acetylcholine, epinephrine, gamma aminobutyric acid (GABA), and others will land at receptor sites on the dendrites. You can think of a receptor site as a boat slip where one would park their boat in a marina and the neurotransmitter would be the boat. Or another common analogy to explain neurotransmitters and receptor sites is the "key and lock analogy." The neurotransmitter is like a key and the receptor site on the dendrite is like the lock. This analogy is useful because it highlights how only certain neurotransmitters fit into certain receptor sites, just as only certain keys fit into certain locks.

Most neurotransmitters are excitatory and therefore tend to make neurons "fire" and send a burst of biochemical electricity down the axon. When the electricity reaches the axon terminal, the neuron will release its neurotransmitters (or sometimes hormones), which in turn may affect other neurons and continue the communication process.

At least one type of neurotransmitter, known as GABA, will make neurons less likely to fire or have what is known as an *action potential*. This GABA-induced inhibitory process is very important in the brain, as we must govern the brain's activity and sometimes prevent activity and us from doing certain things. Disorders such as anxiety may be related to a lack of GABA and inhibitory

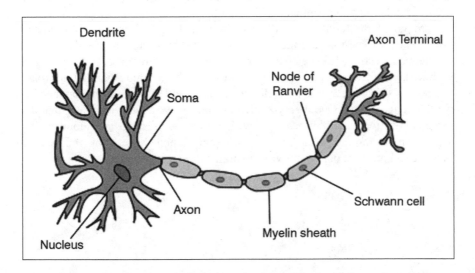

Figure 3. A neuron with its main parts labeled. Public domain image from Wikipedia http://en.wikipedia.org/wiki/Brain

action in some parts of the brain (i.e., the limbic system). Or at the very least, we know that when we give people a drug that mimics GABA's actions (e.g., diazepam), their anxiety symptoms usually decrease. Many drugs used to treat psychological disorders work by affecting the levels of neurotransmitters between the neurons (i.e., in the synaptic clefts). Other psychiatric drugs work because they either mimic a neurotransmitter (known as agonists) or block the action of a neurotransmitter (known as antagonists).

Another part of the neuron that is important in order to understand behavior and especially how our brains change with age is the myelin sheath. Myelin is composed mostly of fatty lipids, which cover most axons. Myelin also serves to insulate the axon as the electrochemical signal travels down it. Myelin makes the signal travel down the axon faster. Signals can travel down the axon at speeds of up to 270 miles per hour, if the myelin is thick enough. The thicker a person's myelin, the faster the signals will travel down the axons, which is usually a very good thing. If someone's brain signals are moving rapidly, that will probably help them think quicker and also help them be able to hold more information in their short-term memory, which is a major component of traditional intelligence tests. The thickness of our myelin increases during childhood (as does our short-term memory capacity) and then our myelin undergoes slow thinning throughout adulthood. As the myelin thins, our reaction times increase (i.e., we become a little slower) and our short-term memory capacity decreases. Some diseases, such as multiple sclerosis, are characterized by abnormal demyelination. A very interesting hypothesis that is discussed in Chapter 5 is that omega-3 fatty acids may be associated with memory and mood benefits because they are involved in helping to maintain healthy myelin.

Throughout this book, we will talk about making new connections in the brain. Much of learning and memory is really just about making new and more efficient connections between our neurons. Neurons will die or become damaged with many of the neurodegenerative diseases associated with aging (e.g., Alzheimer's disease, Parkinson's disease); many will also die or be damaged if we live long enough. One theory known as the *reserve hypothesis* states that the more connections and abilities we have, the more we can lose without having a problem. In the next chapter, we will expand upon these ideas and discuss how we can increase our cognitive (and brain) reserves.

CHAPTER 4

Use It or Lose It:
The Survival of the Busiest Minds

Anyone who stops learning is old, whether at twenty or eighty. Anyone who keeps learning stays young. The greatest thing in life is to keep your mind young. Henry Ford (1863–1947)

USE IT OR LOSE IT

There are many parallels between good physical health and good cognitive health. First of all, they both abide by the "Use It or Lose It" principle. Everyone wants to have good physical health and everyone wants to have a good memory. But from a practical standpoint, just as it is difficult for most people to start and maintain an exercise program, it is often very difficult to start and maintain an effective cognitive exercise program. Previous memory programs have had limited success because they don't have enough depth and breadth to make them interesting and challenging for the long haul. In order to take full advantage of what scientists are learning about the brain and memory, people need to make lifestyle changes. We will discuss such changes at the end of this chapter, but first let's look at the evidence that supports the Use It or Lose It theory of memory and aging.

EVIDENCE SUPPORTING THE USE IT
OR LOSE IT THEORY

One of the first clues that the likelihood of developing Alzheimer's disease might be related to the type of mental activity people engaged in was the finding that people who had more education were less likely to develop the disease. Or at the very least, the symptoms of memory loss were delayed among people with more education (e.g., see Stern, Alexander, & Mayeux, 1992).[1] It is important to note that education, or other cognitively stimulating activities, probably don't

---

[1] There are alternative explanations for the finding that education is inversely associated with the likelihood of showing symptoms of Alzheimer's disease. It may be that people with lower levels of education perform more poorly on tests designed to assess dementia and thus are more likely to be classified as having a memory problem.

prevent Alzheimer's disease, as the onset of the disease (i.e., the malfunction and death of certain types of neurons in the brain) is probably independent of education. However, research indicates that increased education provides people with a "mental reserve" that takes longer to deplete before people begin showing signs of dementia (i.e., an inability to make new memories).

Another line of evidence supporting the Use It or Lose It notion, is that people who have led more cognitively stimulating careers appear to be less likely to have memory problems. A number of studies (e.g., Qiu, Karp, Strauss, Winblad, Fratiglioni, & Bellander, 2003; Stern, Gurland, Tatemichi, Tang, Wilder, & Mayeux, 1994) have generally found that blue collar workers, especially those involved in manufacturing, are more likely to develop Alzheimer's disease and other types of dementia. We cannot conclusively say that less stimulating jobs *cause* dementia. It may be that white-collar workers are less likely to be exposed to toxins that cause brain damage, or they may be less likely to heavily drink and smoke. With that said, the occupational attainment findings are consistent with other observations about the Use It or Lose It theory.

Possibly the most promising findings and recommendations for people concerned about memory loss come from studies that have found a relationship between the number of cognitively stimulating leisure activities people engage in and the likelihood of developing memory problems. People who report engaging in a greater number of mentally stimulating activities are less likely to develop dementia, as compared with their less active counterparts. For example, Wilson and his colleagues published a paper in the *Journal of the American Medical Association*, that included the findings of a four-and-a-half year study. Wilson et al. (2002) surveyed 801 Catholic nuns, clergy, and brothers about the frequency in which they engaged in a number of activities, including listening to the radio, reading newspapers, reading magazines, reading books, playing games (e.g., cards, checkers, crosswords), or going to museums. At the initial assessment, none of the study participants were classified as having dementia. After approximately four-and-a-half years, the participants were reassessed to determine who developed Alzheimer's disease. Unfortunately, 111 of the original 801 people were classified as having developed possible or probable Alzheimer's disease. The researchers wanted to know whether there was a difference between the people who developed Alzheimer's and those who didn't, in terms of the number of cognitively stimulating activities they initially reported doing. Wilson et al. found that the 10% of people who did the greatest number of cognitively stimulating activities were 47% less likely to develop Alzheimer's, compared with the 10% of people who did the fewest.

The results of Wilson et al.'s study are very compelling, especially since they can be used to make practical recommendations to people who are concerned about memory loss. The findings clearly suggest that a more engaging mental life might delay or prevent the dreaded Alzheimer's diagnosis. However, some people have questioned what this study really means. For example, Alzheimer's disease has a very long course. It may be up to 20 years from the time neurons begin dying because of Alzheimer's disease and ultimate death. It may be 10 years from the time an M. D. utters the words "possible Alzheimer's" and ultimate death. Therefore, it may be that some of the people in Wilson's study were actually experiencing subtle effects of the disease at the beginning of the four-and-a-half year study, even though the disease was not detected or diagnosed. It is likely that those participants who had undetected or preclinical Alzheimer's at the beginning of the study were already reducing their cognitive activity level due to their subtle memory problems. Or in other words, it is possible that reduced activity is an early sign of Alzheimer's disease.

Many of the limitations in the above study were overcome when Verghese and his colleagues conducted a study that followed the same older adults for 21 years, from approximately 1980 to 2001. One of the stated purposes of this study was to determine if stimulating activities lower the risk for dementia or if early-stage memory problems lead to reduced participation in stimulating mental activities. By following people for a longer period of time, we are better able to determine whether the lack of cognitive stimulation leads to memory loss or if the lack of cognitive stimulation is the result of memory loss. The researchers repeatedly assessed the frequency with which people read, wrote, did word games, played musical instruments, or participated in organized discussions. After 21 years, some of the original participants developed various types of dementia. Alzheimer's was the most common type of dementia, followed by vascular dementia, which is caused by strokes. The relationship between the number of activities and the likelihood of developing dementia was striking. The people who were in the top 33%, in terms of engaging in the most cognitively stimulating activities, were 63% less likely to develop dementia, as compared with the bottom 33%. I have never seen any intervention, drug, or behavior that could reduce the likelihood of developing dementia by a whopping 63%. In fact, for each additional activity someone did each week, over the course of the study, they were 7% less likely to develop dementia. In a similar study, other researchers found a 12% reduction in the likelihood of developing dementia for each additional cognitively stimulating activity someone did on a weekly basis. Clearly, those who want to prevent memory loss should take notice of these dramatic results.

How is the Use It or Lose It Theory Related to the Idea of Cognitive Reserve?

The "Cognitive Reserve" hypothesis is similar to the Use It or Lose It theory and simply suggests that the more you have, the more you can lose without having a memory or cognition problem. For example, people who have developed more of a mental reserve through education, mentally challenging careers, or other cognitively stimulating activities can sustain more brain damage (either from Alzheimer's-related degeneration or from a more acute brain injury) without showing severe losses in memory and mental functioning (see Katzman, Aronson, Fuld, Kawas, Brown, Morgenstern, et al., 1989). However, the opposite also appears to be true, such that people who led less cognitively stimulating lives showed greater cognitive deficits than one would expect given their brain damage.

Support for the Cognitive Reserve theory comes from the fact that either overall brain size or the size of the hippocampus predicts which people with mild cognitive impairment will remain stable and which will develop Alzheimer's disease (see Chapter 3 for more information about the hippocampus and what happens if it is damaged). Researchers predicted which patients would develop Alzheimer's disease with 70% accuracy when using the size of the hippocampus, and their accuracy rate was 62% when using overall brain volume (Erten-Lyons et al., 2006).

In another study, Heijer et al. (2006) found that older adults who ultimately develop dementia had hippocampal regions that were significantly smaller. In fact, the researchers were able to predict which cognitively healthy older adults would develop dementia over a 6-year period by measuring the size of the hippocampus and nearby structures. These findings regarding the size of the brain or various neurological structures are consistent with the Reserve hypothesis—apparently the more you have, the more you can lose without having problems.[2]

Why would having more education, a larger brain, or a more cognitively challenging occupation be associated with a reduced likelihood of developing memory problems? It has been suggested that education and cognitive activities lead to more neurons and, more importantly, a greater number of connections among one's neurons. Presumably, the more neurons one has, the more they can lose and not show signs of memory problems. Increased synapses or connections among neurons are made when people learn new things and challenge themselves. Those increased synaptic connections provide redundant pathways that can allow informational signals to travel in the brain, even when neurons are being damaged. It is analogous to having a number of ways to drive between two cities. If the main road is closed, then you can take one of the alternate routes. If the first alternate route is closed, you can take another road and still make it to your destination. Similarly, if a neuron dies (and they do die with Alzheimer's disease and other neurodegenerative diseases), the brain signal can still get the information through one of the alternate pathways, if there are enough

[2] Another interesting finding related to education and cognitive ability is that people with more education use different brain regions when engaging in a cognitive task. To further complicate matters, education leads to different brain activity in younger and older adults. Springer, McIntosh, Winocur, and Grady (2005) reported that "in young adults, education was negatively correlated with frontal [lobe] activity, whereas in older adults, education was positively correlated with frontal [lobe] activity" (p. 181). Thus, it appears that more educated older adults are compensating for normal age-related impairment by efficiently recruiting more brain resources.

redundancies. If that alternate pathway is closed because another neuron dies, you can still get the brain signal through another route, if there *is* another alternate route. People who have led less stimulating lives may not have as many alternate pathways to use when or if neurons begin dying.

An interesting observation related to cognitive reserve is that people who have more of a reserve experience a different series of mental symptoms if they develop Alzheimer's. Le Carret, Auriacombe, Letenneur, Bergua, Dartigues, and Fabrigoule (2005) reported that people with more education seem to keep their ability to pay attention and their ability to make new memories longer than one would expect, given severity of their disease process. For example, if you look at the brains of two people with similar Alzheimer's disease symptoms, one who had led a cognitively active life and the other who did not, you would see some striking differences. The more active person's brain would have more of the telltale signs of Alzheimer's diseases (e.g., neuritic plaques and tangles) than you would expect, given their memory and mental symptoms; whereas the less active person's brain would be much less damaged (i.e., fewer neuritic plaques and tangles), even though they were experiencing similar levels of memory impairment.

Apparently, people who have more education and led more stimulating lives have better developed the regions of the brain associated with paying attention. And paying attention is, in my opinion, the most important factor in maintaining good memory ability as we age. The best memory enhancement activities should exercise the attentional centers of the brain. The idea that people have different levels of cognitive reserve may also help explain why people who have led more stimulating lives *appear* to deteriorate faster once getting a diagnosis of Alzheimer's. People who start out with better mental abilities can rely upon their reserves longer, even though the brain is experiencing the ravaging effects of Alzheimer's disease or other types of dementia that slowly damage the brain. Similarly, the idea of cognitive reserve also explains why people with more education don't have the attention problems you would expect, given the state of their brain's deterioration.

100 BILLION NEURONS WITH UP TO 20,000 CONNECTIONS EACH

It may be more important to have a large number of connections between neurons (i.e., synapses) than it is to have a large number of neurons. In fact, we probably had more neurons as newborns than we do now. But with experience and learning, we have made new connections among our neurons. Such interconnectivity may be behind many of the findings that support the idea of Cognitive Reserve.

Dr. Mortimer from the University of South Florida summarized the findings from a recent study by stating that "larger brain size and more education provide extra reserve that allows one to function normally in the presence of a brain disease like Alzheimer's. . . . However, because education is a lifelong process, it is possible that elderly people can delay or even prevent the onset of dementia by keeping their brains active" (Delotto-Baier, 2003).

It appears that people who are intelligent, have more education, or have a large brain, have a reserve that delays the onset of dementia-like symptoms. But it may also be that people can develop a reserve later in life by engaging in stimulating cognitive activities. Or in other words, they can *prehabilitate* their cognitive abilities by exercising their brain and memory.

We conducted a study at Western Oregon University to assess whether older adults who lived in assisted living facilities could benefit from intensive cognitive stimulation (see Winningham et al., 2003). We were aware of previous research findings that showed how people who did the greatest number of cognitively stimulating activities were least likely to develop memory problems later in life. But we wanted to know whether it was possible to increase people's ability to make new memories by intervening and exposing them to cognitively stimulating activities relatively late in life. The average age of our participants was 82 years, and most were residing in an assisted living environment because of some health issue.

We assessed memory and mental functioning of all participants. The group was then split into two. Half of them took part in a cognitive enhancement program, up to three times a week, for three months. The other half served as a control group and did not do anything different than they had been doing. After three months, everyone was tested again using similar tests. The results showed that the cognitive enhancement group increased their ability to make new memories. For example, they scored better on a comprehensive memory test that was designed to assess such things as remembering names, stories, where they put things, routes, and appointments. This was a very promising and optimistic finding because we learned that even people in their 80s can improve their ability to make new memories.

The participants in the cognitive enhancement group also scored higher on a test designed to measure their confidence in their own ability to make new memories. This was another exciting finding. Older adults need to believe they are capable of making new memories, otherwise they will not put the necessary effort and attention into making memories. In Chapter 14 we discuss ways to increase people's confidence and motivate them to make the necessary steps to improve their quality of life.

A leading researcher on cognitive reserve recently wrote, "There is the possibility that directly enhancing CR [cognitive reserve] may help forestall the diagnosis of AD [Alzheimer's disease]" (Stern, 2006, p. S69). In Chapter 12 we will discuss how to develop a memory enhancement program that is based on stimulating older adults' brains and increasing their cognitive reserve. However, one doesn't necessarily need a professionally developed cognitive enhancement program, rather a change in lifestyle and attitude may bring many of the benefits associated with the principles of Use It or Lose It and cognitive reserve, especially for those who are not experiencing significant declines in memory ability. It may be possible to delay memory problems by simply trying new things, learning new skills, and seeking out new experiences. Such activities would certainly make new and more efficient connections among existing neurons and would probably lead to the creation of many new neurons in the brain's hippocampus.

I believe that people should have access to high-quality cognitive enhancement programs, especially if they are living in an institutionalized setting or have significant physical or mobility problems. Although more independent and capable older adults can certainly benefit from an appropriate cognitive enhancement class, I believe they should strive toward living more active and *novel* lives. If at all possible, the younger retirees should take advantage of the Use It or Lose It and cognitive reserve principles by learning about new things and having unique experiences. Independent older adults will be better able to maximize their level of cognitive stimulation if they are doing things that are inherently interesting and worthwhile.

For example, independent older adults can start second careers, take college-level classes, or develop new skills and interests. Such pursuits will be more self-sustaining than trying to engage in prepared paper and pencil mental stimulation activities. For example, a recently retired couple could take Spanish 101 at a local community college for a semester, then take a trip to Mexico or Spain for two weeks, where they try to immerse themselves in the language and culture. Such experiences could dramatically enhance cognitive reserve. The retirees would enhance their verbal abilities and attentional resources, which should prevent future memory problems. "The enemy of mental vitality isn't growing older. The real enemy is the passivity that tends to creep up on us as we age. The fight is not with age—it is with boredom, with routine, with humdrum" (Chernow, 1997, p. 202).

In order to maximize cognitive reserve, it is important to seek novel experiences, which can increase the connections among neurons (i.e., synaptic density) and even create new neurons in the hippocampi. And recall that the larger your hippocampi, the less likely you are to show signs of dementia. There are numerous examples of novel activities that would facilitate better cognitive health: ordering new magazines, reading books in a different genre than you usually do, taking different routes to frequent destinations, or vacationing in new places. See Table 1 for a list of other cognitively stimulating activities that may make your life more interesting and also prevent future memory problems.

Table 1. 46 Cognitively Stimulating Activities that
Middle-Aged and Older Adults Can Do To Maximize
Cognitive Stimulation

Maximize Cognitive Stimulation

1. Read a book
2. Subscribe to a newspaper
3. Do crossword puzzles and other word games
4. Take a class at a senior center
5. Join a club or other organization
6. Visit with friends
7. Take a class at a community college
8. Go to a sporting event
9. Try to develop a new hobby
10. Attend community events
11. Go to a different grocery store
12. Take a trip to a new place
13. Go dancing or take a dance class
14. Begin using e-mail or a new Internet browser
15. Volunteer
16. Write a letter
17. Join a book club
18. Study a foreign language
19. Get a part time job
20. Garden (become a master gardener)
21. Read new magazines
22. Listen to the radio
23. Play (new?) board games
24. Visit museums
25. Elderhostel
26. Try using the bus
27. Cook new recipes
28. Sew
29. Join a chorus or local orchestra
30. Buy furniture that needs assembly
31. Get involved in politics
32. Program your VCR and other electronic devices
33. Learn to juggle
34. Begin journaling
35. Complete jigsaw puzzles
36. Join a Toastmasters public speaking group
37. Attend medical lectures at hospitals
38. Do counted cross-stitch embroidery
39. Try using the self-scan checkout at the grocery store
40. Participate in a play
41. Do jigsaw puzzles
42. Volunteer at a church (e.g., teach Sunday school classes or organize volunteer efforts)
43. Subscribe to daily e-mails (e.g., word of the day or health tip of the day)
44. Play Sudoku
45. Complete word-finds
46. Solve anagrams (jumbled word) puzzles

Ask the Memory Doctor:
Would watching television be considered a cognitively stimulating activity?

Most of the time, when people watch television they are not actively engaged in the process, as it is by nature a passive activity. Therefore, watching television is probably not a cognitively stimulating activity. Watching television may even be a risk factor for developing attention and memory problems. I am not aware of any studies that have looked at middle-aged or older adults and the effects of television on their cognitive abilities. However, we do know that children who watch television are much more likely to develop Attention Deficit Hyperactivity Disorder. One study found that for each hour of television children watched on a daily basis, their risk of being diagnosed with Attention Deficit Hyperactivity Disorder increased by 10% (Christakis, Zimmerman, DiGiuseppe, & McCarty, 2004). The brain processes involved in Attention Deficit Hyperactivity Disorder are very similar to those involved in normal age-related memory impairment. Regardless of age, if someone is unable to concentrate on what they are trying to learn, then they may not ever form a new memory.

But research on children suggests that some television may actually benefit cognitive ability. And I know many older adults claim that some of the game shows challenge their memories. I would also add that if people change how they watch television then it might have some benefits. For example, people can watch a television show together and then discuss what they just saw. Or people could try to write a summary of the show after it is over. Or they could try to remember a certain number of facts while watching a nonfiction show.

CHAPTER 5

Nutrition

Food for thought: An apple a day keeps the doctor away (and maybe Alzheimer's too).

This chapter will look at recent research that suggests certain types of foods and possibly supplements can improve memory ability in adults. Nutrition is an important lifestyle factor that affects cardiovascular health, the chance of getting diabetes, and the likelihood of developing clinical depression. But nutrition also affects our memory ability and our chance of being diagnosed with Alzheimer's or other types of dementia. This chapter includes information about antioxidants, omega-3 fatty acids, and nutritional supplements.

The section on antioxidants will expose the reader to the idea that certain foods can prevent damage to our cells and particularly to our neurons, which are essential in making, storing, and retrieving memories. By understanding that certain foods may help keep neurons healthy and alive, people should be more motivated to improve their diet. I will also discuss research that suggest diets high in omega-3 fatty acids might decrease the chance of developing Alzheimer's. Foods high in omega-3, such as fish, nuts, and olive oil, may also keep our neurons healthy. The reader will learn more about neurons, specifically the natural process of thinning that occurs in the fatty insulation on our neurons. When this insulation, called the myelin sheath, gets thin, the individual's brain will not process information as quickly or efficiently.

This chapter will also contain information, some of it contradictory, about supplements and their effects. This information is provided so the reader can make more informed decisions and better understand the plethora of nutritional information and advice that we are being exposed to. There will be a short section on diabetes and memory. Finally, the reader will be given lists of foods that are high in omega-3 fatty acids and antioxidants.

In the previous chapter, there was compelling information about how increasing our cognitive reserves will allow us to lose synaptic connections among our neurons or even entire neurons without noticing a cognitive deficit. In addition to increasing our reserves by participating in cognitively stimulating activities, we can also protect our neurons and other cells through good nutrition. In this chapter we will explore how our diet affects our ability to think.

Nutrition is another important lifestyle factor that not only affects our cardio-vascular health, our chance of getting diabetes or cancer, and the likelihood of developing clinical depression, but it also affects our memory ability and our chance of being diagnosed with Alzheimer's or other types of dementia. In fact, due to changes in absorption and metabolism, it is thought that older adults constitute the largest population who are at risk for nutritional deficiencies. This chapter will include information about antioxidants, omega-3 fatty acids, nutritional supplements, diabetes, and obesity.

Before we continue, it should be noted that it is often very difficult to *prove* that certain nutritional deficiencies are *causing* memory problems. For example, cognitive impairment might affect people's diets, thereby making it difficult to determine what's going on when we see that people with dementia have certain nutritional deficiencies. People who eat well probably also engage in other behaviors that promote good health and better memory functioning (e.g., physical exercise). In addition, advanced age or an institutional living environment may affect people's diets *and* cognitive ability. Moreover, when people have poor nutrition, they often are lacking numerous dietary requirements, which makes it difficult to determine which nutritional deficiencies are causing the memory problems. And it is known that supplements are often not as effective as getting one's nutrients from food. With all these possible limitations in mind, some trends seem to be emerging from the research, and I think we are in a position to make some dietary recommendations for those interested in maximal brain health.

WHAT ARE ANTIOXIDANTS?

Over time, many of our neurons die or become damaged. If enough neurons are damaged or killed, we would expect to see deficits in thinking and memory ability. In fact, Alzheimer's and Parkinson's diseases are both examples of neurodegenerative diseases that damage neurons, which leads to cognitive deficits. It therefore makes sense that we want to prevent our neurons from being damaged and thereby prevent cognitive impairment. And antioxidants can prevent damage to our cells, including our neurons.

Our bodies are constantly exposed to harmful molecules called free radicals. These free radicals come from the environment as well as our own bodies. A free radical is any molecule that has a single unpaired electron in an outer shell. These molecules are very unstable because they may take an electron from a molecule in a living cell, which may cause the molecule that was just robbed to steal from another molecule, leading to a potentially dangerous chain reaction. In addition, there may be a secondary process that damages our brain cells through inflammation. Over time, damage from free radicals can cause our cells to function abnormally or die. The same process also causes iron to rust, peeled apples to turn brown, and cooking oils to become rancid. In fact, one theory of why we age suggests that the cumulative damage from free radicals causes our bodies to deteriorate and wear out. Some theorists believe that aging processes are largely driven by damage from free radicals. The theory would suggest that the longer we live, the more damage our cells sustain from the insidious free radicals. Regardless of whether free radical damage is the primary cause of aging processes, it is probably the case that free radicals are a factor in aging and may be associated with conditions such as cancer, arthritis, athero-sclerosis, and diabetes. Antioxidants, such as vitamins A, C, and E, may counter-act the effects of free radicals by absorbing them.

We know that diets high in antioxidant foods such as fruits and vegetables are associated with a lower risk for cancer, heart disease, stroke, cataracts, Parkinson's disease, and arthritis. There are also strong associations between antioxidants and the likelihood of developing Alzheimer's or other memory problems. Researchers have looked at blood serum levels of various antioxidants to see whether those levels are related to memory ability. A number of studies have found that vitamins E, C, and beta-carotene levels were lower in people with Alzheimer's. Another study found that vitamins C and E were associated with reduced dementia after strokes but not reduced Alzheimer's. However, another study found that vitamin C and E supplements might actually slow the progress of Alzheimer's. Researchers have also found that dietary supplements from fruit and vegetable extracts slowed age-related declines in neuronal and cognitive function in rats. Another study found that dogs experienced less cognitive decline when fed food that has been fortified with antioxidants.

But not all researchers have found that antioxidants help memory and prevent dementia. Moreover, a study published in 2007 found that taking supplements containing beta-carotene, vitamin A, and vitamin E, either alone or in com-bination, actually reduces one's life expectancy. The researchers combined data from 68 published studies, with almost 250,000 participants. All of the studies were designed to assess the effects of supplements on mortality. Surprisingly, the researchers reported that "Beta carotene, vitamin A, and vitamin E given singly or combined with other antioxidant supplements increase mortality" (Bjelakovic, Nikolova, Gluud, Simonetti, & Gluud, 2007, p. 848). This study was published in the *Journal of the American Medical Association*.

These disparate findings are frustrating and leave the health-conscious person bewildered, but researchers will continue to try to figure out the relationship between antioxidants, mental functioning, and the effects of supplements on overall functioning. In the meantime, it is my opinion that we should try to increase our intake of fruits and vegetables that are high in antioxidants. I don't advocate taking mega doses of vitamins, as that may cause damage to other bodily systems. On the whole, it appears that the research findings do not sup-port the use of antioxidant supplements such as vitamins A, C, and E (but that consensus can, and probably will, be modified as more is learned). With all that said, it does appear that getting antioxidants from food sources is highly advisable. Some of the food that are highest in antioxidants include prunes, raisins, berries, spinach, brussels sprouts, and grapes.

GOOD FAT VS. BAD FAT

Omega-3 fatty acids are another important nutritional factor that may affect the likelihood of developing dementia. To date, only a handful of studies have looked at the relationship between dementia and consuming either fish or omega-3 fatty acid supplements. In a recent review of the literature, researchers found that four out of five studies supported the idea that omega-3 fatty acids decrease the chance of getting dementia (Issa et al., 2006). In fact, one study found that people who had early- or mid-stage dementia experienced improved cognition when their omega-3 consumption increased. In addition to these studies, work with animals has shown that diets high in omega-3 fatty acids are associated with better learning and memory and a number of positive physiological changes to the brain. For example, animals fed diets high in omega-3s have been shown to have increased levels of neurotransmitters, more growth in the hippocampus (the part of the brain needed to make new memories), and less damaged neurons. It appears that people in developed countries are getting too much bad fat (i.e., omega-6 fatty acids) and not enough good fat (omega-3 fatty acids). The average person in North America has a bad fat to good fat ratio of approximately 10:1, and nutrition experts recommend having a 4:1 ratio. Apparently, we are consuming two to three times more bad fat relative to good fat than we should be. This is problematic because fatty lipids are absolutely necessary for proper functioning of our cells, particularly our neurons. Moreover, our bodies may not be able to efficiently utilize as much of the good fat it consumes if there are also high levels of bad fat in our diet.

In one of the most compelling human studies on omega-3 fatty acids and memory, researchers simply looked at self-reported fish consumption and the likelihood of developing Alzheimer's (Morris et al., 2003). The researchers looked at thousands of older adults and found that people who ate fish at least once a week were 60% less likely to be diagnosed with Alzheimer's. And the people who ate more fish than 80% of the other study participants were 70% less likely to get Alzheimer's. Moreover, it appears that the effects of omega-3 consumption on the likelihood of having cognitive problems are dose-dependent. In other words, it appears that people are getting more of a protective effect as the consumption of omega-3 fatty acids increases.

Further support for the role of omega-3 fatty acids in preventing dementia comes from observing the fatty acid levels of people with various types of dementia. Researchers have found that people who have Alzheimer's, other types of dementia, or cognitive impairment that isn't bad enough to be diagnosed as dementia all had lower levels of omega-3 fatty acids in their blood plasma as compared with people of similar ages who didn't have memory problems. In addition, results from animal studies have found that a diet high in omega-3 fatty acids can reduce some of the telltale signs of Alzheimer's disease in the brains of rats by more than 70%.

We are unsure of the exact mechanisms involved in the protective effects that omega-3 fatty acids appear to have on the brain. Moreover, many of the studies did not directly manipulate how much omega-3 fatty acids people consumed. Therefore, we can't conclude, with 100% confidence, that omega-3 fatty acids cause people to be less likely to develop dementia. We can't rule out that some unknown variable (e.g., socioeconomic status) is causing people to both have a higher level of omega-3 fatty acids and better memory ability. However, with all that said, I strongly recommend that people increase their omega-3 consumption and take advantage of its potential protective properties. I base this recommendation on the assumption that the risk of eating most types of fish is very minimal and the potential benefits of doing so are great (see the Ask the Memory Doctor box about mercury and fish). In addition, we know that omega-3 fatty acids can lead to more healthy cholesterol levels and a decreased number of depressive symptoms for people who have depression (see Chapter 7 for more information about omega-3 fatty acids and depression).

Ask the Memory Doctor:
I want to add more fish to my family's diet, but I am concerned about mercury and other pollutants. Won't the pollutants in fish cancel out any positive effects from the omega-3 fatty acids?

It is possible to develop mercury poisoning by eating too much fish, especially larger fish. However, for middle-aged and older adults, the health benefits of eating at least 12 ounces of fish per week far outweigh the risks. Children, pregnant women, and women considering having children should be more cautious and avoid certain types of fish. Larger fish generally have higher levels of methylmercury and other toxins. The toxins accumulate in fish as food moves up the food chain. The larger fish, such as shark, have the highest levels of mercury, because their diet is based on mercury-contaminated food and they generally live a long time. Some experts believe we may have gone too far in scaring people away from fish due to possible mercury poisoning. For example, recent research indicates that it may be more likely that children will have behavioral and learning problems if their mothers didn't get enough fish while they were pregnant. Another study showed that mothers who ate fish in the second trimester had children who were significantly more intelligent later on. Most older adults can certainly tolerate more than 12 ounces of the right kind of fish each week. Salmon, pollock, light tuna (not Albacore), and shrimp are relatively low in mercury and older adults can safely consume these fish several times a week. Here are some guidelines posted by the Environmental Protection Agency:

> By following these three recommendations for selecting and eating fish or shellfish, women and young children will receive the benefits of eating fish and shellfish and be confident that they have reduced their exposure to the harmful effects of mercury.

> 1. Do not eat shark, swordfish, king mackerel, or tilefish because they contain high levels of mercury.
> 2. Eat up to 12 ounces (two average meals) a week of a variety of fish and shellfish that are lower in mercury.
> 3. Check local advisories about the safety of fish caught by family and friends in your local lakes, rivers, and coastal areas. If no advice is available, eat up to six ounces (one average meal) per week of fish you catch from local waters, but don't consume any other fish during that week.

> Follow these same recommendations when feeding fish and shellfish to your young child, but serve smaller portions.

> From: http://www.epa.gov/waterscience/fishadvice/advice.html

FAT AND DEMENTIA

A group of Swedish researchers collected data from a large group of middle-aged and older adults regarding their fat consumption. The researchers assessed the participants' consumption of both polyunsaturated fats (including omega-3 fatty acids) and saturated fats (e.g., fat from butter, lard, coconut oil, cottonseed oil, and palm kernel oil, dairy products, and meat). The researchers followed the participants for 21 years to see whether there was a relationship between the type and amount of fat they consumed and their chance of developing dementia. The researchers reported that moderate consumption of polyunsaturated fat actually decreased the chance of getting dementia. On the other hand, saturated fat consumption was associated with an increased risk of developing dementia, especially for people who inherited the genes associated with an increased risk of developing Alzheimer's disease (i.e., ApoE- E4). This latter finding reminds me of the extra protective effect seen from physical exercise among those who are genetically at risk of developing Alzheimer's. Although it appears to be true for everyone, people who have an increased risk of developing Alzheimer's due to their genes, should take comfort from the fact that they can reduce the chance of developing Alzheimer's by exercising more and eating less bad fat and more good fat.

Why does the link exist between saturated fat consumption and increased dementia? According to Laitinen et al. (2006), there are a number of possible explanations. For example, it may be that eating saturated fats increases the chance of cardiovascular events (e.g., strokes or heart attacks), which could impair cognitive functioning. It is also possible that saturated fat or omega-6 fatty acids negatively affect the health of our cells, particularly our neurons (e.g., cell membranes, neuronal regeneration, and the efficiency with which new neuronal connections are made). Another possibility is that saturated or bad fat may be related to cell damage through oxidative stress (which is what we can limit by eating fruits and vegetables). Laitinen et al. also suggested that good fat or unsaturated fats may protect against inflammation; inflammation in the brain may increase the chance of developing dementia. Also, it could simply be that the good fats help our cells function better.

Can Blood Sugar Levels Affect Memory?

In addition to getting more good fat and antioxidants in our diet, we also need to be concerned about blood-glucose levels. We know that diabetes is a risk factor for dementia; therefore, researchers have begun looking at "pre-diabetes" or "impaired glucose tolerance." We now know that when blood-glucose levels are elevated, people's ability to make new memories decreases. The American Diabetes Association estimates that 41 million Americans have pre-diabetes, which appears to put them at risk for developing dementia even before they develop full-blown diabetes. Pre-diabetics have a slower glucose metabolism, which leads to elevated glucose levels and poorer memory functioning. The good news is that pre-diabetes is usually reversible through diet, exercise, and weight loss. Pre-diabetics can dramatically reduce both their risk of memory impairment and full-blown diabetes by reducing their weight, changing their diet, and exercising more. The American Diabetes Association recommends that everyone maintain a healthy diet in order to prevent diabetes. They recommend that people eat lots of fruits and vegetables, choose whole grain products whenever possible, eat fish two to three times per week, limit sugar-laden beverages, and watch portion sizes.

OBESITY AND CALORIC INTAKE

We know that in some studies, people who are obese or have diabetes are more than four times as likely to develop Alzheimer's disease. But the relationship between weight and dementia is complex and differs depending on age. According to a study conducted by Luchsinger, Patel, Tang, Schupf, and Mayeux (2007), people under the age of 76 who were very underweight were more likely to be diagnosed with probable Alzheimer's disease. However, after the age of 76, people with the largest waistlines were more likely to develop vascular dementia. Other studies have generally concurred with these findings.

We also know that being obese during one's midlife years increases the chance of developing dementia later in life. Whitmer, Sidney, Selby, Johnston, and Yaffe (2005) followed people over time and found that obese middle-aged adults had a 74% increased chance of developing dementia, while overweight people had a 35% increased chance of developing dementia as compared with those with a normal weight. The take-home message appears to be that people in the normal weight range for their height have a reduced chance of developing Alzheimer's disease or vascular dementia.

Clearly, if people want to reduce their chance of developing dementia, they should maintain a healthy weight and lifestyle while in their middle age and early older adulthood years. However, the trend of increasing obesity rates in every state of the union and in almost every demographic group is particularly concerning as we watch tens of millions of baby boomers enter their golden years. Not only are people who struggle with their weight more likely to develop dementia, but they are also more likely to have more than one health problem and a decreased quality of life. Hopefully, the above findings will motivate people to take the weight off and keep it off, especially for those who are already at an increased risk of developing dementia due to their genes.

Ask the Memory Doctor:
Should I be taking ginkgo biloba for my memory?

Probably the most widely purchased supplement to improve memory and cognition is ginkgo biloba. But does it work? Well, it depends. It depends on which study you are looking at, who is taking it, how much they are taking, what tests are used to measure its effectiveness, and what you mean by improvement. The good news is that some studies have shown that it has a small but statistically significant effect on helping people make new memories. The bad news is that the effect is quite small and not all studies have found that it helps.

Some research suggests that it helps older adults, especially those with memory problems, more than younger adults. When researchers find that ginkgo biloba helps cognition, the amount it helps is usually quite small, maybe half as much as a currently available Alzheimer's drug (i.e., an acetylcholine esterase inhibitor such as Aricept). One study found that it only helped prevent dementia in people who took it regularly (Dodge, Zitzelberger, Oken, Howieson, & Kaye, 2008), but that effect could be related to the possibility that people who take their medications and supplements regularly probably have better cognitive functioning.

When researchers have found a positive effect for the herb, they generally report that it affects people's ability to pay attention, which can indirectly help memory performance. An interesting development in ginkgo biloba research is that it appears to reduce anxiety in some older adults, which may indirectly help memory (see Woelk, Arnoldt, Kieser, & Hoerr, 2007).

The typical dose in the researchers' studies has been 120 to 240 milligrams per day. A number of studies have shown there is a dose-dependent effect, such that the more you take, the better it works, up to a point. Very high doses (i.e., above 500mg) are not recommended due to possible side effects or unknown complications. Side effects appear to be mild and rare, but there is evidence for gastrointestinal problems, headaches, dizziness, tinnitus (ringing in the ears), bleeding, and skin rash. A recent study did find an increase risk of strokes in people who had been randomly assigned to take a ginkgo biloba extract (Dodge et al., 2008). Moreover, although most studies have not reported significant side effects, we are never entirely sure how herbal supplements will interact with other medications people might be taking.

We also are not sure why ginkgo biloba might help. Some have suggested that it has a neuroprotective effect through its antioxidant properties. It may affect certain chemical systems in the brain that are involved with memory (i.e., acetylcholine). Or it may reduce stress, which may increase memory ability. Another big unknown is whether the effect is short-lived and only seen immediately after ingestion or if the effect is long term. Clearly, there are still a lot of unanswered questions about ginkgo biloba and the research will continue.

DRUGS AND DEMENTIA

Regardless of age and memory ability, many drugs can affect our ability to learn and make new memories. In general, drugs that make people tired or sedated usually have a negative effect on memory ability. We generally find that narcotic painkillers that are derived from opium or synthetic opium have a negative effect on memory. Benzodiazepines are a class of drugs that are generally used to treat anxiety, insomnia, agitation, seizures, and muscle spasms. These drugs can produce considerable sedation and can significantly impair memory ability.

Alcohol and Cognition

The relationship between alcohol consumption and the likelihood of developing memory problems is complex. Long-term chronic alcohol consumption that is associated with malnutrition because people get so much of their caloric intake from alcohol and their bodies have difficulty absorbing nutrients can lead to a form of dementia known as Korsakoff's syndrome (see Chapter 11 for a discussion of Korsakoff's syndrome). In addition, some believe that large quantities of alcohol could lead to oxidative damage to one's body, which could damage or even kill neurons over time. But, paradoxically, moderate alcohol consumption is associated with better cognitive functioning, a reduced likelihood of developing dementia, and slower rate of progression from mild cognitive impairment to dementia.

One of the first large-scale studies to assess the relationship between alcohol consumption and the likelihood of developing dementia was published by Mukamal, Kuller, Fitzpatrick, Longstreth, Mittleman, and Siscovick (2003) in the

Journal of the American Medical Association. These researchers found that abstainers were twice as likely to develop dementia as compared with older adults who consumed one to six drinks per week. It is important to note that the above study and others have observed that people who have the genetic makeup associated with Alzheimer's disease (i.e., APOE E4) did not have a protective effect from moderate alcohol consumption; moreover, they were at significantly higher risk of dementia if they consumed more than seven drinks per week. At this point, it appears that alcohol consumption and the risk of developing dementia has a u-shaped function, such that complete abstinence and very high consumption rates increase the risk (see Figure 1 to view a graphic representation of the hypothetical relationship between alcohol consumption and the likelihood of developing dementia).

There is also evidence that very moderate consumption of alcohol might slow the rate of progression from mild cognitive impairment to dementia. Solfrizzi et al.

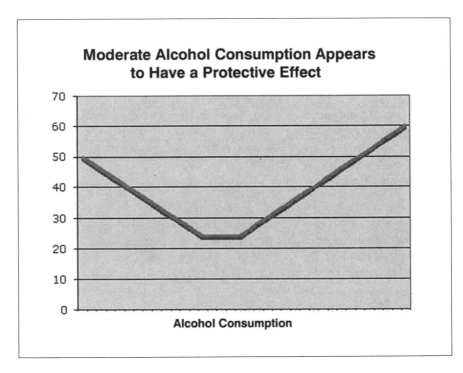

Figure 1. Research suggests that moderate levels of alcohol consumption may lower the chance of developing dementia, however high levels of alcohol consumption will probably increase the chance of developing dementia.

(2007) studied 1,445 people between the ages of 65 and 84 years. They found that people with mild cognitive impairment who averaged less than one drink per day had a much slower rate of memory decline and progression toward dementia than did people who completely abstained from alcohol. However, people who averaged one drink or more per day did not differ in their rate of progression as compared with the abstainers. As is the case in these types of studies, it is difficult to conclude that having one drink on most days of the week *causes* a decrease in dementia. We can't rule out other mechanisms; for example, maybe people who occasionally drink one glass of wine are getting the antioxidant benefits (the study was done in Italy, where red wine is the most common alcoholic beverage). Or it could be that people who occasionally have a drink socialize more and therefore have the benefits of the social support and cognitive stimulation. Or it could be that people who occasionally have a drink generally live moderate and healthy lives. Or given that moderate alcohol consumption has been shown to have positive effects on people's cardiovascular health, the effect may be mediated by better cardiovascular health and cholesterol levels. Regardless, it is worth noting that very moderate alcohol consumption might be associated with better memory functioning.

Marijuana and Cognition

It is estimated that seven million Americans smoke marijuana at least weekly. Marijuana use certainly affects people's short-term memory functioning and ability to encode new memories while intoxicated, but does it have lasting effects on memory ability? Researchers have documented impaired cognitive functioning among very heavy users, even after 28 days of abstinence (e.g., see Bolla, Brown, Eldreth, Tate, & Cadet, 2002). The level of impairment appears to be related to how much people have used. However, as of right now, we are not sure whether there will be any permanent effects from chronic marijuana use after people have abstained for a while.

Stimulants and Cognition

Amphetamine or methamphetamine has been associated with impaired executive functioning (e.g., attention and inhibition). Many studies have documented brain changes after chronic use of the above drugs. Unfortunately, it appears that some of the deficits persist, even after extended periods of abstinence (e.g., see Volkow et al., 2001). In general, the deficits seen in chronic amphetamine or methamphetamine abusers are related to frontal lobe functioning (but other areas also appear to be affected), which leads to difficulty paying attention, inhibiting attention, and controlling behavior. In addition, we have known for a while that chronic use of stimulants can lead to a form of psychosis, often referred to as amphetamine psychosis, which can persist after the person stops using the drug. Anecdotally, many former "meth addicts" have been described as having serious attention and impulse control problems, which is consistent with the research that shows these types of stimulants affect the frontal lobes. But it is difficult to know if the drugs are leading to attention and impulse-control problems or if the impulse-control problems are leading to the addiction or both (my vote is for the latter).

Cocaine

Chronic cocaine abusers score lower on traditional measures of cognitive ability, with more impairment seen in making new memories rather than attentional processes (although some studies have also found attention deficits). The amount of lifetime abuse is correlated with the levels of impairment. Chronic cocaine users generally have poorer visual memory and less cognitive flexibility. Shortly after cessation, we see an improvement in verbal processes and cognitive flexibility but not spatial ability (Lundqvist, 2005). The research is very sparse on the long-term outcomes after people have quit using for a longer period of time. I would predict that the stress, poor nutrition, and possible cardiovascular consequences of long-term cocaine abuse could lead to some permanent impairment in some people, but that is just an educated guess.

Heroin and Opiate Painkillers

There is no doubt that heroin, less potent derivatives of the opium poppy, or synthetic opioids have an acutely negative effect on memory and cognitive ability. People who take narcotic painkillers to deal with their chronic pain are probably going to experience some cognitive deficits as a result. But what are the long-term effects of using painkillers and being addicted to heroin? It appears that long-term use can lead to impairment of impulse control, but several studies failed to find other negative effects in executive functioning (e.g., attention) (see Lundqvist, 2005 for an excellent review).

Pharmaceuticals

Pharmaceuticals can certainly be a source of memory impairment. However, one has to always balance the person's therapeutic need and potential side effects. For example, we know that hypertensive drugs, which are used to treat high blood pressure, can impair memory performance. However, untreated hypertension can kill or lead to a stroke, which is one of the most common ways of getting dementia (i.e., vascular dementia). So a balance is needed between treating one's condition and limiting side effects.

Many times, a patient and doctor may decide to try a different medication. For example, if a patient starts an antidepressant and notices a decrease in memory ability, a new medication can be tried. But once a medication and a dose are decided upon, it still needs to be monitored. The patient may start a new medication that may interact with the old one. It is also important to note that as patients get older, their bodies may become less efficient at metabolizing the drug(s). As a result, older adults may be more susceptible to drug side effects.

Mason and Smith (2005) provided a very thorough lists of drugs that may cause confusion or impair cognitions. In general, people should try to be aware of changes to their memory and cognitive ability when taking new medications. Loved ones and people close to the patients may also notice a change in cognition after a new medication is prescribed. People should be particularly vigilant when taking sedatives, tranquilizers, anticholinergic medications, and narcotic painkillers.

Ask the Memory Doctor:
I understand that eating fish may be good for my brain. But I don't like fish. Is there anything else I can eat that will have a similar effect?

Yes. Many studies are finding the omega-3 fatty acids found in fish are good for the brain, cardiovascular health, memory ability, cholesterol levels, mood, and may even reduce the chance of getting cancer (although the cancer research currently appears to be inconclusive). Most types of seafood have high levels of omega-3 fatty acids, and it looks like we should increase our consumption of certain types of seafood, assuming we don't consume too many heavy metals (e.g., mercury) associated with polluted fish.

However, some people don't like seafood. Moreover, there are probably millions of people who have seafood allergies, which could cause a dangerous condition known as anaphylaxis or even worse, anaphylactic shock, which could cause death. Moreover, many types of seafood are expensive. Fortunately, there are other sources of omega-3 fatty acids besides seafood and fish oil pills. For example, you can buy cooking oils such as canola and olive oil, which are higher in omega-3 fatty acids than vegetable oil. You can also use ground flax seed, which many people put on cereal. Flax seeds have one of the highest levels of omega-3 fatty acids of any botanical food. However, it is recommended that people consume ground flax to maximize absorption during the digestive process. Walnuts are also very high in omega-3 fatty acids.

There are actually a number of different types of omega-3 fatty acids, and they are often referred to by their acronyms, such as EPA, DHA, ALA, and DPA. It is probably the case that different types of foods have different levels of the various types of omega-3 fatty acids. For example, coldwater fish (e.g., salmon) appear to be high in EPA and DHA, whereas flax appears to be highest in ALA. The good news for people who don't like or can't consume fish is that ALA appears to be converted into EPA and the DHA after it is consumed. However, only a small percentage actually gets converted, apparently requiring greater consumption of the nonseafood sources of omega-3 fatty acids.

Many different kinds of foods have varying levels of omega-3 fatty acids. Moreover, what we feed our farm animals affects the omega-3 levels of their meat and eggs. Grass-fed cattle have twice as much omega-3 fatty acids as grain fed cattle. Chickens fed a diet of greens and insects produce eggs that are higher in omega 3 fatty acids, as compared with chickens fed soybeans and corn. Some other foods besides seafood that contain various types of omega-3 fatty acids include cauliflower, cabbage, broccoli, brussel sprouts, squash, spinach, and kale. So there are many options available for people who want to try to get some of the many benefits associated with omega-3 fatty acids but are unable to consume fish. However, if someone just doesn't like seafood and they are not allergic to it, I would suggest taking a fish oil capsule to maximize the above health benefits.

SUGGESTED WEBSITE

American Heart Association www.americanheart.org

CHAPTER 6

Physical Exercise: Improving Memory May Be Just Steps Away

Walking is the best possible exercise. Habituate yourself to walk very far.
Thomas Jefferson (1743–1826)

Physical exercise is an important component of any holistic attempt to maintain one's cognitive abilities in older adulthood. Although some previous research on the effects of physical exercise on cognitive ability has been murky, consistent and robust findings are emerging. We are now in a position to say that any attempt to maximize memory ability in older adulthood requires considering physical exercise. This chapter will look at the overall health benefits of physical exercise and then show how many of those benefits (e.g., reduced obesity, reduced hypertension, reduced stress, reduced diabetes) indirectly reduce the chance of developing dementia. This chapter will also look at what types of exercise are most important and who benefits the most from a memory standpoint. As seen in previous chapters, I will present current ideas about *why* physical exercise appears to help memory and cognition, in order to motivate people who are interested in improving their memory to engage in as much physical activity as is reasonable. Finally, I will present 10 ways that all adults can increase their overall level of physical activity and a diverse list of activities that can be done to increase overall activity levels.

HOW MUCH DO WE EXERCISE?

A report from the U.S. Surgeon General concluded that more than 60% of adults do not achieve the recommended amount of regular physical activity. Moreover, 25% of all adults are not active at all. The report also found that inactivity increases with age and is more common among women than men and among those with lower income and less education than among those with higher income or education. These statistics are concerning, given recent research that shows that people who are physically active have better cognitive abilities and are less likely to develop dementia, especially dementia of the Alzheimer's type.

Increasing one's level of physical activity is something that almost all of us have wanted to do at some time or other. However, it is difficult for many people to maintain a physical exercise program for a long period of time. The good news is that it becomes easier to exercise shortly after one begins doing so and, at that point, exercise becomes more reinforcing and less punishing. Regardless, it is important to be aware of the difficulties people have in motivating themselves to exercise. There are two general ways to help people increase their motivation to exercise. One is to help them increase their belief or self-efficacy that they can begin and maintain an exercise program. You can help older adults increase their self-efficacy for exercising by pairing them with other older adults who are exercising. This will help them become aware that it is possible for older adults to begin and maintain an exercise program. You can also help increase self-efficacy for exercise by having people exercise in a group setting (see Chapter 14 for more information about helping people to increase their motivation).

The other way to increase motivation to get adequate physical exercise is to inform people, and then frequently remind them, of the benefits of physical exercise. Many of these benefits will be specific to the individual. For example, if someone has recently had knee surgery, then certain types of exercise will facilitate recovery and help prevent future problems. Or a diabetic may be motivated to engage in physical exercise to help reduce dependency on insulin and increase life expectancy. Or someone may simply want to lose some weight, and they know that a combined aerobic and weight resistance program will increase metabolism and help burn calories. But many of the benefits of physical exercise are just now being discovered. The next section will review some of the benefits of physical exercise for older adults. This information can be shared with older adults in an attempt to help increase activity levels and the likelihood that they will begin and maintain a well-rounded exercise program.

What is the Benefit of Exercising in Middle and Late Adulthood?

There is a staggering number of health benefits associated with regular physical exercise (see Box 6.1 to view a list of 19 health benefits). Consider using this information to help motivate people to begin and maintain an exercise program. In this next section, we will discuss the myriad health benefits associated with physical exercise and present some ideas as to why exercise is associated with the various health benefits.

Increasing physical activity has been shown to decrease depression, which should indirectly lead to improvements in memory and cognitive ability, especially in people who struggle with depression. For example, Strawbridge, Deleger, Roberts, and Kaplan (2002) published a large-scale study of almost 2000 adults with an average age of about 63 years and who were a good representation of American demographics in terms of ethnicity, gender, and socioeconomic levels.

Strawbridge and his colleagues found that the people who reported more frequent participation in activities such as walking, jogging, swimming, or taking part in active sports were less likely to be diagnosed as being depressed. Similar studies have also found that exercise appears to protect people from depression. It may be that physical exercise leads to increases in certain brain chemicals associated with better moods (and memory ability). It may also be that people who exercise more are less likely to develop chronic illnesses, which are often associated with increased depression. Regardless of the mechanism, it appears that physical exercise can help people increase their overall mood and decrease their chance of debilitating depression.

Being physically fit is even associated with greater life expectancy. A group of Norwegian researchers recruited 1,960 male participants to ride a stationary bike for a set amount of time. The researchers measured how much energy the participants expended while on the bike. They then followed these men for the next 16 years and found that the men who expended the most energy (those in the top 25%) were 54% less likely to die during the course of the study than the men who expended the least amount of energy (the bottom 25%). The researchers even controlled for cardiovascular health, as that would certainly affect how hard they could ride a bike and the likelihood of dying. These dramatic results show that how physically fit middle-aged adults are predicts how long they will live, which should be motivation enough to start exercising more.

Older adults who begin exercise programs can also experience significant improvements related to their overall mobility, balance, and their likelihood of falling. In one study done by Marigold, Eng, Dawson, Inglis, Harris, and Gylfadóttir (2005), it was found that older adults who had experienced chronic strokes, and thus were at great risk for a debilitating fall, had significant improvements in their postural reflexes and balance after beginning an exercise program. Many participants in memory enhancement classes have experienced strokes, and often times those strokes have caused a decrease in memory ability and mobility. It appears that physical exercise may help older adults improve both their memory and their ability to get around, thereby helping them maintain a much higher quality of life.

Clearly there are many benefits to getting more physical exercise, but one of the most intriguing findings was that exercise leads to faster healing of wounds. Charles Emery and his colleagues at Ohio State University conducted a study to assess whether adults (mean age 61 years) would heal faster if they had been and were exercising (2005). The researchers randomly assigned participants to either an exercise group or a nonexercise control group. After the exercise group had become accustomed to the exercise program, superficial wounds were inflicted on all participants. The researchers reported that the exercise participants healed quicker (29 days on average) than the control group (39 days on average). The list of positive health benefits associated with exercise is constantly getting longer (see Table 1 to view a list of benefits associated with exercise). Next, we will look

Table 1. 19 Health Benefits Associated with Physical Exercise[a]

1. Reduces the risk of dying prematurely.
2. Reduces the risk of dying from heart disease.
3. Reduces the risk of developing diabetes.
4. Reduces the risk of developing high blood pressure.
5. Helps reduce blood pressure in people who already have high blood pressure.
6. Reduces the risk of developing colon cancer.
7. Reduces feelings of depression.
8. Reduces feelings of anxiety.
9. Helps control weight.
10. Helps build and maintain healthy bones, muscles, and joints.
11. Helps older adults become stronger and better able to move about without falling.
12. Promotes psychological well-being.
13. Reduces stress.
14. Reduces chance of dementia.
15. Increases neural plasticity.
16. Increases the speed of wound healing.
17. Reduces nicotine craving for people who are trying to quit smoking.
18. Increases speed of reflexes and improves balance for those who have experienced a stroke.
19. Helps older adults maintain their driving ability.

[a]This list was compiled from information in a report from the U.S. Surgeon General about physical exercise and recently published research findings.

at the effects of physical exercise on older adults' cognitive ability and their likelihood of developing dementia.

PHYSICAL EXERCISES DURING MIDDLE AGE REDUCES THE CHANCE OF DEMENTIA

Rovio et al. (2005) found that exercising during midlife reduces the chance of getting a number of types of dementia, especially Alzheimer's disease. Rovio et al.'s study is unique in that they followed the same people for up to 26 years. They asked middle-aged adults (mean age 51 years) how many times per week they engaged in physical activity for at least 20 to 30 minutes that caused breathlessness and sweating. They found that 40% of the participants reported exercising at least twice a week and 60% did not and were classified as sedentary. Then, approximately 20 years later, the participants were contacted again to see who developed dementia. Unfortunately, 117 had dementia and 76 of those were dementia of the Alzheimer's type.

The researchers reported that the people who were classified as being sedentary in midlife were 50% more likely to have developed dementia, and they were 60% more likely to develop dementia of the Alzheimer's type! Another interesting finding is that people who had genes associated with an increased risk of Alzheimer's (i.e., an APOE-4 allele) experienced even greater protective effects against Alzheimer's when they were physically active. The fact that people are much less likely to develop Alzheimer's if they stay physically active, especially if they have a genetic vulnerability, should prove to be very motivating for those who are concerned that they might have a genetic vulnerability. It may also give them hope that they can actually do something to reduce their risk of developing Alzheimer's disease.

Does Physical Exercise Help Memory?

Physical activity is indeed related to better cognitive performance among older adults. It appears that exercise leads to increases in executive functioning, our ability to concentrate, plan, and effectively use our mental resources. This is an important finding because much of what leads to decreases in older adults' memory ability (e.g., the ability to make new memories) is related to decreases in executive functioning, particularly the ability to pay attention. Although executive functioning is the type of mental functioning that most benefits from physical exercise, researchers have also documented reliable increases in speed of processing and spatial abilities, both of which are vulnerable to the effects of aging.

In 2003 Colcombe and Kramer published one of the most comprehensive studies on the effects of exercise on older adults' cognition. These researchers combined the results of 18 studies published between 1966 and 2001 in order to get a more complete picture of how physical exercise affects older adults' cognitive ability. They reported that older adults who do both aerobic and strength training had better cognitive ability than those who only did aerobic exercise. It is interesting to note that cardiovascular researchers have also found that a combination of aerobic and strength training leads to better outcomes than either of them alone. Another finding from Colcombe and Kramer's study was that exercise programs that last longer than six months were associated with better outcomes than shorter programs. In addition, it appears that exercise sessions lead to maximal benefits when they are 31 to 45 minutes in duration; however we have seen significant improvements for older adults who simply engage in

30-minute walking sessions. Another finding that emerged when Colcombe and Kramer combined the results of 18 studies was that people 66 to 80 years of age appeared to benefit more from physical exercise than did people who were 55 to 65 years old.

STRENGTH TRAINING IS ASSOCIATED WITH BETTER COGNITIVE FUNCTIONING

When people think of physical exercise, I suspect that aerobic exercise comes to mind first for most people. However, a growing body of research is finding that strength training, also known as resistance training, has a number of positive effects on health. Most researchers have focused on the effects of aerobic exercise. However, Lachman, Neupert, Bertrand, and Jette (2006) conducted one of the first studies to assess the effects of resistance training by itself on cognitive functioning.

Lachman and her colleagues randomly assigned older adults to either a resistance-training group or a control group. They measured short-term or working-memory ability after 3 and 6 months. The researchers did not find a reliable difference between the two groups; however, when they looked at their resistance exercise group they found that those who improved their strength more (and presumably exercised more) had significant improvements in their working-memory capacity. This is an important finding given that working-memory capacity is an excellent predictor of how well someone will function in everyday situations (see Chapter 2 for a discussion of working or short-term memory).

Why Does Exercise Help Cognitive Ability?

There are many possible reasons why physical exercise is associated with better cognitive functioning. One of the most intriguing hypotheses is that physical exercise increases levels of growth hormones in the brain, which may cause increased connections among neurons and possibly creation of new neurons. Some research suggests that physical exercise might also cause new neurons to be created in the hippocampus, which is used in making new memories. This is an exciting finding because the larger an older adults' hippocampus is, the less likely they will develop Alzheimer's disease.

Other explanations for the link between exercise and improved thinking is that exercise reduces stress and possibly the by-products of stress. When we are stressed out, we usually don't think as efficiently, and we are less likely to make new memories. Stressful thoughts can distract us and prevent us from paying attention to what we want to remember. In addition, research shows that stress by-products, such as cortisol, have been linked to impaired memory functioning, particularly working-memory capacity, which is already vulnerable in the aging brain, and can prevent them from making new memories. Any activity or coping strategy that reduces stress should lead to improvements in memory ability, and it appears that exercise might just do that.

There could still be other reasons why exercise helps older adults to think and remember better. Exercise is associated with reduced obesity and reduced likelihood of developing diabetes. Given that obesity and diabetes are risk factors for severe memory problems, it may be that exercise acts to reduce these risk factors. Another intriguing hypothesis is that exercise reduces the buildup of amyloid protein. It appears that high amyloid levels in neurons lead to Alzheimer's disease and the death of neurons needed to effectively think and remember. Recent research suggests that physical exercise may be helpful in reducing the likelihood of developing Alzheimer's, possibly because exercise reduces amyloid buildup. Regardless of why physical exercise helps older adults' cognitive ability, it is clear that it does, and we should do whatever we can to help older adults get more exercise and thereby maintain or increase their quality of life.

Exercise Can Be Very Beneficial for the Oldest or Frailest

It is clear that exercise has many health and cognitive benefits, regardless of age. However, the oldest and most frail adults often benefit the most from physical exercise. Physical exercise helps people maintain their leg strength and balance ability, which are crucial in reducing the chance of falling.

Numerous researchers have found that people who are having cognition problems, especially those related to attention and executive functioning, are more likely to have a fall (e.g., see Liu-Ambrose, Pang, & Eng, 2007). People who are at risk of falling need to improve their attentional capacity by being mentally stimulated, but they should also get as much physical activity as possible so they have better lower-body muscle strength and mobility. A recent study even showed that an exercise intervention program can lead to better obstacle avoidance, which is crucial in reducing the risk of falling. Someone without attention or memory impairment can easily navigate their environment, step over or around obstacles, while simultaneously doing a cognitive task such as talking on a phone or listening to the television. However, if someone's attentional abilities are impaired, they may divert attention from navigating around obstacles in order to do a cognitive task, which can lead to a disabling fall.

BRINGING IT ALL TOGETHER

Physical activity, nutrition, and memory ability are all related and affect each other. In my opinion, the best prescription for memory improvement requires consideration of all three of these lifestyle factors. We already know that cognitive exercise and learning new things will lead to new connections in our brains and an increase in cognitive reserve. But it could be that physical exercise improves the efficiency with which new connections are made because of increased growth hormones in the brain. And it could be that omega-3s in our diet will help the efficiency with which new neurons are made in the hippocampus when we learn new things. Regardless of the exact mechanisms involved, it is clear that nutrition, physical exercise, and cognitive exercise are important aspects of maintaining and promoting a high quality of life. All three of those components need to be considered if one wants to truly maximize cognitive health, physical health, and quality of life. Moreover, unlike many pharmaceutical interventions, the above activities have a very low risk of causing harm relative to their potential benefits.

If you are involved in running memory classes for older adults, please consider incorporating some light exercise into your program. It is often difficult for many people to begin and sustain a rigorous physical exercise program. See Table 2 to view some ideas about how people can increase their overall activity levels.

If someone has difficulty beginning an exercise program, then encourage them to start small. Make a goal of walking an extra 10 minutes a day or parking at the perimeter of parking lots. Then, slowly increase the goals. If one has a gym membership but doesn't go as often as they would like, they could make a goal of going to the gym for just 15 to 20 minutes twice a week. Once they experience some success, they can increase their goals.

Table 2. Ways to Increase Overall Physical Activity Levels

1. Take the stairs instead of the elevator.
2. When at an airport, walk instead of using the moving walkways.
3. Try to take a 30-minute walk during the evening.
4. Plant a garden.
5. Walk or ride a bicycle to run errands, if possible.
6. Join a gym.
7. If you already have a gym membership, schedule some time with a personal trainer to change your workout.
8. Swim.
9. Ask a friend or spouse to exercise with you.
10. Buy an MP3 player and put audio books or interesting podcasts on it so your workout goes quicker.

CHAPTER 7

Mood and Social Support

The simple solution for disappointment depression: Get up and get moving. Physically move. Do. Act. Get going. Peter McWilliams (1949–2000)

Depression is a very serious disorder that can negatively affect many aspects of an older adult's life. We know that sad or depressed older adults have 30% greater increased mortality rates (Cooper, Harris, & McGready, 2002). Suicide rates are much higher in older adults as compared with younger groups of people. In addition, depression and social support are both related to the likelihood of developing memory problems. Older adults who are depressed are less likely to engage in physically or cognitively stimulating activities, which also increases their risk of experiencing significant memory problems. Clearly, depression is a risk factor for memory problems that needs to be addressed in order to maximize people's ability to maintain good cognitive health. In this chapter we will look at how those who are at risk for developing dementia are often also at risk for developing depression. In order to maximize the likelihood of detection and treatment, the reader will be given a list of risk factors for depression among older adults, as well as some of the diagnostic criteria. We will also discuss treatment options available for depressed older adults.

Social support is related to a number of health outcomes, including depression, cardiovascular health, and immune functioning. However, many older adults, especially those living in institutionalized settings, often have inadequate social support networks (see e.g., Winningham & Pike, 2007), which appears to increase mortality rates and decrease life expectancy.

This chapter will show how social support is related to quality of life and even memory ability. There will be a list of activities and programs that can be adopted by residential care facilities to help facilitate meaningful social interactions among residents. Such social support interventions are easy to implement and can be an integral part of a group-based cognitive enhancement program.

HOW COMMON IS DEPRESSION AMONG OLDER ADULTS?

Do older adults experience depression at a higher rate than younger adults? The answer to that question depends on the age of older adults, their health status, and living environment. For example, one survey found that men are the happiest after age 65 and the least happy between 18 and 29 years old. Another survey found that people are most likely to be depressed in their 40s (Blanchflower & Oswald, 2008). These findings seem to suggest that younger people are at a greater risk of developing depression. However, if older adults have a chronic health condition, experience chronic pain, cognitive impairment, or live in an institutionalized setting, their chances of developing depression increases, possibly higher than any other group.[1]

Stroud, Steiner, and Iwuagwu (2008) found that 21% of people who came to a geriatric outpatient clinic complaining of memory problems had a significant number of depressive symptoms. Li and Conwell (2007) reported data from 18,000 older adults as they were admitted to community-based long-term care programs. They found that almost 25% had "probable depression," which is much higher than we usually see in younger populations, but it isn't as high as the percentage of people in skilled nursing facilities, which has been estimated to be as high as 49%. Regardless of the rates for different groups of people, depression should not be viewed as a normal part of aging.

---

[1] Caregivers of people who have dementia, especially family members, have extremely high rates of depression. In one study, 32% of caregivers had probable depression (Covinsky et al., 2003) and other researchers have reported even higher rates. If the person who is being cared for has aggressive or anger symptoms, the likelihood that the caregiver will experience depression increases. In addition, the lack of financial resources also predicts greater likelihood of experiencing caregiver depression. However, other negative outcomes are also associated with caring for people with dementia. Mausbach, Patterson, Rabinowitz, Grant, and Schulz (2007) cited research showing that caregivers are more likely to have impaired immune functioning, hypertension, and cardiovascular disease. Caregivers who report significant strain associated with caring for someone with dementia are 64% more likely to die in the next four years, as compared with similar people who were not caregivers. Clearly, caring for people with dementia is a very challenging job. Caregivers often are very sleep deprived because of the frequent night wakings common in dementia patients. Moreover, caregivers often report a difficulty staying asleep because they are listening to make sure their loved one doesn't wake up and do something potentially dangerous. I strongly encourage family caregivers to schedule respite care or some home health care so they can have a break. Caregivers need time to rest, run errands, socialize, and reduce their stress levels; doing so will make them healthier and allow them to continue to be good caregivers.

RISK FACTORS FOR DEVELOPING DEPRESSION IN OLDER ADULTHOOD

Based on these findings, it appears that it is too simplistic to say that older adults experience higher rates of depression. What is probably more informative for people who work with older adults or are concerned about a loved one is to be able to recognize the symptoms and risk factors associated with depression (see Table 1 to view a list of risk factors for geriatric depression). Given that geriatric depression is underrecognized and undertreated (Mulsant & Ganguli, 1999), it is important that we know the symptoms, signs, and risk factors. One risk factor for depression is the presence of memory problems. In addition, many times what appears to be dementia turns out to be depression. Approximately one-third of patients referred for dementia actually have depression, not dementia (Maynard, 2003).

Stroud et al. (2008) found that the best predictor of depression among a group of older adults who were complaining about memory problems was the number of medications they were taking. It is hard to determine whether the medications are directly causing the depression. One possibility is that people with poor health take more medications, and the depression might be related to the common observation that chronic illness is associated with a greater likelihood of being depressed. In addition, we know that if people perceive themselves as being unhealthy, regardless of actual health, they are more likely to be depressed; it could be that people who take a lot of medication perceive themselves as being less healthy.

A very surprising finding from Stroud et al.'s research was that moderate alcohol consumption was associated with a reduced likelihood of being depressed. This finding may seem counterintuitive as other studies have found that heavy alcohol consumption is associated with a greater likelihood of being depressed. But once again, it is difficult to determine cause and effect. One possibility, according to Stroud et al., is that people who consume moderate levels of alcohol are also engaging in an active lifestyle by doing things such as attending social events and hosting get-togethers. Moreover, other research has shown that very moderate levels of alcohol consumption are associated with a reduced chance of developing dementia.

APATHY

Apathy can be seen in many older adults who appear to be very unmotivated, lack initiative, and don't engage in goal-directed behavior. As many as 80% of people with dementia show signs of apathy, and between 27% and 36% of community-dwelling older adults are considered apathetic (as cited in Onyike et al., 2007). Apathetic individuals, who are in the normal range for cognitive ability, perform worse than nonapathetic individuals on neuropsychological tests.

Table 1. Risk Factors for Geriatric Depression

- Left-hemisphere stroke (Robinson, Kubos, Starr, Rao, & Price, 1984)
- Chronic illness (Alexopoulos, 2005)
- Multiple medications (Stroud et al., 2008)
- Negative perceptions of one's health status (Tsai, Yeh, & Tsai, 2005)
- Being female (Tsai et al., 2005)
- Living in an institutionalized setting (Bergdahl et al., 2005)
- Painful conditions (Cuijpers & Van Lammeren, 1999)
- Disability (Alexopoulos, 2005)
- Cerebrovascular disease (Krishnan, Hays, & Blazer, 1997)
- Poor social support (Cuijpers & Van Lammeren, 1999)
- Dissatisfaction with living conditions (Tsai et al., 2005)
- Low economic status (Wilson, Chen, Taylor, McCracken, & Copeland, 1999)
- Perceived income inadequacy (Tsai et al., 2005)
- Relocation (Armer, 1993)
- Stress (Maddock & Pariante, 2001)
- Alzheimer's disease (Alexopoulos, 2005)
- Memory problems (Alexopoulos, 2005)
- Parkinson's disease (McDonald, Richard, & DeLong, 2003)
- Diabetes (Anderson, Freeland, Clouse, & Lustman, 2001)
- Caregiver burden (Covinsky et al., 2003)
- Hypothyroidism (Hendrick, Altshuler, & Whybrow, 1998)
- Sleep disturbances (Ford & Cooper-Patrick, 2001; Perlis et al., 2006)

I believe that older adults who are apathetic are at great risk of developing future problems. It appears that apathy is a precursor to dementia and should be viewed as an early warning sign (Onyike et al., 2007). But the problem is that, by definition, apathetic people are going to be less likely to do what is necessary to produce positive changes in their lives. I also worry that apathetic individuals are less likely to have an engaging lifestyle that includes cognitive stimulation, physical exercise, and proper nutrition. Moreover, the apathetic individual may be less likely to maintain a good social support network, which would serve as a buffer for a number of negative outcomes.

It is difficult to motivate an apathetic individual, but there are a number of techniques that can be used to increase someone's motivation to do a specific behavior. See Chapter 14 for a section on motivating older adults to increase certain behaviors that may help improve their health or quality of life. In addition, it is important that the apathetic individual is evaluated and, if necessary, treated for depression.

Just because someone doesn't meet the official criteria for depression, doesn't necessarily mean that their depressed mood isn't negatively affecting their quality of life. For example, apathy and reduced engagement in activities the person previously found enjoyable can have a huge impact on quality of life and possibly even cognitive ability. I hope that older adults who are not experiencing optimal quality of life due to subclinical depression begin doing some of the nonpharmacological interventions discussed later in this chapter, such as increasing physical exercise, increasing omega-3 fatty acid intake, and engaging in a more active social life. These behaviors will help enhance mood, quality of life, and very probably quantity of life.

DEPRESSION, COGNITION, AND MEMORY

There is a strong relationship between depression and cognitive impairment in older adults, which often makes it difficult to accurately diagnose dementia, depression, or the presence of both. People with certain types of dementia (e.g., vascular dementia, Alzheimer's disease, and Parkinson's-related dementia) are at a much greater risk of developing depression. Moreover, older adults who don't have dementia but are depressed often have problems with attention, concentration, and slower mental processing speeds (Alexopoulos, 2005).

Another way to view the depression-dementia link is to consider depression a strong risk factor for the development of future memory problems. Many times depressive symptoms precede the development of dementia. Moreover, people who have more mild forms of cognitive impairment *and* depression are likely to develop full-blown dementia within a few years, especially if nothing is done to ameliorate the situation. A study published in 2003 found that people who had depression or a family history of depression were more likely to develop Alzheimer's disease. This was especially true if the depression first appeared within a few years before the onset of Alzheimer's. However, even depression that appeared 25 years before the patients' Alzheimer's diagnosis increased the likelihood of developing Alzheimer's (Green et al., 2003).

What happens when the depressed patient seeks treatment? One good piece of news is that depressed older adults generally benefit as much as depressed younger adults do when antidepressants are introduced (Alexopoulos, 2005). Doraiswamy et al. (2003) found that older adults whose depression improved following 12 weeks of pharmacological therapy with a typical antidepressant also experienced significant improvement in their memory ability. This encouraging finding definitely gives us hope that depressed older adults can regain some of their lost abilities, if they seek and adhere to a treatment plan. However, another study found that older adults whose depression was in remission still had some residual cognitive impairment, especially in terms of their processing speed and executive functioning (Thomas & O'Brien, 2008). The authors of this study also stated that depressed older adults might be more likely to have a damaging cardiovascular event, which might lead to long-term cognitive impairment. Therefore, it is imperative that depressed older adults seek treatment as soon as possible and strictly adhere to a treatment plan.

Ask the Memory Doctor:
I know someone who is beginning to have memory problems, but they are unmotivated to do anything about it. Is there anything I can do to help them?

Motivating people to take the necessary steps to improve their memory can be difficult. I would first ask you whether you think your friend is suffering from depression. Depression increases people's chances of experiencing memory problems. Depression is also a risk factor for Alzheimer's disease. Research has shown that clinically depressed older adults usually experience an improvement in their memory and cognitive ability a few weeks after they begin taking a selective serotonin reuptake inhibitor (e.g., sertraline, nortriptyline, and fluoxetine). Regardless of mood and the number of depressive symptoms someone has, there are a few techniques that can be helpful in motivating people to do things to improve their quality of life. Albert Bandura suggested that whether or not someone is motivated to do something is determined by two factors. One factor is the person's level of self-efficacy, which is the belief that one has the capability to manage the demands of a challenging situation in such a way as to attain a desired outcome. In other words, people need to believe that they can successfully engage in a program to improve their memory. There are several ways to help people increase their self-efficacy:

- Experiences in mastering new skills and overcoming obstacles will increase self-efficacy. Try to help the person set a number of attainable goals (e.g., eat fish at least once a week, walk at least one mile three days a week, and take a class at the senior center).
- Vicarious experiences provided by successful models who are similar to oneself can also increase people's self-efficacy.
- Tell the individual about similar people you know who have succeeded at doing the target behaviors.
- Use verbal encouragement and persuasion to increase the person's belief that they can do the target behaviors.
- The other factor that affects motivation is knowing what the expected gains or outcomes are of doing the target behavior. For example, what are the expected benefits of changing one's diet, increasing physical activity, or doing more cognitively stimulating activities? Help people become aware of

the benefits, which should increase their motivation and the chance that the person will begin doing the target behaviors. Throughout this book, you can find information about the benefits of doing (or not doing) certain behaviors. Also consider whether any of the following would be affected if the individual began doing some behavior:

- Being able to work
- Being able to parent
- Being able to attend school
- Being able to continue caring for pets
- Being able to live with one's spouse
- Being able to continue or begin a hobby
- Being able to live independently

There is no silver bullet that will help increase people's motivation to make positive changes in their lives, but the above suggestions can be very effective.

DEPRESSION AND PARKINSON'S DISEASE

Over 1 million people in the United States have Parkinson's disease, and it is the second most common neurodegenerative disease, second only to Alzheimer's disease (McDonald et al., 2003). Approximately half of people with Parkinson's disease also have depression (Dooneief, Mirabello, Bell, Marder, Stern, & Mayeux, 1992), although that estimate varies widely between studies (McDonald et al., 2003). It is very difficult to diagnose depression in people who have Parkinson's disease because many of the symptoms used to diagnose depression are also common among people who have Parkinson's, including sleep disturbance, fatigue, concentration problems, apathy, and a general withdrawal from social activities (McDonald et al., 2003). It is important that people who work with older adults are aware of the very high rate of depression among Parkinson's patients, especially since people with Parkinson's are already at increased risk of developing dementia. We want to identify and treat depression as soon as possible in order to prevent further apathy and withdrawal, which could further increase the likelihood of developing dementia. Many medical doctors are prescribing antidepressants to people with Parkinson's disease and depression, however there are concerns about the side effects of the antidepressants, which may exacerbate Parkinsonian symptoms. It appears that a careful analysis of the potential side effects, relative to the potential benefits of antidepressants, must be done by the patient, medical professional, and possibly the family. In addition, I believe it is very important that people with Parkinson's disease consider doing many of the nonpharmacological interventions that can help their cognitive ability as well as decrease the likelihood of depression. For example, I believe people with Parkinson's (as well as others) should eat omega-3 fatty acids, antioxidants, get regular physical exercise, socialize, and try to maximize their level of cognitive stimulation.

DEPRESSION AND STROKES

An estimated 15 million people suffer strokes worldwide each year, and the chance of suffering a stroke increases dramatically for those over the age of 85. Each year, people over 85 have a 1 in 50 chance of experiencing a stroke, whereas the annual chance of having a stroke for people 55-64 years of age is less than 1 in 600 (Bonita, 1992). Having a stroke puts older adults at increased risk of developing depression (and cognitive impairment).

There are two types of depression that are related to cardiovascular health, although I don't believe we should make too much of the distinction because both are probably on the same continuum (Newberg, Davydow, & Lee, 2006) and probably have the same underlying causes. With that said, one type of depression is called *vascular* depression, which refers to depression that generally begins late in life and is associated with the presence of vascular risk factors. The other type of depression is known as *post-stroke* depression, which refers to depression that develops after a stroke. Both types of depression share common risk factors. For example, people are more likely to develop either type of depression if they are female, score high on neuroticism, are older, have a history of anxiety or mood disorders, have recently experienced a negative life event, or have poor social support (as cited in Newberg et al., 2006).

Another commonly cited risk factor for post-stroke depression is a left hemispheric stroke (Robinson et al., 1984). You can often tell the presence of a left hemispheric stroke because it is likely to affect motor function on the right side of the body. It is possible to develop depression if strokes occur in the frontal lobe regions (CME Institute of Physicians Postgraduate Press, Inc., 2007). As an aside, left hemispheric strokes are also more likely to lead to language problems, either comprehending speech, producing speech, or both.

It appears that left hemispheric strokes in particular and all strokes in general are most likely to be associated with depression in the first six months after the stroke occurred. But it is important to note that most people will not develop depression after a stroke. Robinson (2003) combined all the available research data that had been published on the topic and found that approximately 19% of stroke patients who are in a rehabilitation hospital or in-patient facility have major depression and about 19% have minor depression. That is a very high rate compared with people who haven't had a stroke. However, an optimist might point out that 62% of stroke patients do not have a significant number of depressive symptoms and that the above rates tend to go down six months after the stroke.

Fortunately, the symptoms associated with post-stroke depression and vascular depression can usually be reduced with antidepressant medication. Some studies have found that the typical antidepressants (e.g., Prozac) are helpful for post-stroke patients. But one study (as cited in Newberg et al., 2006) found that nortriptyline was better than Prozac. Nortriptyline is known as a second-generation tricylcic antidepressant. Other studies have also found the antidepressant citalopram was better at treating post-stroke depression. In addition, it appears that most non-pharmacological forms of therapy (e.g., talk therapy) are also effective in treating post-stroke depression, however they haven't been studied very extensively for people who have had strokes. Next we will review antidepressant medication for geriatric depression in general, not just post-stroke depression.

ANTIDEPRESSANTS FOR OLDER ADULTS

Pharmacological therapy is probably the most common treatment intervention for depression. The most common class of antidepressants is known as selective serotonin reuptake inhibitors (SSRIs). SSRIs work to increase levels of the neurotransmitter serotonin that are outside of neurons so they can act to increase the activity of neurons. SSRIs actually block the reuptake or recycling of the serotonin back inside neurons, which makes more serotonin available to make neurons communicate. There is another class of drugs that blocks the reuptake of both serotonin and another neurotransmitter known as norepinephrine; these drugs are sometimes referred to as tricyclics, which is a reference to their molecular structure. Given that tricyclics affect two neurotransmitter systems, most experts believe they have a greater likelihood of leading to side effects, although a recent review of published studies showed that SSRIs and tricyclics had similar rates of side effects, but the side effects associated with tricyclics were potentially more serious as they can sometimes lead to cardiovascular side effects (Shanmugham, Karp, Drayer, Reynolds, & Alexopoulos, 2005). SSRIs are more likely to cause side effects related to nausea, loss of appetite, and sexual dysfunction. Side effects are usually seen within one to four weeks after beginning the antidepressant medication. See Table 2 to view a list of possible anti-depressant side effects.

In their review of the published scientific literature, Shanmugham et al. (2005) found that more than half of the geriatric patients treated with antidepressants experienced at least a 50% drop in the number of depressive symptoms. Apparently, a partial therapeutic response to antidepressants is common among older adults. Some older adults don't experience a significant decrease in their depressive symptoms after taking antidepressants, therefore it is important to consider other types of antidepressant medication as well as other nonpharmacological intervention strategies.

Table 2. Possible Side Effects of Antidepressant Medication

- Bone fractures
- Loss of libido
- Dry mouth
- Urinary retention
- Blurred vision
- Constipation
- Sedation (can interfere with driving)
- Sleep problems
- Weight gain
- Headache
- Nausea
- Gastrointestinal disturbance/diarrhea
- Abdominal pain
- Inability to achieve an erection
- Inability to achieve an orgasm
- Agitation
- Anxiety

Ask the Memory Doctor:
My mom and aunt had Alzheimer's disease. Should I be worried that I will get it?

One could argue that there are two main factors that determine whether or not someone will develop Alzheimer's disease. One factor is their genetic make-up. There is in fact a genetic component to Alzheimer's (and many other forms of dementia). If a family member that you are genetically related to has Alzheimer's disease, you probably do have a higher risk of developing the disease yourself. However, it is important to point out that many (but not all) studies have found that early-onset Alzheimer's (i.e., beginning before the age of 65) has a stronger heritability rate, and fewer than 10% of Alzheimer cases are of the early-onset variety. That is good news for over 90% of people who are related to someone who has or had Alzheimer's. Clearly, just because someone has one or more close family members with the disease doesn't mean they will get it.

One study estimated that 12% to 19% of women and 6 to 10% of men over the age 65 will develop Alzheimer's disease. Not surprisingly, the longer someone lives, the greater their chance of developing Alzheimer's disease. It appears that genetics account for a little over half of the risk.

The other factors that determine someone's chances of developing Alzheimer's are their behavioral and lifestyle choices. We can't do anything about our genetics (at least not yet); what we can control is our lifestyle and most of the nongenetic risk factors. We can get adequate physical exercise, eat antioxidants and omega-3 fatty acids, continue to exercise our brains, keep a healthy weight, maintain a healthy cardiovascular system, and avoid diabetes. Those factors will reduce the likelihood of developing dementia, regardless of one's genetic make-up, and that is what this book generally stresses. More importantly, the above risk factors are largely within our control.

NON-PHARMACOLOGICAL INTERVENTIONS FOR DEPRESSED AND APATHETIC OLDER ADULTS

Given that there are often significant side effects associated with various antidepressant medications and the fact that antidepressant drugs don't always work for everyone, it is important to offer depressed individuals an array of choices for treating depression. Moreover, many studies have found that the best results for treating depression come from an approach that includes both pharmacological and nonpharmacological interventions. Options available to people include cognitive therapy (i.e., counseling), support groups, physical exercise, and increasing omega-3 fatty acid intake.

Physical Exercise

According to Motl, Konopack, McAuley, Elavsky, Jerome, and Marquez (2005), "Physical activity might be one of the most important behavioral interventions for preventing depression among older adults" (p. 385). Numerous researchers have found that depressed older adults experience a reduction in the number of depressive symptoms after beginning an exercise program. The physical exercise leads to changes in brain chemistry associated with better mood. Moreover, physical exercise, regardless of the presence of depression, tends to lift mood and lead to more euphoric feelings.

Blumenthal et al. (1999) randomly assigned depressed middle-aged and older adults to one of three groups: an aerobic exercise program group, an antidepressant medication group, or combined exercise and medication group. After 16 weeks, all groups experienced a decreased number of depressive symptoms. Interestingly, there were not any differences between the three groups after 16 weeks. However, the authors reported that people who were in the medication-only group experienced the quickest improvement in mood. In addition, people in the medication and exercise group who were the most depressed did not see improvement as fast as those who were less depressed. Results from this study and others clearly show us that physical exercise is a viable treatment option for depressed individuals; but does exercise improve the mood of people who don't meet the diagnostic criterion for depression?

Motl et al. (2005) assigned nondepressed older adults to either a walking group or a resistance/flexibility training group for six months. Before the exercise intervention began, participants took depression tests that measured the number of depressive symptoms they had. After six months of the exercise intervention, participants in both groups experienced a similar reduction in the number of depressive symptoms. However, the most exciting aspect of their results was that the improved mood was maintained 6 and 54 months after the official intervention ended. So it appears that even nondepressed individuals' mood can benefit from increased physical exercise.

COUNSELING FOR DEPRESSION

Another nonpharmacological therapy for older adults is psychotherapy or counseling. There are a number of types of psychotherapy or talk therapy that have been found to be effective in treating depression (Mackin & Areán, 2005). The most common type of talk therapy is probably cognitive behavior therapy or behavioral therapy. Cognitive behavior therapy begins with the premise that depression is largely caused by an inability to cope with life stressors, regulate one's emotions, social isolation, and difficulty solving problems. Therefore, cognitive behavior therapy is used to teach people methods for regulating their emotions, staying engaged in enjoyable activities, and changing the behaviors and modes of thinking that lead to depression (Wyman, Gum, & Areán, 2005).

Mackin and Areán (2005) reviewed the published literature on the effects of cognitive behavior therapy relative to control groups and found that the therapy was indeed helpful for depressed older adults as compared with not getting talk therapy. In addition, they found evidence that the treatment gains are maintained over long periods of time. In addition, cognitive behavior therapy also appears to be useful in treating dysthymia or low-grade depression, which isn't severe enough to meet the diagnostic criteria for major depression.

Other types of talk therapies have also been found to be effective, but they generally have not been researched as much as cognitive behavior therapy. An example of a potentially effective therapy that hasn't been researched very much is reminiscence therapy, sometimes called life review, which involves looking back at one's life events, facilitating additional recall, and promoting the perception of control over future events. Various forms of reminiscence therapy are frequently offered in assisted living and skilled nursing facilities, but there is a great deal of variability in how it is conducted.

Surprisingly little research has been conducted on the effects of combining talk therapy with antidepressants to treat geriatric depression, however the research that has been done (e.g., Thompson, Coon, Gallagher-Thompson, Sommer, & Koin, 2001) has found it to be effective in reducing depression. Talk therapies may teach people better coping skills, which will help the individual long after the therapy is over; medication alone probably doesn't have the same sort of long-term benefits.

One potential problem with treating geriatric depression is dealing with cognitive impairment. Cognitive impairment is common among depressed geriatric patients and may be caused by the depression, or it may be caused by a neurodegenerative disease, or both. Regardless of the cause, very little research has been done on the effects of talk therapies with cognitively impaired older adults. Presumably, the therapy would need to be done at a slower pace and the cognitively impaired patient would need a greater number of opportunities to practice new skills and strategies.

Another challenge in treating depression with psychotherapy is obtaining access to therapists who specialize in working with depressed older adults. People who live in rural areas may be able to undergo psychotherapy via the telephone, which has been shown to be effective.

OMEGA-3 FATTY ACIDS AND DEPRESSION

One of the most exciting recent developments in depression research is the finding that depression is related to dietary intake of omega-3 fatty acids. There are two types of fat that we must get from our diet because our body is unable to make them; they are omega-3 fatty acids (sometimes referred to as "good fat") and omega-6 fatty acids (sometimes referred to as "bad fat"). Omega-6 fatty acids come from cereals, whole-grain breads, most vegetable oils, eggs, poultry, animals that are fed grain (e.g., corn), and baked goods. Omega-3 fatty acids are high in seafood, nuts, canola oil, and olive oil. Many foods have both omega-3 and omega-6 fatty acids in them.

As discussed in Chapter 5, it appears that most people living in Western countries have a disproportionately high intake of omega-6 fatty acids relative to omega-3 fatty acids. Estimates vary, but many researchers think that we historically have had four units of omega-6 fatty acids to every one unit of omega-3 fatty acids. However, the average person living in Europe or North America now has up to 20 units of omega-6 fatty acids to each unit of omega-3. If these estimates are accurate, our ratio of these two different types of fat may be up to 500% out of line with what our bodies need (i.e., 4:1 vs. 20:1). Some researchers have even proposed the idea that our modern diet, with its very high levels of omega-6 fatty acids relative to omega-3 fatty acids, may be driving the increased prevalence of depression seen during the past century (Owen, Rees, & Parker, 2008).

The evidence for omega-3s being linked to mood disorders comes from many sources. For example, we know that countries whose citizens have, on average, higher consumption of fish tend to have much lower rates of depression (Hibbeln, 2002) and bipolar depression (Noaghiul & Hibbeln, 2003). Other studies have found that people who are depressed have higher omega-6 to omega-3 ratios, as compared with similar people who are not depressed (Ross, 2007). Researchers have even begun assessing the effectiveness of omega-3 supplements (usually made from fish oil) on people who have major depression. Although there have been some inconsistent findings, the majority of the studies have found that omega-3 fatty acid supplements lead to greater improvements in mood as compared with placebos (Lin & Su, 2007). Given the side effects associated with antidepressants, the possibility that omega-3 fatty acids may serve as an alternative treatment for some people is very exciting. Given that omega-3 fatty acids have very few potential side effects, and the possible benefits of taking them are potentially very significant, I believe we are in a position to recommend that people who are concerned about depression and memory consider taking them. Omega-3 fatty acids have also been associated with better memory ability, as discussed in Chapter 5. People should consult their primary-care physician before adding any nutritional supplements to their diet, as they may affect other medications or medical condition.

DEPRESSION AND SOCIAL SUPPORT

Nearly all older adults experience a series of losses and disruptions to their social support networks. It is common for social support networks to change when people retire and have less contact through work. At some point, most older adults stop driving for safety or health reasons, which further limits their ability to socialize (and opportunities for cognitive stimulation and new experiences). Disruptions to social networks often continue due to the death of a spouse and close lifelong friends. At some point, many retirees need to move closer to family if their health deteriorates to the point of requiring additional care. Or they may need to move to an assisted living or skilled nursing facility. These disruptions to social support networks can negatively affect physical, cognitive, and mental well-being. People with poor social support networks are more likely to experience depression, cardiovascular health problems, impaired immune system functions, less cognitive stimulation, poorer cancer prognoses, and reduced life expectancy. Older adults and those who work with them need to be aware of these social changes and try to mitigate the negative effects they might have. See Table 3 to view a list of risk factors that have been associated with poor social support.

Selective Optimization

Many younger people believe that older adults need more friends and opportunities to socialize. That may or may not be the case, depending on the situation.

Table 3. Risk Factors for Poor Social Support in
Older Adult Populations[a]

Risk factors	References	Mean age
Depression	Cuijpers & Van Lemmeren (1999)	84.5
	Cummings & Cockerham (2004)	84.4
	Cummings (2002)	83.7
	Gurung, Taylor, & Seeman (2003)	76.5
Low self-efficacy	Gurung et al. (2003)	76.5
Impaired cognition	Bassuck, Glass, & Berkman (1999)	≥ 65
	Gurung et al. (2003)	76.5
	Seeman, Lusignolo, Albert, & Berkman (2001)	~74.5
Gender	Cummings (2002)	83.7
	Kaye & Monk (1991)	63% over 75
	Gurung et al. (2003)	76.5
Marriage status	Gurung et al. (2003)	76.4
	Wister (1990)	≥ 65
Number of visits	Gurung et al. (2003)	76.5
	Pinquart & Sorensen (2001)	≥ 60
Extraversion	Krause, Liang, & Keith (1990)	68.7
Physical health	Bassuk et al. (1999)	≥ 65
	Berkman, Leo-Summers, & Horwitz (1992)	≥ 65
	Pedersen, Van Domburg, & Larsen (2004)	61.0
	Seeman et al. (2001)	~74.5

[a]This table has been adapted from Winningham and Pike (2007).

It is actually quite normal to have increasingly fewer friends throughout adulthood, but at some point (probably in the 80s) our social support network becomes too small.

I believe that many older adults, particularly those who are living in more institutional settings, are at risk of negative physical and mental health outcomes because they lack social support. I have seen firsthand how little socialization takes place in many assisted living and skilled nursing facilities. I believe we can do a lot to increase social support and thereby increase overall quality of life and possibly the level of cognitive stimulation people receive.

SOCIAL SUPPORT IN FACILITY-BASED COMMUNITIES

I am particularly concerned that we develop programs, interventions, and policies to help older adults living in residential retirement communities and assisted living facilities develop and maintain social support and connections. The act of moving into an assisted living facility is often preceded by a decrease in overall health and functioning. In addition, many older adults who move into assisted living facilities are often required to move a great distance to a facility closer to adult children, thereby leaving their social support networks behind. These social factors converge into a dangerous combination that puts many older adults at risk for loneliness, isolation, and possibly depression. We need to do more to facilitate meaningful social interaction in many residential communities. Next, I will present some ideas that may help the social environment in residential communities.

STRATEGIES TO FACILITATE SOCIAL SUPPORT AND DECREASE LONELINESS

One of the most effective ways to change the social environment in facility-based communities is to have a resident ambassador program. Programs like this vary, but they all have a small number of residents play a crucial role in facilitating social interactions and creating a warm environment. Resident ambassadors can be volunteers, paid, or receive money off their monthly bills (most are probably volunteers).

Resident ambassadors can do things such as greet people entering the facility during business hours and directing them toward people or staff, which provides a warm feeling for visitors and also adds a measure of security. Resident ambassadors can also facilitate social interaction among residents. For example, they can introduce themselves to new residents. I also suggest that the resident ambassadors write short notes about new residents and distribute them to the people who live close to the new resident (e.g., on the same floor or in a certain section of the building). The notes might also include a picture of the new resident. Neighbors are more likely to make eye contact, say "hi," know each other's names, and begin conversations if they are introduced to each other with the notes from resident ambassadors. Resident ambassadors can also work on newsletters, help with activities, socialize with residents who appear isolated, bring books from the library to people, distribute mail, distribute refreshments at events or before meals, and bring more coffee or water to residents during meal times. I have seen some facilities even purchase special jackets or blazers and professionally produced nametags for the ambassadors. Having volunteers serve as resident ambassadors is a win-win situation, because the other residents benefit from their work, the interactions they have, and the positive changes to the overall environment. The ambassadors benefit from the work also, as it is cognitively stimulating, and they will probably benefit from the knowledge that they are helping others and playing a vital role. In addition, the ambassadors usually engage in physical exercise while doing many of their duties.

Many retirement communities adopt the "aging in place" model, whereby people can move from independent living to assisted living to skilled nursing facilities all on the same "campus." These aging-in-place campuses provide an ideal opportunity to volunteer and help people who are more impaired or require additional services. People from the independent living area can go into the assisted living or skilled nursing facilities and volunteer their services. Similarly, many people from the assisted living areas are capable and willing to go to the skilled nursing areas to help, even if it just sitting and talking with someone. Some aging-in-place campuses also have child daycare facilities, in which some of the older adult residents can volunteer to help. See Table 4 for a list of activities that volunteers can do.

One of the best sets of activities to facilitate social interaction among residents involves using standardized questions that each resident can answer and other residents can learn in a group setting (see Table 5 for the Good Neighbor Activity sheet, which contains the questions). This activity can be modified for different levels of cognitive functioning by using recognition (easiest; "Which of these states is Helen's place of birth?"), cued recall (moderate; "In what state was Helen born?"), or free recall (difficult; "What do you know about Helen's childhood?"). This activity could be called the "memory game." I recommend focusing on one question at a time, or during one memory class, or as a warm-up for other activities such as Bingo. You can also revisit previous questions and see how well people remember the information. After the people have gone through a few questions and learned things about other residents, an activity director or a volunteer can make crossword puzzles or word-find puzzles using the information. There are excellent puzzle makers available online and for purchase. The software is usually easy to use and the customized puzzles can be a lot of fun for residents.

IS IT POSSIBLE TO FACILITATE SOCIAL SUPPORT AND DECREASE LONELINESS IN CARE FACILITIES?

My colleagues and I wanted to see if older adults who live in assisted living facilities could actually experience an increase in perceived social support and a decrease in loneliness by taking part in activities like the ones I have described above. We went into seven assisted living facilities and measured residents' perceived social support and loneliness using three different tests. Half of the volunteers participated in a program that combined cognitive exercises with

Table 4. Activities that Volunteers Can Do for Residents

- Help conduct simple physical exercise classes
- Help conduct small group craft programs
- Decorate the building or a bulletin board for a holiday
- Develop a photograph project where residents' pictures and names are posted
- Help organize or maintain the library
- Help maintain raised flower and vegetable gardens
- Enter computer data for the facility
- Help residents care for their pets
- Distribute mail to residents
- Escort residents to and from events or meals
- Help with outings or field trips
- Play games
- Distribute word games or Sudoku puzzles to residents
- Bring residents extra coffee, tea, or water during mealtimes
- Read to residents
- Dictate letters for residents
- Lead discussion groups or book clubs
- Visit with residents
- Get residents to sign a get-well card for someone who is recovering in a hospital or rehabilitation facility
- Go to the local library or the facility library to get books for residents

various activities that were designed to facilitate social interaction and the other half served as the control group and were not exposed to anything different. The results were exciting: we found that the people who participated in the program reported increased social support and decreased loneliness, as compared with the control group (Winningham & Pike, 2007).

In Figure 1, you can see how the loneliness score decreased in the cognitive enhancement group, as compared with the trend toward increased loneliness in the control group. In Figure 2, you can see how perceived social support increased for the group that received the intervention. The interventions lasted only three months; notice the trend toward increased loneliness and decreased social support in the control group. Given that the average assisted living resident resides in their home for about two years, I am very concerned that in

Table 5. The Good Neighbor Activity Sheet

The Good Neighbor Activity Sheet

1. What is your first name? _____
2. What was your childhood nickname? _____
3. In what city (or state) were you born? _____
4. What was your favorite vacation? _____
5. What was your most embarrassing moment? _____
6. Who is your favorite musical artist? _____
7. What is your favorite color? _____
8. What is your favorite season? _____
9. What is currently your favorite activity or hobby? _____
10. What is your all-time favorite movie? _____
11. What was/is your favorite pet? _____
12. What is your favorite food item? _____
13. What is your favorite dessert? _____
14. What is your all-time favorite book? _____
15. What is your favorite play? _____
16. How many grand or great-grandchildren do you have?

the absence of a concerted effort to improve aspects of residents' social lives, they will be experiencing very significant decreases of this important aspect of quality of life.

OTHER ACTIVITIES TO FACILITATE SOCIAL INTERACTIONS AND SUPPORT

Many times assisted living facility residents, or even residents in more independent living environments need to go to the hospital or a rehabilitation facility for a while. It is extremely rare that the residents ever hear from their neighbors while they are recovering or rehabilitating. Such a glaring absence of concern from others can be depressing and reduce the recovering patient's motivation to work hard during the rehabilitation process. Resident ambassadors or staff members can make a huge impact on the recovering resident and motivate them to do what is necessary to improve their physical health and get back home. Staff may even consider contacting the rehabilitating resident or their family and

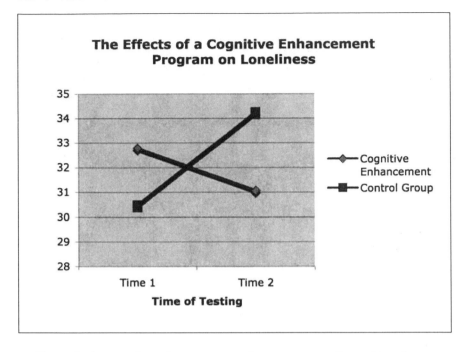

Figure 1. A group-based program can decrease perceptions of loneliness. Average scores from Winningham and Pike (2007). Time 1 refers to participants' scores on the loneliness scale before the intervention and Time 2 refers to their scores 3 months later. Higher scores indicate higher levels of loneliness.

ask whether the facility bus driver can bring some of their friends and neighbors over to the rehabilitation facility or hospital for a short visit. At the very least, residents can sign a get well card and possibly send it with some flowers or maybe some cognitively stimulating materials from their memory class.

Consider pairing residents with similar interests and cognitive functioning. For example, many times older adults have assigned seats in the dining room. It is imperative that people with similar cognitive abilities are paired at tables. Also, consider organizing "Family Days" at your facility. Invite residents' family to come and take part in a day of games, entertainment, and dining. Older and younger people can take part in games and activities. The event may help to facilitate interactions among residents. Such an event could also include a chance to play one of the popular video games (e.g., Wii) that are becoming increasingly ubiquitous at residential care facilities and senior centers.

Some facilities have chosen to give people nametags. The residents don't have to wear them but many do. When residents know and use each other's names,

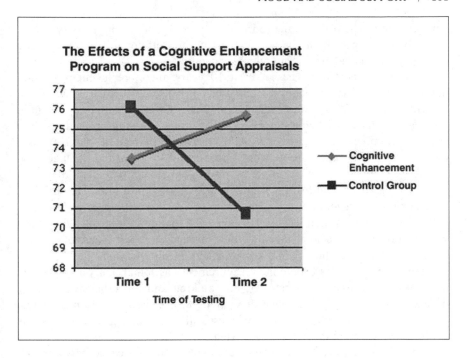

Figure 2. A group-based program can increase perceptions of social support. Average scores from Winningham and Pike (2007). Time 1 refers to participants' scores on the social support scale before the intervention and Time 2 refers to their scores 3 months later. Higher scores indicate higher levels of perceived social support.

the social milieu is altered for the better. Some communities have set up Resident Council Programs, in which certain residents serve in an advisory capacity for the facility and management. Book clubs are another great way to simultaneously stimulate minds and facilitate meaningful interactions. Trips to the local senior center for regular classes are another great opportunity to stay active and engaged.

Ask the Memory Doctor:
I have a friend who recently retired and he doesn't do much except play golf. Is my friend at risk for developing memory problems?

Unfortunately, the answer to your question is probably yes. There are some potentially fabulous cognitive benefits associated with regular golfing. For example, the physical exercise can lead to cognitive benefits and possibly decreased chance of dementia (especially if you don't use a golf cart for every hole). In addition, the social interactions can be cognitively stimulating and may also facilitate the development and maintenance of a good social support network. However, if that is the retirees' only hobby or regular activity, then I would be concerned that he is not challenging himself cognitively by learning new things or challenging his attentional capacity.

The average retirement lasts at least 10 years, therefore health promotion during retirement is crucial for maintaining good health and quality of life (Wilson & Palha, 2007). Moreover, many retirees have more time to engage in physical exercise, socializing, traveling, and learning new things. And research shows that retirees have lower stress levels than working-age people. However, the time right after retirement is crucial, as a major life transition is underway. People are more likely to have problems transitioning into retirement if they have a very strong attachment to work, perceive a lack of control over the transition, have anxiety about retirement, or have low self-efficacy (Solinge & Henkens, 2005). Very little research has been done on the topic, but it appears that those whose work was the central focus of their life and their self-image often have the greatest time transitioning into a healthy and fulfilling retirement.

The research that has been done on retirement has found that walking is the most common activity after retiring, but walking and other physical activity declines with advancing age. Swenson et al. (2005) as cited in Wilson and Palha (2007), found recreational activity increases after retirement and then levels off for a while before declining again. Men begin decreasing their activity after the age of 70. Caucasian women begin decreasing their physical activity after 63, and Hispanic women don't decrease their physical activity until about 70 years of age. Although we will have to see if these patterns continue as the boomers go through their 60s and early 70s, the bottom line is that we should strive to be and remain active in a variety of activities as long as we can.

SUGGESTED READINGS FOR PEOPLE
WHO ARE INTERESTED IN SELF-HELP BOOKS
ON DEPRESSION

Bieling, P. J., Antony, M. M., & Beck, A. T. (2003). *Ending the depression cycle.* Oakland, CA: New Harbinger Publications.

Burns, D. (1999). *Feeling good: The new mood therapy.* New York: HarperCollins Publishers.

Lewinsohn, P. (1992). *Control your depression.* New York: Fireside. (Original work published 1978.)

Pettit, J. W., Joiner, T. E., & Rehm, L. P. (2005). *The interpersonal solution to depression: A workbook for changing how you feel by changing how you relate.* Oakland, CA: New Harbinger Publications, Inc.

Williams, M. G., Teasdale, J. D., Segal, Z. V., & Kabat-Zinn, J. (2007). *The mindful way through depression: Freeing yourself from chronic unhappiness.* New York: The Guilford Press.

Yapko, M. D. (1997). *Breaking the patterns of depression.* New York: Doubleday.

CHAPTER 8

Stress and Memory

Worry gives a small thing a big shadow. Swedish proverb

This short chapter will look at the effects of stress on memory. Surprisingly, stress does not always impair memory and cognitive performance, but many times it does. This chapter will discuss the positive and negative effects of stress. Readers will better understand why stress and anxiety about their own memory ability can actually become a self-fulfilling prophecy. I will also present basic information on the biology of stress, especially how it might decrease the life expectancy of our cells. The relationship between stress, depression, and immune functioning will also be discussed. Finally, recommendations about how to reduce stress will be provided.

Stress is a difficult term to define. Psychologists have not all agreed upon a single definition of stress, possibly because the term refers to a number of different things. One group of researchers wrote the following, "Our daily lives are full of emotionally arousing experiences, ranging from small annoyances to major life events like the loss of a spouse. Collectively, these potential threats of our bodily homeostasis are referred to as stress" (Joëls, Pu, Wiegert, Oitzl, & Krugers, 2006, p. 152). Whether something is stressful depends, to a large extent, on the individual. One person may perceive a situation as being very stressful, whereas another person might perceive the same situation as a welcomed challenge. It turns out that stress is largely in the eye of the beholder. In this chapter, we will discuss the negative effects of stress, especially on memory and learning. We will also look at ways to reduce stress.

GOOD STRESS

Before we discuss all the negative effects of stress, it is important to discuss the idea that not all stress is bad. Stress has important roles in our lives. Stress can be motivating. We often are "stressed" by things we need to do, which motivates us to actually do them. When we complete the task, the stress is taken away, which is reinforcing and increases the chance of doing the needed behavior

103

next time we have stress about incomplete tasks. Another example of how stress can sometimes motivate us to action might be seen in why some people are reading this book. If someone is concerned about declining memory abilities, that may have motivated them to get this book and read it. Hopefully they would also engage in some of the suggestions in the book. If they did so, they would be doing what they can to improve memory, and at the same time, reduce the level of stress about their own memory ability.

Stress can also increase our level of arousal, which, up to a point, may actually improve performance. I see this with my students at the university; when I say, "this would make a great exam question," they usually snap to attention, experience some mild stress, begin paying closer attention, write more class notes, and ask questions to help clarify their understanding. Adding a small amount of stress can actually help students. However, sometimes students who are prone to becoming distressed can become so overwhelmed by the stress of thinking about an upcoming exam that they have difficulty paying attention to the lecture.

The idea that stress and arousal can help performance up to a point, and then greater levels of arousal can impair performance, is generally known as the Yerkes-Dodson Law. A graphic representation of the Yerkes-Dodson Law can be seen in Figure 1. It is important to note that the inverted U-shaped function, which is synonymous with the Yerkes-Dodson Law, might only be true for difficult tasks. When tasks are easy, boring, or require stamina and perseverance, the relationship is more linear, such that more arousal helps, and even greater levels of arousal don't hurt performance. One possible reason that performance on challenging or difficult tasks is impaired with the highest levels of arousal is that the increased arousal might affect people's ability to pay attention to the appropriate aspects of the task. For example, if someone is stressed that they won't be able to remember driving directions while they are simultaneously listening to the directions, then they won't be able to devote the necessary resources to actually remember the directions. Instead, they will be thinking about how they might not remember the directions, how they should be writing down the information, and how they hope they will be able to find someone else to give them directions when they get lost again.

A similar situation might arise if people are stressed about their own memory ability and how they don't want to make embarrassing mistakes or be forgetful. Just the act of worrying about one's memory performance while they should be paying attention to the situation or remembering some information can become a self-fulfilling prophecy. People will experience a reduction in their available cognitive resources (their ability to understand and remember something if they are simultaneously worrying about a possible memory failure.

There is another mechanism by which stress may actually improve memory. If the experience of stress and the associated brain chemicals (e.g., cortisol and noradrenaline) are not present in elevated levels before an event (e.g., in the hour that precedes the event) or long after the event (e.g., the next day), but only at

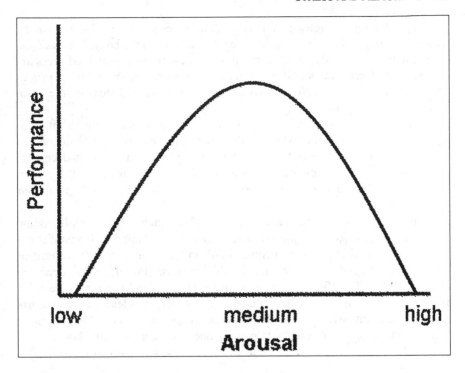

Figure 1. The Yerkes-Dodson Law states that there is an inverted U-shaped function (curvilinear) between arousal and performance, such that low levels of arousal produce fairly low levels of performance, moderate levels of arousal produce the highest level of performance, but additional arousal will impair performance. Recent research suggests that the above effect is most pronounced when the task is difficult. Public domain image from *Wikipedia*, found at http://en.wikipedia.org/wiki/Yerkes-Dodson_law.

the time of the event, then we generally see improved memory for the arousing or stressful event (Joëls et al., 2006). The above mechanism was probably very adaptive in helping our ancestors remember acute stressors (e.g., an encounter with a bear in a certain cave). However, the type of stress many people experience today is present for longer periods and in many cases is chronic, which won't help overall memory ability. Moreover, chronic stress may impair the system that helped our ancestors remember acutely stressful events.

BIOLOGY OF STRESS

Stress causes a cascade of chemical changes in the brain that affects hormonal levels and cognitive ability. One of the mechanisms by which stress impairs memory is through the release of a class of hormones known as glucocorticoids, especially cortisol. These hormones have many effects on the body. For example, we know that cortisol can weaken the immune system, increase blood pressure, and possibly depress mood. Glucocorticoids also act on the frontal lobe cortices and the hippocampi, which are two of the most important areas of the brain involved in making memories.

Sauro, Jorgensen, and Pedlow (2003) combined the results from 88 different stress and memory studies and found that stress increases cortisol levels, which in turn impairs cognitive ability. Sauro et al. reported that stress and cortisol negatively affected the hippocampal regions of the brain and inhibited the activity of neurons, which could, in part, explain why stress and cortisol impair our memory ability.

People vary in how much stress negatively affects their memory ability. Some people use more effective coping strategies, which may limit the effects of stress on memory. In addition, some people focus on things they can do to limit or remove the stressors from their lives, which reduces the effects of stress on memory ability. The effects of stress on memory may also have a more negative impact if the person is not healthy, developing memory problems, depressed, has cardiovascular disease, poor social support networks (Sauro et al., 2003), or has a neurotic and negative personality (Crowe, Andel, Pedersen, & Gatz, 2007).

FLIGHT NON-ATTENDANTS[1]

Cho et al. (2000) conducted an interesting study in which they looked at the effects on cortisol levels and cognitive performance of crossing time zones. Cho et al. assessed whether flight attendants who crossed multiple time zones had different levels of cortisol and cognitive performance as compared with ground crew who didn't regularly cross time zones. They also looked at employees with one, two, three, and four years of experience to see whether the effects were cumulative. Cho et al. reported that flight attendants who crossed time zones had higher levels of cortisol, which indicates that the experience is stressful for the body. They also reported that flight attendants who didn't cross time zones had lower levels of cortisol, thereby ruling out the possibility that flying caused increases in cortisol. However, not all the flight attendants who traveled across time zones and therefore had elevated cortisol levels performed more poorly on cognitive tests. Only the flight attendants with four years of experience had impaired cognitive functioning, which indicates that the stress and cortisol effects may be cumulative. Of course, the people with four years of experience would be

---

[1] I first saw the creative title "Flight Non-Attendants" in an article published by www.nature.com on March 15, 2000. David Adam wrote a short article that described the study by Cho, Ennaceu, Cole, and Suh (2000). The online article is no longer available.

slightly older than the people with less experience, but most participants were under 30 years of age and therefore shouldn't have been experiencing significant age-related cognitive deficits. The researchers also looked at another group of flight attendants, from different airlines, who also had higher levels of cortisol due to crossing time zones, but they didn't have the negative cognitive effects. Cho et al. (2000) noted that the latter group was given longer breaks between flights, which may have allowed them to recover.

The cognitive effects of crossing time zones for several years include slower reaction time, reduced working memory, and possibly impaired attention, which are exactly the type of problems we see in normal age-related memory impairment. Therefore, it is very important that older adults, who are concerned about declining memory ability, do what they can to limit stress and cortisol release.

STRESS AFFECTS THE LIFE EXPECTANCY OF OUR CELLS

Every time our cells divide, which is necessary in order to make new cells or overcome the effects of damaged cells, the cells' telomeres become a little bit shorter. Telomeres cap our chromosomes, which make up our DNA, and thus our telomeres promote cellular stability. The reason all of this is important to aging and health is that once a given cell's telomeres are gone, the cell's lifespan has come to an end.[2] Researchers believe that our cells can be damaged and require cell division if the cells are exposed to physical stress. However, it also appears that psychological stress can also damage our cells and lead to shortened telomeres and a reduced life expectancy for our cells and organs, including brain cells. In animal studies, shorter telomeres have been associated with increased chance of developing cancer. How does stress affect human cells?

Epel and her colleagues published an important study in 2004. They assessed whether stress in younger women, average age 38 years, was associated with the length of their telomeres. Some of the participants in this study were raising children with chronic illnesses and were therefore thought to have a higher than average degree of chronic stress. There were also women in the study who were of similar age but were not raising chronically ill children. All participants had their telomeres measured and completed a questionnaire about their perceived stress levels. Epel et al. reported that the women who were experiencing the greatest stress had the shortest telomeres. Even among the women who were not raising chronically ill children, their level of perceived stress predicted the length of their

---

[2] One of the theories of aging is that our biological longevity is determined by the length of our telomeres. Our genetics probably determine the length of the telomeres we are born with. Support for this theory of aging comes from the fact that one of the best predictors of how long we will live is how long our parents lived.

telomeres. The researchers estimated how much shorter our telomeres become each year; using this data they estimated that the women with the greatest stress and thus the shortest telomeres possessed cells that had aged the equivalent of 9 to 17 years. In other words, a 38-year-old woman who was under a great deal of stress had cell damage equivalent to what we would expect to see in a 55-year-old.

STRESS AND DEPRESSION

Stress and depression are closely linked. We know that people who are depressed tend to generate more daily stressors in their lives, which can further exacerbate their depression (Hammen, 1991). We also know that the risk factors associated with developing depression are very similar to the risk factors associated with developing an anxiety disorder (Vink, Aartsen, & Schoevers, 2008). Many researchers have also found evidence that stress might actually cause people to develop depression (Maddock & Pariante, 2001). Experiencing depression as a result of stress may be another mechanism whereby older adults' memory abilities are compromised. Depression wreaks havoc on older adults' memory and cognitive abilities, and that depression may be a by-product of stress. But there are other pathways and mechanisms through which stress can lead to impaired cognitive functioning, and we will explore these ideas next.

STRESS AND MEMORY

Clearly, stress has many negative effects on people's physical health. But stress also affects our cognitive abilities. Through a number of different pathways, stress reduces our ability to make memories, store them, and retrieve them when needed. In addition, stress appears to increase our chance of developing dementia (Crowe et al., 2007).

Interference

Much of the research that has assessed the relationship between stress and cognitive impairment has focused on the physical effects of stress, such as increased cortisol levels, neuronal atrophy, and damage to the hippocampi. These biological factors are important to consider, but there are also psychological mechanisms associated with stress that impair our cognitive ability. As we discussed in Chapter 2, most age-related deficits in cognitive ability can be traced back to an impaired executive functioning, such as reduced ability to concentrate, pay attention, and suppress irrelevant or off-task thoughts. Another way to view this situation is to recognize that an inability to suppress off-task thoughts will reduce one's short-term or working-memory capacity, thereby leaving fewer cognitive resources to help make memories, recall information, or comprehend information. Recall the bookshelf analogy used in Chapter 2. Our short-term memory is like a bookshelf that holds only a small number of books at one time. If we put another book (thought) on our bookshelf (short-term memory), we have less space for other books and any new book on the bookshelf will push off a book that was already on the shelf. In addition, older adults' bookshelves become a little smaller with age, meaning that they can't hold as much information in their short-term memory at one time.

Researchers are finding evidence that one of the main reasons stress impairs older adults' cognitive ability is that they have a harder time suppressing stressful thoughts while simultaneously trying to do a cognitive task. These intrusive thoughts are put onto the already shrunken bookshelf, leaving very little space to think about and remember information about the task at hand. Stawski, Sliwinski, and Smyth (2006) conducted an important study, which found that many older adults have difficulty suppressing stress-related thoughts and that difficulty was associated with reductions in their working-memory capacity (i.e., size of their bookshelves). Stawski et al. also reported that intrusive and stressful thoughts reduced older adults' ability to make new memories and reduced their processing speed. Once again, it appears that the effects of stress on memory are significant and need to be considered when trying to help older adults improve their overall cognitive ability.

Daily Stressors and Memory

Neupert, Almeida, Mroczek, and Spiro (2006) conducted an interesting study in which they had older adults maintain a diary for eight consecutive days, answering questions about their daily stress levels and their memory ability. The researchers found that as the number of stressors increased, the number of memory problems also increased. One interesting finding was that interpersonal stressors (e.g., related to friends and family) were associated with increased memory problems for the day there was the interpersonal stress. This finding is consistent with other studies that have found that stressful experiences can cause cognitive interference and intrusive thoughts. It may be that older adults (and possibly younger ones) spend time thinking about ways to solve the problem at hand which reduces the mental resources available for making new memories and remembering things that one is suppose to do.

STRESS AND DEMENTIA

Crowe et al. (2007) measured how much people react to stress, as some people are not affected by stress as much as others. Then they assessed whether there was a relationship between reactivity to stress and the likelihood of developing dementia more than 30 years later. They reported that people who were more reactive to stress were more likely to develop dementia. Crowe et al. suggested that the damage that stress and cortisol cause to neurons might play a key role in promoting dementia. They also pointed out that their results were consistent with findings from other studies, which have shown that people who score high on tests of neuroticism (i.e., they are prone to negative emotions, anger, and anxiety) are much more likely to develop dementia. It could be that people who are more neurotic also experience more damage to their neurons, which may make them prone to developing dementia.

PERSONALITY, STRESS, AND MEMORY

Stress is in the eye of the beholder. What is stressful to one person may be perceived as a welcome challenge by another person. Numerous researchers have converged on the finding that personality traits affect how we perceive potentially stressful situations. Psychologists have identified a personality trait known as "distress proneness," which is related to neuroticism. People who are prone to distress tend to worry, feel tense, easily become angered by how others treat them, and often feel helpless and at the mercy of others to help them (Wilson, Bennett, de Leon, Bienias, Morris, & Evans, 2005). In one study of over 4000 older adults with an average age of 74 years, it was found that the more prone to stress people were, the more their cognitive ability declined during a 5-year period (Wilson et al., 2005). These findings are consistent with the research reviewed above about the damaging effects that stress has on people's central nervous systems. The level at which someone is prone to distress is relatively stable over one's lifetime, therefore we may be looking at the cumulative effects of stress in older adults who report being more easily distressed.

RECOMMENDATION FOR STRESS REDUCTION

Clearly, there are many negative consequences associated with stress, but fortunately there are things people can do to reduce stress in their lives. Earlier, I wrote that stress is in the eye of the beholder, which referred to the fact that the same situation could be very stressful to one person but not at all so for someone else. One way to reduce stress is to change how we view the world. This is much easier said than done, but that is what cognitive therapy attempts to do (i.e., change how people think about situations so their perceptions of life don't cause them as much distress). If someone is struggling with stress to the point that it is negatively affecting their health, cognitive ability, relationships, or other areas of life, then I strongly encourage them to seek help from a psychologist or other qualified mental health professional.

Just as people vary in how prone they are to experience stress, people also vary in the techniques and interventions that are most effective for reducing or eliminating stress reactions. Some people turn to exercise, others prefer meditation, or talking with friends. Regardless of the techniques employed, reducing stress can have many physical and cognitive health benefits. Next, a list of possible stress-reduction techniques will be presented.

Exercise

One of the most immediate and effective ways to reduce stress is to exercise. Exercise helps to metabolize the chemical by-products of stress and can lead to the release of endorphins, which can make a person feel better. In addition, exercise can improve mood, raise confidence, and help alleviate anxiety. I strongly recommend a physical exercise program that includes both aerobic and resistance training (see Chapter 6 for more information about physical exercise).

Yoga

There are many different types of yoga, but they generally help train people to better control both their minds and bodies. Yoga that is frequently practiced in Western culture generally focuses on stretching and breathing. This is a great way to gain better control of one's thought processes, which in my opinion, is a necessary skill with which to manage stressful thoughts. Consider taking a yoga class as a way to alleviate stress and improve overall well-being. Yoga classes as well as Tai Chi classes are becoming increasingly popular at health clubs and even senior centers.

Meditation

Meditation is a wonderful way to gain better control of thoughts and therefore control anxiety and reduce stress. There are many forms of meditation, and many books and articles give advice about how to meditate. One goal of meditation is to quiet both the body and the mind. Find a comfortable position to sit, close your eyes, take several deep breaths, and let your thoughts come into and go out of your mind. Visualize a single object, such as a rose. Repeat the word "rose" in your mind. Keep doing this for several minutes. Next time try to do it a little longer, and work your way up to 15 to 20 minutes (Engs, n.d.). If people work at learning how to mediate and control their thoughts, they will be able to reduce intrusive and stressful thoughts. In addition, people who have a hard time falling asleep because they can't "turn their mind off," will also benefit from practicing meditation.

Progressive Muscle Relaxation

Progressive muscle relaxation is a widely used technique that allows people to gain better control of muscle tension and learn how to relieve it. Although is was first developed by physician Edmund Jacobson back in the 1920s, it is still widely used by therapists today. Here are instructions for the technique:

Sit in a comfortable chair—reclining armchairs are ideal. Lying on a bed is OK too. Get as comfortable as possible—no tight clothes or shoes and don't cross your legs. Take a deep breath; let it out slowly. Again. What you'll be doing is alternately tensing and relaxing specific groups of muscles. After tension, a muscle will be more relaxed than prior to the tensing. Concentrate on the feel of the muscles, specifically the contrast between tension and relaxation. In time, you will recognize tension in any specific muscle and be able to reduce that tension.

Don't tense muscles other than the specific group at each step. Don't hold your breath, grit your teeth, or squint. Breathe slowly and evenly and think only about the tension-relaxation contrast. Each tensing is for 10 seconds; each relaxing is for 10 or 15 seconds. Count "1,000 2,000 . . ." until you have a feel for the time span. Note that each step is really two steps—one cycle of tension-relaxation for each set of opposing muscles.

Do the entire sequence once a day until you feel you are able to control your muscle tensions. Be careful: If you have problems with pulled muscles, broken bones, or any medical contraindication for physical activities, consult your doctor first.

1. Hands. The fists are tensed; relaxed. The fingers are extended; relaxed.
2. Biceps and triceps. The biceps are tensed (make a muscle—but shake your hands to make sure not tensing them into a fist); relaxed (drop your arm to the chair). The triceps are tensed (try to bend your arms the wrong way); relaxed (drop them).
3. Shoulders. Pull them back (careful with this one); relax them. Push the shoulders forward (hunch); relax.
4. Neck (lateral). With the shoulders straight and relaxed, the head is turned slowly to the right, as far as you can; relax. Turn to the left; relax.
5. Neck (forward). Dig your chin into your chest; relax. (Bringing the head back is not recommended—you could break your neck.)
6. Mouth. The mouth is opened as far as possible; relaxed. The lips are brought together or pursed as tightly as possible; relaxed.
7. Tongue (extended and retracted). With mouth open, extend the tongue as far as possible; relax (let it sit in the bottom of your mouth). Bring it back in your throat as far as possible; relax.
8. Tongue (roof and floor). Dig your tongue into the roof of your mouth; relax. Dig it into the bottom of your mouth; relax.
9. Eyes. Open them as wide as possible (furrow your brow); relax. Close your eyes tightly (squint); relax. Make sure you completely relax the eyes, forehead, and nose after each of the tensings.
10. Breathing. Take as deep a breath as possible—and then take a little more; let it out and breathe normally for 15 seconds. Let all the breath in your lungs out—and then a little more; inhale and breathe normally for 15 seconds.
11. Back. With shoulders resting on the back of the chair, push your body forward so that your back is arched; relax. Be very careful with this one, or don't do it at all.

12. Butt. Tense the butt tightly and raise pelvis slightly off chair; relax. Dig buttocks into chair; relax.
13. Thighs. Extend legs and raise them about 6 in. off the floor or the footrest, but don't tense the stomach; relax. Dig your feet (heels) into the floor or footrest; relax.
14. Stomach. Pull in the stomach as far as possible; relax completely. Push out the stomach or tense it as if you were preparing for a punch in the gut; relax.
15. Calves and feet. Point the toes (without raising the legs); relax. Point the feet up as far as possible (beware of cramps—if you get them or feel them coming on, shake them loose); relax.
16. Toes. With legs relaxed, dig your toes into the floor; relax. Bend the toes up as far as possible; relax.

Now just relax for a while. As the days of practice progress, you may wish to skip the steps that do not appear to be a problem for you. After you've become an expert on your tension areas (after a few weeks), you can concern yourself only with those. These exercises will not eliminate tension, but when it arises, you will know it immediately, and you will be able to "tense-relax" it away or even simply wish it away. (From: http://en.wikipedia.org/wiki/Progressive_relaxation)

Take a Deep Breath

One way to refocus one's attention and relieve stress is to simply take a few deep breaths. In addition, one may try diaphragmatic breathing, which can be a great way to relieve stress. Here are instructions for a common diaphragmatic breathing exercise:

1. Sit or lie comfortably, with loose garments.
2. Put one hand on your chest and one on your stomach.
3. Slowly inhale through your nose or through pursed lips (to slow down the intake of breath).
4. As you inhale, feel your stomach expand with your hand. If your chest expands, focus on breathing with your diaphragm.
5. Slowly exhale through pursed lips to regulate the release of air.
6. Rest and repeat
   (From: http://en.wikipedia.org/wiki/Diaphragmatic_breathing)

Reduce Exposure to Stressful Situations

One obvious way to reduce overall stress in anyone's life is to simply reduce one's exposure to situations that are stressful. For example, many people experience stress when unavoidable traffic delays cause them to be late for appointments. If that is a possibility, then try to leave for the appointment earlier and bring something to read or some cognitive exercises to do while you wait, if you happen to arrive early. If someone is stressed by the fact that they have too much to do, then they need to learn to say "no" when asked if they would be willing to help out or do something. However, people should not engage in "avoidance coping," which occurs when people avoid thinking about or actually doing something about a life stressor as a way of coping with stress. Avoidance coping may increase the number and intensity of daily hassles people experience in the future and it may increase the likelihood of becoming depressed (Holahan, Moos, Holahan, Brennan, & Schutte, 2005).

Table 1. Additional Stress Reduction Techniques

- Stretch
- Take a warm bath
- Stand up and smile
- Sleep
- Learn to say "no"
- Switch to decaffeinated beverages (do so gradually if you consume a lot of caffeine)
- If things are out of your control, admit that and accept it
- Eat healthier food
- Listen to your favorite music
- Look at photos of family and friends
- Organize your time
- Make a list of things that need to be done
- Talk to a friend
- Take a nap
- Read a book
- Watch a television show or movie
- Make two lists, one that contains all the stressors you can change and another of the stressors you can't change. Determine to change what you can and not worry about what you can't change.
- Try using the aroma-therapy oils, especially those that are calming, such as basil, bay, chamomile, eucalyptus, lavender, peppermint, rose, and thyme
- Avoid being stressed by traffic and unavoidable delays by leaving early for trips or appointments.
- Recognize that life is a work in progress and that not everything will be done exactly as you had hoped or planned.
- Don't avoid doing things that need to be done as a way of reducing stress, as recent research shows that can increase stress in the long run.

Many people overbook themselves running from one event to another. How many times have you heard retirees say, "I am so busy now; I don't know how I ever found time to work?" Well, many people can become too busy, and that can lead to stress. Given the physical and cognitive health risks associated with high levels of stress, I believe it is imperative that people who are experiencing high levels of stress do what is necessary to reduce their overall levels of stress and become more calm. See Table 1 to view additional stress-reduction techniques.

SUGGESTED READINGS

Exercise: Rev up your routine to reduce stress by MayoClinic.com. Available at: http://www.mayoclinic.com/health/exercise-and-stress/SR00036

Braza, J. (1997). *Moment by moment: The art and practice of mindfulness*. Boston: Tuttle Publishers.

Carlson, R. (1997). *Don't sweat the small stuff*. New York: Hyperion.

Davis, M., Eshelman, E. R., & McKay, M. (2000). *Relaxation & stress reduction workbook*. Oakland, CA: New Harbinger Publications.

Honore, C. (2004). *In praise of slowness*. San Francisco: Harper.

Leyden-Rubenstein, L. A. (1998). *The stress management handbook*. New Canaan, CT: Keats Publishing, Inc.

Kabat-Zinn, J. (1994). *Wherever you go, there you are: Mindfulness meditation in everyday life*. New York: Hyperion.

Nhat Hanh, T. (1992). *The miracle of mindfulness: A manual on meditation*. Boston: Beacon Press.

Ruiz, D. (1997). *The four agreements*. San Rafel, CA: Amber-Allen Publishing.

Sapolsky, R. M. (1998). *Why zebras don't get ulcers*. New York: W. H. Freeman and Co.

Wallace, A. (2006). *The attention revolution: Unlocking the power of the focused mind*. Boston: Wisdom Publications.

Wheeler, C. M. (2007). *10 Simple solutions to stress: How to tame tension and start enjoying your life*. Oakland, CA: New Harbinger Publications.

CHAPTER 9

Sleep and Memory

Sleep is the interest we have to pay on the capital which is called in at death; and the higher the rate of interest and the more regularly it is paid, the further the date of redemption is postponed. Arthur Schopenhauer (1788–1860)

Many older adults suffer from insomnia and other sleep problems. Sleep disorders can negatively affect memory ability and lead to other health problems. This chapter will look at the prevalence of sleep problems among older adults and how sleep patterns change as we age. I will discuss different types of insomnia, as well as sleep apnea. Then I will present information about the effects of poor sleep on memory and other cognitive abilities. Generally speaking, insomnia appears to lead to memory impairment, especially when it comes to learning new things, paying attention, and ignoring distracters. Recently, researchers have asserted that insomnia is yet another risk factor for developing memory problems. Moreover, sleep problems may be a risk factor for memory problems that can be dealt with through simple behavioral changes. As we have seen in other chapters in this book, if we can remove or reduce risk factors for memory impairment and dementia, we should be able to delay or even prevent cognitive deterioration. Identifying and treating sleep problems is another important intervention tool in preventing dementia.

There are well-established recommendations for those who are suffering from insomnia. After we discuss sleep and the effects of insomnia on memory, I will present and explain 15 recommendations to improve sleep quality without the aid of pharmaceuticals. These invaluable strategies can be used by anyone and can dramatically improve people's sleep and quality of life. Finally, I will review the latest information on pharmaceuticals designed for people with sleep problems, as the invention of several new sleep aids, many with reduced side effects, increases the options for people suffering from insomnia.

INSOMNIA

Sleep disturbance is one of the most common health problems among older adults. Older adults spend more time in bed than younger adults, but older adults actually get less sleep. Insomnia affects only about 9% of people between the ages of 20 and 30, but 35% to 50% of people over the age of 65 report having sleep problems (Haimov, 2006). Nearly half of people over the age of 65 complain about chronic sleep problems (Campbell, Murphy, & Stauble, 2005). Sleep disturbances can affect almost every aspect of one's life, including quality of life and mortality rates (see Table 1 for a list of negative consequences associated with insomnia or poor sleep).

INSOMNIA AND MEMORY

Clearly insomnia and sleep disturbance can have a dramatic and negative effect on an older adult's life. But sleep problems may also be contributing to memory and cognitive problems for people of all ages, especially older adults. Many studies have documented the negative effects of poor sleep on cognitive ability in younger adults. For example, we know that young insomniacs are more likely to have attention difficulties, decreased daytime functioning, greater difficulty with concentration and memory tasks, and diminished ability to cope with

Table 1. Possible Negative Consequences Associated with
Insomnia or Poor Sleep

1. Increased mortality risk (Kripke, Garfinkel, Wingard, Klauber, & Marler, 2002)

2. Decreased quality of life (Haimov, 2006)

3. Increased cardiovascular risk (Ayas et al., 2003; Foley, Ancoli-Israel, Britz, & Walsh, 2004; Haimov, 2006)

4. Increased risk of obesity (Foley et al., 2004)

5. Increased risk of Type 2 diabetes (Foley et al., 2004)

6. Increased anxiety and perceived stress (LeBlanc et al., 2007)

7. Increased depression (Foley et al., 2004; LeBlanc et al., 2007)

8. Increased risk of motor vehicle accidents (Horne & Reyner, 1999; Pandi-Perumal et al., 2006)

9. Decreased ability to identify odors (Killgore & McBride, 2006)

10. Higher levels of the stress hormone corticosterone, which may impair memory and immune system functioning (Mirescu, Peters, Noiman, & Gould, 2006)

11. Fewer new neurons made in the brain (Mirescu et al., 2006)

12. Decreased ability to inhibit aggression (Kahn-Greene, Lipizzi, Conrad, Kamimori, & Killgore, 2006)

13. Reduced language abilities (Pilcher et al., 2007)

problems (e.g., see Golan, Shahar, Ravid, & Pillar, 2004). Even though there have been fewer studies on the effects of insomnia on older adults, as compared with younger adults, a number of studies are converging upon consistent findings: primarily that insomnia leads to difficulty with attention and memory encoding.

Haimov (2006) found that older adults with insomnia take more time to make new memories. Yoo, Hu, Gujar, Jolesz, and Walker (2007) found that if people miss just one night of sleep, their ability and likelihood of recognizing things they had seen since the sleepless night decreased from 86% to 74%. One might therefore infer that insomniacs who didn't sleep much the night before would have approximately a 12% reduction in their ability to make new memories.

Turner, Drummond, Salamat, and Brown (2007) had 40 younger participants sleep only 26 minutes per night over a four-day period. Participants' cognitive abilities were tested before, during, and after the sleep deprivation period. On the final test, the average working-memory span of the sleep-deprived group had dropped by 38% relative to the control group. Working-memory capacity is very important in making new memories (see Chapter 2 for an extensive review of the importance of working-memory for encoding new memories). Moreover, working-memory capacity decreases throughout adulthood and especially in later adulthood. Therefore, it is important that older adults who are experiencing declining memory ability get good sleep and are well-rested.

Attention and memory are very closely related. If one is having difficulty paying attention, they won't be able to hold as much information in their working-memory, which in turn would decrease memory and comprehension abilities. Sustained attention is probably the cognitive process that researchers have most often observed to be impaired by sleep deprivation (Haimov, 2006). This is also concerning for older adults because much of the age-associated declines in cognitive ability are driven by impairments in attention. This finding further bolsters the idea that older adults, especially those who are concerned about declining memory ability, learn proper sleep hygiene (i.e., behaviors that are recommended to increase sleep time and sleep quality), which will be discussed later in this chapter.

It is important to note that recent research has shown that there is a fair amount of variability in how much sleep deprivation actually hurts various people's cognitive ability. Van Dongen, Baynard, Maislin, and Dinges (2004) found that some younger adults (18-38 years of age) did not show much impairment from sleep deprivation and that effect appears to stay constant in people over time, but other people did show significant cognitive declines with sleep deprivation and that trait also stayed constant within individuals. Therefore it may be that some older adults are not affected by sleep deprivation as much as others, but research designed to test that, to my knowledge, has not been conducted.

Another potential negative effect from insomnia is that people who are sleep deprived may be less able and motivated to engage in cognitively stimulating activities. As was discussed in Chapter 4, cognitively stimulating activities can act as a powerful protective buffer against cognitive decline. Moreover, this relationship could explain some of the connection between insomnia and reduced cognitive ability. However, I suspect that the majority of the relationship between insomnia and memory ability is related to attention and concentration.

SLEEP BASICS

By understanding sleep, you will be better equipped to help yourself and others improve total sleep time as well as overall sleep quality. In particular, understanding and recognizing wake-sleep cycles and their causes can help you create more effective behavioral changes to improve sleep.

SLEEP STAGES

There are two general types of sleep: rapid eye movement (REM) sleep and non-rapid eye movement (NREM). It appears that both REM sleep and NREM sleep are needed to consolidate or cement new explicit memories into place. Adults spend about 80% of their sleep time in NREM sleep. There are four stages of NREM sleep. During Stage 1 and Stage 2, people are sleeping lightly. They are most likely to experience hypnic jerks or muscle twitches during Stage 1 (these twitches are more likely to occur when people are sleep deprived). Stage 3 and Stage 4 are considered slow wave sleep, as the activity level of the brain slows down. Stage 4 is the deepest sleep, when the brain is least active.

REM sleep occurs approximately every 90 minutes, and the length of REM episodes get longer throughout the night. The brain is actually quite active during REM sleep, and when researchers measure brain waves in REM sleep, they look like those of someone who is awake. Therefore, we sometimes refer to REM sleep as paradoxical sleep, as the person is asleep, but the brain is very active. Most dreams occur during REM sleep.

The percentage of time that we spend asleep and in REM sleep decreases dramatically through infancy, childhood, adulthood, and even older adulthood. Newborns spend about 16 hours a day sleeping, 50% of that time is in REM sleep. Two year olds spend about 12 hours a day sleeping, about 25% of that time is in REM sleep. Middle-aged adults spend less than eight hours a day sleeping, and approximately 20% of that time is in REM sleep. People in their 80s spend less than seven hours a day sleeping, and approximately 20% of that time is in REM sleep. Sleep also becomes more fragmented for older adults; they are more likely to frequently wake up during the night.

Circadian Rhythms

We have a number of cycles that affect our overall wakefulness throughout the day. First, we have a circadian rhythm, which is our night and day rhythm and is usually on a 24-hour cycle. The word "circadian" comes from the Latin "circa," which means "around," and "diem" or "dies," which means "day," therefore the word "circadian" translates into "around a day." That is a fitting translation because the cycle really is around a day. Researchers have found that if people don't have any night-day cues (e.g., if they spend several weeks in an underground laboratory), they usually adjust to a 25-hour cycle or around a day. The circadian rhythm is largely controlled by the hormone melatonin, which is released by the pineal gland.

Melatonin is largely controlled by light. Researchers recently discovered photo-receptors in the back of our eyes, which, when activated by light, are involved in turning off melatonin secretion. Conversely, when the photoreceptors are not activated by light, the pineal gland releases melatonin and the person becomes sleepy. This entire system can be disrupted by artificial light, which is ubiquitous in modern life. If the body is inhibiting melatonin release because the environment is brightly lit, the person may have a hard time falling asleep. Therefore, to maximize the ease with which one falls asleep, it would be advisable to decrease the overall light levels before bedtime. See Figure 1 for information about how the circadian rhythm affects people and their melatonin release.

Research on the effects of light exposure at night has led to mixed results. It may be that fairly large doses of light are needed to lead to dramatic sleep disruption. But one consistent and robust finding is that if older adults are not exposed to enough daylight during the day, their night sleep may be impaired.

Ultradian Rhythm

We not only cycle through being more awake and less awake in a 24-hour period, but we also have a subrhythm that we cycle through every 90 minutes. This subrhythm is known as an ultradian rhythm. For example, if you are wide awake at 8:00 a.m., you are likely to be a little less awake at 8:45 a.m., and then more awake again at 9:30 a.m. (i.e., 90 minutes after 8:00 a.m.). You may have noticed the effect of ultradian rhythms in your life. For example, have you ever had to get up very early, say 4:00 a.m., and you naturally awoke at 3:15 a.m.? If so, you might have thought, "Well, I could fairly easily get up now, but I better get an extra 45 minutes of sleep." Then, when your alarm went off at 4:00 a.m., you could hardly get out of bed. You may have wondered why you naturally awoke earlier but after a little more sleep you felt more tired. The answer to that apparent conundrum is that your ultradian cycle was making you more awake earlier and less awake later.

We can use our ultradian cycles to help us fall asleep. For example, don't wait until you are at the bottom of your ultradian cycle (i.e., most tired) before getting ready to go to bed because by the time you get ready for bed you will no longer be at the bottom of your ultradian cycle. Moreover, 45 minutes after you

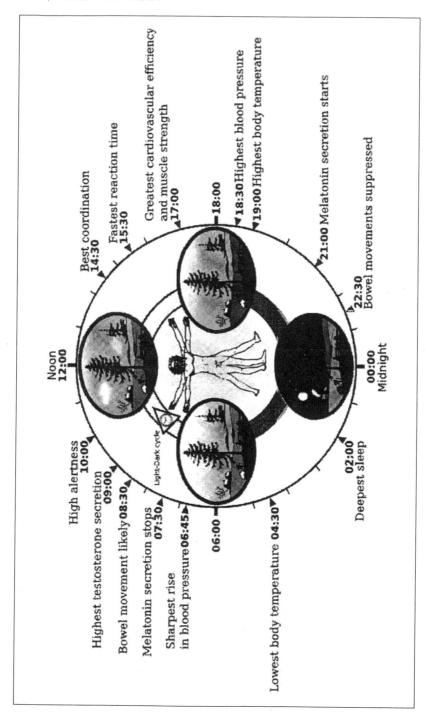

Figure 1. The human circadian rhythm. Public domain image from http://en.wikipedia.org/wiki/Circardian_rhythm

hit the bottom of the ultradian cycle you will be at the top and that may be when you are staring at the ceiling feeling frustrated that you can't fall asleep.

Consider calculating when your optimal time to go to sleep is. To do this you must note when your body naturally wakes up in the morning. For example, if you naturally awoke (i.e., without an alarm or other disturbance) at 8:00 a.m., we can infer that 12 hours later (eight ultradian cycles) you should be relatively awake at 8:00 p.m. and less awake at 8:45 p.m. and every 90 minutes afterwards. So optimal times to be in bed and ready to fall asleep would be 8:45 p.m., 10:15 p.m., and 11:45 p.m., if you naturally awoke at 8:00 a.m.

INSOMNIA: TYPES AND POSSIBLE CAUSES

Insomnia affects 30% to 40% of adults in the United States. William Dement, a leading sleep researcher and the person who coined the term "rapid eye movement" said, "Sleep deprivation is a major epidemic in our society. . . . Americans spend so much time chasing the American dream, that they don't have much time left for actual dreaming" (as cited in Weiten, 2002).

Insomnia can have many different contributing and underlying causes. We know that some mental health disorders and issues are associated with sleep disturbances. For example, depression, bipolar disorder, neuroticism, high levels of perceived stress, and anxiety are more common in insomniacs than people who report good sleep (LeBlanc et al., 2007). It is always difficult to know which condition is causing which condition. For example, is a predisposition to anxiety causing insomnia or is the lack of sleep making people more anxious? With that said, it does appear that depression may be directly leading to an increase in the chance of developing insomnia, such that insomnia makes people three to four times more likely to develop depression (Perlis et al., 2006). In addition, there is evidence that older adults and women may be more vulnerable to developing depression if they are experiencing insomnia. Given that depression can wreak havoc on older adults' cognitive ability, we need to be cautious of the possibility that chronic insomniacs may develop depression. Other medical conditions, especially those associated with chronic pain, are associated with increased risk of sleep problems. In addition, many pharmaceuticals can disrupt sleep patterns.

SLEEP APNEA

Sleep apnea is a sleep disorder associated with pauses in breathing during sleep. Apnea translates into "without breath." The breathless pauses last at least 10 seconds, and in the more severe cases, the long pause causes a significant drop in blood oxygen levels. However, even in the less serious cases, the pause in breathing causes the individual to briefly awaken. Given that many cases of sleep apnea are related to obesity, sleep apnea is fairly common in industrialized countries; between 20% and 24% of middle-aged and older adults in the United States and United Kingdom have at least occasional sleep apnea. The rates climb even higher for older adults living in a more institutionalized setting.

There are two types of sleep apnea: central and obstructive. Central sleep apnea is less common and is associated with an impaired ability to regulate breathing and adjust to low oxygen levels or high carbon dioxide levels. People with central sleep apnea don't make an effort to breath during the breathless episode but will often breath faster afterwards. The more common type of sleep apnea is known as obstructive sleep apnea, which is associated with the soft tissue in the throat becoming relaxed during sleep, which in turn obstructs the breathing pathway for many people. This problem is made much worse if the individual is obese, especially if they have a lot of fat in the neck and face. However, it should be noted that nonobese individuals can also have obstructive sleep apnea.

Sleep apnea can lead to some very serious medical problems, including hypertension, arrhythmias, cardiovascular disease, and cardiopulmonary disease (Cohen-Zion, Stepnowsky, Johnson, Marler, Dimsdale, & Ancoli-Israel, 2004). In addition, the impaired quality and quantity of sleep may be contributing to cognitive deficits, not to mention possible negative effects associated with hypoxia (low oxygen saturation levels) in the most severe cases.

Cohen-Zion et al. (2004) reported that sleep-breathing disorders are asso-ciated with poorer performance on various neurocognitive measures. Moreover, they found that the severity of the sleep-breathing disorder was correlated with the severity of the cognitive impairment. Other researchers have documented impaired executive functioning, decreased attention, and impaired memory ability among sleep apnea patients.

It is possible to treat sleep apnea in many cases, however many people don't know they have sleep apnea and don't remember the difficulties they have breathing during the night. Oftentimes, a loved one is the first to notice the sleep apnea or notice it worsening. The most common symptom observed by loved ones is loud snoring, followed by breathless pauses, followed by gasps for breath. The sleep apnea sufferer is most likely to notice extreme drowsiness during the day, often associated with an inability to stay awake even while doing normal daytime activities such as carrying on a conversation. Other symptoms include headaches, trouble paying attention, irritability, memory problems, anxiety, depression, weight gain, night sweats, and frequently getting up to urinate. A proper diagnosis usually requires an overnight stay in a sleep clinic to monitor breathing and sleep patterns.

People need to be aware of sleep apnea, the risk factors for the condition, and symptoms associated with it, because the repercussions can have a dramatic and negative effect on people's overall health, quality of life, and their cognitive ability. Moreover, sleep apnea is usually treatable. Many times simple lifestyle and behavioral changes may improve the condition. Changes such as avoiding alcohol and sedative drugs (e.g., benzodiazepines), losing weight, or quitting smoking can improve the condition. People can change their sleeping position or use a mouthpiece designed to keep the airway open. If those interventions don't work, the person's doctor may recommend wearing a device that blows a continuous stream of air into the person's mouth. And in the most severe cases, surgery is often used to open the airways.

SNORING

Clearly, snoring is not as detrimental to one's health as sleep apnea. But some studies have found that snorers are more vulnerable to cognitive decline (e.g., Quesnot & Alperovitch, 1999), while other studies have not found such a relationship. Regardless, it is clear that snoring can negatively affect one's sleep and the sleeping partner's ability to get a good night's rest. Snoring appears to be more common in men and also appears to increase after the age of 60 (Lugaresi, Cirignotta, Coccagna, & Piana, 1980). Some of the more conservative treatments for sleep apnea may also be used to treat excessive snoring. Both the snorer and their sleeping partner are likely to get better sleep and therefore maximize their cognitive ability. Factors that increase the likelihood of snoring or snoring more loudly include alcohol consumption, being overweight, or having a cold. Sleeping on one's side may limit snoring relative to sleeping on one's back.

SLEEP AND AGING

Older adults' sleep patterns are somewhat different from younger adults. Older adults spend less time in deep sleep (Stages 3 and 4) and more time in lighter stages. They often experience more nighttime awakenings and more fragmented sleep, often waking up every 90 minutes as dictated by their ultradian cycle. Older adults also spend a little less time in REM sleep. One interesting and common change in sleep patterns is that older adults become tired earlier in the evening and get up earlier in the day, which is known as a *phase advance in circadian rhythms*, and may be caused by the hormone melatonin being released earlier in the night. It is interesting to note that the opposite change occurs in adolescents, which causes them to stay up later and sleep in later.

WAYS TO IMPROVE SLEEP AND
OVERCOME INSOMNIA

There are many well-established recommendations to help people decrease the amount of time it takes to fall asleep, decrease the chance of frequent night wakings, increase sleep quality, and increase overall sleep time (see Table 2 to view a list of recommendations). I will review a few of the recommendations.

Table 2. Fifteen Ways to Improve Sleep

1. Keep regular hours.

2. Exercise everyday but not in the evening. Stretching and moderate exercise in the morning seems to be most beneficial in decreasing how long it takes to fall asleep and how long people stay asleep.

3. Don't drink too much alcohol after dinner; it will impair the quality of sleep.

4. Avoid nicotine and caffeine, which are both CNS stimulants. Jefferson et al. (2005) found that insomniacs were more likely to smoke cigarettes as compared with non-insomniacs. Some studies have found that caffeine consumption, especially later in the day, causes people to fall asleep slower and stay asleep for shorter periods of time.

5. Take a nap during the day. This recommendation is different from what has been suggested during the past 30 years, but new research (e.g., Campbell et al., 2005; Lai, 2005) shows it generally increases total daily sleep duration and quality of night sleep.

6. Unwind in the evening. "The lamb and the lion may lie down together but the lamb won't be very sleepy" (Woody Allen). This mechanism is adaptive if there is a danger or threat, but it has had a negative affect on modern people whose lives are often full of chronic stressors.

7. Don't go to bed starved or stuffed.

8. Don't associate the bedroom with wakefulness. Don't eat, drink, or watch television in bed. If you can't go to sleep, get up and do something else besides worrying about not going to sleep.

9. Don't ruminate in bed. If you have thoughts that you would like to remember, jot them down and stop thinking about them.

10. Use the ultradian cycles to predict optimal times to go to sleep.

11. Control light and thus melatonin release.

12. Be sure to make the sleeping environment as comfortable as possible (e.g., bedding, temperature)

13. Make sure the sleeping environment meets your standards of tidiness.

14. Get more exposure to natural light during the day.

15. Try to reduce noise exposure during the night.

Napping

Should people take naps to increase overall sleep? This has been a somewhat controversial question among sleep experts and gerontologists. In the past few decades, many medical professionals have advised against napping, citing that it would negatively affect nocturnal sleep duration and quality. However, based on recent studies, that perspective is changing.

Older adults obtain, on average, one hour less sleep per night than their younger counterparts. Given that sleep-deprived individuals are often less alert, have poorer attention, and memory ability, it is easy to wonder whether napping could help older adults' cognitive ability. A recent study done by Campbell and his colleagues (2005) yielded some promising findings. Campbell gave older adults a two-hour napping opportunity each day and measured how it affected their nighttime sleeping and their cognitive performance. Campbell et al. reported that napping was associated with better performance on a number of cognitive and psychomotor tasks, including the Stroop Test (see Chapter 13 for more information about the Stroop Test, as it is an excellent measure of cognitive ability and can be used in cognitive enhancement programs). Campbell et al. also reported that the cognitive improvements associated with napping were present after the nap and continued into the next day. Other researchers are also finding that napping can lead to improvements in cognitive ability, which is great news for anyone who wants to improve their memory ability. But did the daytime napping, which for most people occurs between 2:00 p.m. and 4:00 p.m., lead to poorer sleep at night?

Campbell et al. (2005) reported that daytime napping did not lead to shorter sleeping durations at night, as some professionals had feared. Moreover, when you add the time spent napping, the older adults total time spent asleep during a 24-hour period increased to an average of 7.4 hours. Other researchers (e.g., Lai, 2005) have reported similar findings. However, I should mention that a minority of researchers has found that napping does not always help, but few studies reported that napping significantly impairs overall sleep.

The above findings are exciting because they give people another tool to improve their quality of life and their cognitive ability. However, just as some people are morning people and others are evening people, it appears that some people are good at napping, while others are less so.

Exercise and Sleep

Physical exercise can be used to help individuals improve their sleep. Researchers have found that individuals who are physically fit tend to fall asleep quicker at night and have a better quality of sleep. A number of studies have looked at the effects on people's sleep of starting an exercise program. One study found that after four months of exercising, people reported having improved sleep quality, falling asleep quicker, and sleeping for longer periods of time

(King, Oman, Brassington, Bliwise, & Haskel, 1997). Other researchers have reported similar findings.

In another study, researchers found that older women who have problems sleeping had fewer sleep complaints if they did light exercises in the morning. In addition, those who also stretched in the morning had better overall sleep quality. In a study done by Tworoger et al. (2003), post-menopausal women age 50-75 were randomly assigned to one of several exercise or stretching interventions that lasted one year. The researchers found that among women who exercised in the morning, those who engaged in moderate exercise at least 225 minutes a week had less difficulty falling asleep than women who exercised less than 180 minutes a week. But the results were opposite among evening exercisers such that the women who exercised the most (i.e., more than 225 minutes per week) were more likely to report difficulties falling asleep as compared with those who exercised less than 180 minutes a week. One hypothesis as to why evening exercise disrupts sleep is that the body is too warm and takes approximately four hours to cool to the point that is optimal for falling asleep. Some sleep experts recommend taking a hot shower after evening exercise because that will engage the body's natural cooling mechanisms, cool the body faster, and allow for sleep in about half the time.

Alcohol and caffeine consumption can negatively affect sleep quality. Although alcohol will often make people sleepy and more likely to fall asleep, alcohol (and other central nervous system depressants) will cause the sleep to become more fragmented and increase the number of mid-night wakings, which would be particularly problematic for people who struggle staying asleep at night. Jefferson et al. (2005) found that insomniacs were more likely to drink alcohol before bed as compared with non-insomniacs. Not surprisingly, caffeine can also disrupt sleep.

Caffeine consumed later in the day leads to poorer sleep quality, changes in brain wave patterns during sleep, and longer time intervals between going to bed and actually falling asleep. Some studies have found that overall sleep time is reduced when caffeine is consumed in the evening. In one smaller study, researchers reported that overall sleep times for people who consumed caffeine was 336 minutes (5.6 hours), whereas the non-caffeine group slept 415 minutes (6.9 hours). Other studies have consistently found that caffeine is associated with more awakenings during the night. Clearly, caffeine consumption, especially later in the day, should be kept to a minimum if people are having the above sleep problems.

It is imperative that the bed and bedroom don't become associated with wakefulness. People can become classically conditioned to become more awake in their bed if they have had problems falling asleep. It is like Ivan Pavlov, who trained dogs to salivate to a tone. At first, the tone did not produce any salivation. But after the tone and food were repeatedly paired together, the tone soon elicited salivation in absence of food. The same thing can happen with bed and wakefulness. At first, the bed doesn't cause people to become more awake. But insomniacs will often lie in bed, watch the minutes and hours go by, and become increasingly distressed by the fact that they can't fall asleep and how tired and ineffective they will be the next day. If those type of nights are repeatedly paired with the bed, then the bed alone might cause stress and wakefulness. In order to prevent the bed from becoming a classically conditioned stimulus, one should get up and do something else until they are tired again. Many times, just 20 minutes of reading in another room will be enough to make someone tired enough to fall asleep.

Many people will think about things they need to do when they are trying to fall asleep. Many times such thoughts can be mildly distressing and inhibit people's ability to fall asleep. An effective solution is to keep a notepad by one's bedside. If something comes to mind that must be done later, they can simply write it down and (hopefully) be done with the thought and go to bed.

It is also important to control light and thus melatonin release in the evening. Begin to dim lights before bedtime. It may be more difficult for the brain to release melatonin if the environment is brightly lit. Also, when someone gets up and leaves their bed because they can't sleep, they should maintain a fairly dim environment (e.g., just enough light to comfortably read by). See Table 2 to view 15 ways to improve sleep.

Ask the Memory Doctor:

A nurse once told me that you shouldn't take naps because they might make you sleep more poorly at night. I am also worried that people will think I have some sort of problem if I take naps.

In the relatively recent past, medical professionals generally did not recommend napping as it was thought that it might lead to or exacerbate symptoms of insomnia. The suggestion to not nap was a common "sleep hygiene" recommendation. However, the tide is turning. Based on recent research, it appears that napping, regardless of age, does not lead to shorter sleep periods at night. Some studies have even found that napping is associated with better sleep quality at night. Moreover, it appears that napping can improve overall cognitive functioning in older adults, especially in the evening. However, the cognitive benefits associated with napping even continue into the next day.

Throughout recent history, we have seen cultures change their attitudes toward napping as they have gone from an agrarian economy to an industrialized economy. Napping while working in a factory or office building isn't feasible for most people. With those cultural and occupational changes, it seems that some people viewed napping as a negative behavior, possibly associated with being old or being lazy. However, given that older adults often don't get as much sleep as they need and that many people, regardless of age, are sleep deprived, I believe it is time to change our attitudes toward napping and recognize the many possible benefits associated with "taking a siesta."

SLEEPING MEDICATIONS

There are quite a few options available if it is determined that a pharmacological approach to treating insomnia is appropriate. Barbiturates were the first class of drugs available to treat insomnia, however these powerful drugs had significant side effects, which limited their therapeutic effectiveness. Then benzodiazepines became available and were widely used by people who had anxiety disorders or sleep problems. Some benzodiazepines became household names in the 1970s and 1980s, drugs such as diazepam (Valium), lorazepam (Ativan), triazolan (Halcion) and oxazepam (Serax) rapidly became the drugs of choice to treat insomnia. Benzodiazepines work by reducing the excitability of certain brain cells, which tends to have a sedating or calming effect. However, these drugs can be habit forming and when the drug is stopped, people experience rebound anxiety or rebound insomnia, such that they would have more anxiety or insomnia symptoms after stopping the drug therapy than they had before. Moreover, many people had significant residual effects from taking benzodiazepines that caused them to be sleepy and sluggish the next day. For older adults, an increased likelihood of falling is also a concern whenever they are taking strong sedatives. Older benzodiazepines can also dampen attention and cognitive ability if taken in moderate dosages. There is now a new class of sleeping medication available that has fewer side effects and may be less addicting.

So called Z-drugs are now the most common class of drugs used to treat insomnia. They are called Z-drugs because their nontrade names begin with "z" (and zzz's are associated with sleep): *zolpidem* (Ambien), zaleplon (Sonata), and eszopiclone (Lunesta). Z-drugs are not technically benzodiazepines, but they have similar effects in the brain. Z-drugs are metabolized by the body more rapidly and therefore don't have the same "hangover" effects the next day as we see with the older benzodiazepines. Some Z-drugs, such as zaleplon (Sonata) are very rapidly metabolized by the body and therefore are useful in treating insomnia associated with having a difficulty falling asleep. Zaleplon (Sonata) is metabolized so quickly that people taking it are very unlikely to feel any residual effects the next day, however the drug will do little to prevent frequent awakenings. The other Z-drugs are not metabolized as rapidly as zaleplon, therefore they should prevent frequent or early awakenings, but they are more likely to have some residual effects, albeit less severe than traditional benzodiazepines.

Although the Z-drugs are probably less likely to cause impairments in attention, memory, and balance, they may still do so, especially in the evening after they are taken (Allain, Bentué-Ferrer, Polard, Akwa, & Patat, 2005). The dosages of Z-drugs are usually halved in older adults (Wilson & Nutt, 2007). The good news about these new drugs is that they are generally well-tolerated by older adults and possibly less addictive (Conn & Madan, 2006). See Table 3 to view a list of possible side effects for benzodiazepines and Z-drugs.

Table 3. Side Effects from Common Sleeping Medications:
Benzodiazepines and Z-Drugs

Benzodiazepines can cause a range of side effects, including:

- reduced attention and alertness
- stumbling or falling
- memory loss
- drowsiness
- light-headedness
- a hangover effect (i.e., feeling the effects the next day)
- lethargy
- loss of behavioral control leading to irritability and agitation
- increased insomnia after the person stops taking the medication

Z-drugs cause fewer side effects or reduced severity of side effects, but they can cause:

- drowsiness
- nausea
- memory loss
- some people report a short period (i.e., one or two days) of rebound insomnia after the person stops taking the medication, but many do not experience this
- unpleasant taste in the mouth for a minority of patients

Patients given the Z-drugs tend to fall asleep quicker, stay asleep longer, and have fewer nighttime awakenings. In a recent study, researchers gave insomniacs either eszopiclone (Lunesta) or a placebo for 6 months. Those who took the actual drug experienced enhanced quality of life, reduced severity of their insomnia, and had fewer work limitations (Walsh et al., 2007). In a related study, insomniacs taking eszopiclone (Lunesta) took less time to fall asleep, had fewer awakenings, better sleep quality, increased daytime alertness, and a better sense of well-being after taking the medication (Roth, Walsh, Krystal, Wessel, & Roehrs, 2005).

The sales of these new generation sleeping medications have skyrocketed. In 2006 sales of Ambien and Lunesta exceeded $3 billion. And the use of all newer types of sleeping medications has increased by more than 60% since 2000. In 2005 there were 43 million prescriptions filled for this new class of drugs, which generated $2.7 billion in revenue for pharmaceutical companies (McKenzie et al., 2007).

What are the Side Effects Associated with Z-Drugs?

In March of 2007 the *New York Times* reported that the U.S. Federal Drug Administration was requiring pharmacies to put strong new warnings on many of the newer sleeping medications (e.g., Ambien and Lunesta) due to reports of bizarre nighttime behavior. Supposedly, a small percentage of people were eating, baking, buying things on the Internet, making phone calls, having sex, and even driving in the middle of the night when they took the medication. It appears that alcohol, even fairly small amounts, played a role in the vast majority of these cases.

SLEEP IN RESIDENTIAL CARE FACILITIES AND NURSING HOMES

Older adults living in institutionalized settings (e.g., assisted living facilities and nursing homes) have higher rates of sleep problems than independent older adults (Conn & Madan, 2006). As many as two-thirds of older adults living in institutionalized settings report having sleep disturbances. It is worth looking at possible reasons why this population is at greater risk for sleep problems, as those risk factors can be reduced or even eliminated. The net benefit is that the older adults will have better sleep, improved quality of life, and possibly improved cognitive ability. Excessive noise and bright lights are some of the primary environmental reasons that older adults experience greater levels of sleep impairment in institutionalized settings. In a study of 10 nursing homes, Cruise, Schnelle, Alessi, Simmons, and Ouslander (1998) found that noise and light accounted for 50% of the cases in which residents were awoken during the night. Many times, it was staff who were talking in normal conversational voice rather than a hushed whisper, linen carts, or slammed doors that awoke residents. Many of these auditory intrusions could be limited. Another problem for assisted living and nursing home residents is that most do not get enough physical activity, which can in turn lead to impaired sleep. Nor do they receive enough nonartificial light. We should strive to get people to exercise more, go outdoors as much as possible, and reduce nighttime auditory distractions as much as possible.

CHAPTER 10

Practical Tips to Improving the Ability to Make New Memories

I have the worst memory ever so no matter who comes up to me—they're just, like, "I can't believe you don't remember me!" I'm like, "Oh Dad I'm sorry!" Ellen DeGeneres (1958–)

This chapter will present general information about how to improve memory. We will simply go through a series of 12 suggestions about how anyone can improve their memory. These suggestions are not mnemonics but are based on human memory research and theories. Then we will discuss mnemonics, which are strategies to help enhance memory ability. I generally don't explicitly encourage the use of most mnemonic strategies for older adults, especially those who are already beginning to experience significant cognitive decline. Mnemonic strategies usually require a great deal of attention and cognitive resource, which are often impaired in geriatric populations. With that said, a lot of research has found these strategies to be useful for older adults, especially younger older adults. We will discuss some of the research and the strategies that have been found to be helpful. At the end of the chapter, there are recommended readings in which the interested reader can find books devoted to mnemonic strategies.

PAY ATTENTION

It sounds obvious and possibly a bit condescending to state this, but the most important factor in creating new memories is to pay attention. If one doesn't pay attention and concentrate on the to-be-remembered material, the information is unlikely to ever transfer from working memory to long-term memory. Unfortunately, advancing age tends to decrease our ability to pay attention (see Chapter 12 for activities to enhance attention). There are also external factors that can affect attention. For example, many people's cognitive resources, which are required to make new memories, think, and problem solve will be reduced by music with words, people talking, or having the television on. This effect is known as the *unattended speech effect* (Salamé & Baddeley, 1989), because speech that we don't intend to pay attention to gets automatic access to our short-term or working memory (or our mental bookshelf if we use the analogy from Chapter 2). However, it is interesting to note that not everyone is equally affected by the unattended speech effect. People who have an internal locus of control (i.e., they take responsibility for the outcomes in their life) are less affected by the unattended speech effect. Conversely, people who have an external locus of control (i.e., they think that things outside of them such as luck or the behavior of others are responsible for the outcomes in their lives) experience greater cognitive disruption from the unattended speech effect.

So if you want to maximize your ability to pay attention and maximize new memories, I encourage you to minimize the distracters in your environment. For example, if you are having an important conversation with someone, you don't want to have the television on in the background. Some of the words from the television will end up on your mental bookshelf, thereby reducing the available cognitive resources for the conversation. However, if you want to exercise your cognitive ability, especially the ability to pay attention and ignore irrelevant stimuli, I recommend doing cognitive exercises (e.g., Sudoku or other activities in Chapter 12) with the television on. Doing a cognitive exercise with the television on will require even greater attention; it would be like walking with extra weights around your ankles.

REDUCE STRESS

Stress can also disrupt people's attention. Many times people who are experiencing stress will have intrusive thoughts that interfere with their ability to pay attention. The stressful and intrusive thoughts gain access to their working memory, thereby reducing their ability to pay attention and remember what they want to (Stawski et al., 2006). In addition to the attention-robbing effects of stress, it generally reduces memory ability as well. See Chapter 8 for a more detailed discussion of the effects of stress on memory and what you can do to reduce it.

RELAX: TAKE A DEEP BREATH

Anxiety about one's memory ability can negatively impair many people's ability to make new memories. The thought that one might not be able to remember something will use up precious cognitive resources, which will actually reduce the ability to remember something. For this reason, I recommend that people try to relax when trying to remember something. It is difficult to sit down and do a 10-minute progressive relaxation session before trying to remember someone's name or some things you need to pick up at the store. Therefore, I recommend that people simply take a deep breath, breath in through the nose using one's diaphragm, hold it for a second or two, let the stress melt away, and then make a concerted effort to remember what you want to remember.

GET ENOUGH SLEEP

Sleep deprivation can also negatively affect attention and thus memory ability. Turner, Drummond, Salamat, and Brown (2007) found that sleep deprivation reduced participants' working-memory capacity by 38%. Sustained attention is probably the cognitive process that researchers have most often observed to be impaired by sleep deprivation (Haimov, 2006). Given the importance of attention in making new memories, it is crucial that people get adequate quantity and quality of sleep (see Chapter 9 for more information about the effects of sleep on cognition and suggestions as to how sleep can be improved).

BE CAREFUL WITH SIMPLE CARBOHYDRATES AND SUGARY FOODS

Low blood sugar levels can also negatively affect attention. Many people experience low blood sugar levels shortly after consuming food that is high in simple carbohydrates (e.g., refined sugar found in many sweets). Their blood sugar levels rise quickly and then fall quickly, which can make paying attention very difficult. In addition, people with diabetes and even pre-diabetes appear to be at an increased risk of developing memory problems or even dementia; these people clearly need to be very cognizant of their sugar consumption and their blood glucose levels.

REHEARSAL

Rehearsing the to-be-remembered material is one of the best ways to improve future memory performance. However, it is important to note that not all rehearsal is equal. Strive to rehearse information in a deep and meaningful way. Try to connect the information to other things you know. Try to create a visual image of the to-be-remembered material. When trying to remember something, spend a few seconds looking for noteworthy details about the to-be-remembered information. Try to mentally or verbally state what you are noticing, as that will facilitate a deeper level of processing and more efficient encoding of new memories.

Try to use a mnemonic technique. For example, if you need to remember three names of people you just met, try to use the first letter of their names and create a meaningful acronym. If you met Scott, Dan, and Dave, you could rearrange the first letters to create a potentially meaningful acronym—DDS (Doctor of Dental Surgery). Even if you are unable to think of a good mnemonic, just the act of thinking about it will be a fairly deep level of rehearsal, which will increase the chance of remembering the information.

USE EXPANDING REHEARSAL

The timing of the rehearsal is important. We know that it is better to space rehearsal out rather than do it all at one time. It is even better if you have increasingly longer intervals between rehearsal trials. I frequently use expanding rehearsal, with excellent success, when I teach memory classes for older adults. For example, I will give the memory class a fact of the day. We will talk about it briefly, during which time I encourage them to process the information at a deeper level (which is easier said than done). Then, I ask the participants what the fact of the day was 1 minute, 4 minutes, 10 minutes, 20 minutes, and 50 minutes after the initial presentation of the fact of the day. Using this technique, the majority of people with mild cognitive impairment and even some people with early-stage dementia can remember the fact of the day after five or six rehearsal trials. Researchers have also found support for this technique. Neuschatz, Preston, Toglia, and Neuschatz (2005) wanted to see if expanding rehearsal was more helpful than an imagery technique when people are trying to remember names of people. They reported that expanding rehearsal technique was indeed a more superior technique than imagery. Ironically, the biggest challenge to using this memory technique is to *remember* to rehearse the information, which is why it is most useful in a memory class when the instructor can plan to prompt the participants to remember at the appropriate intervals. However, if you really want someone who is experiencing some significant memory problems to remember something, you can try this technique and query them about the information yourself using expanding rehearsal.

TAKE YOUR TIME

It is important to take your time when trying to make new memories. Too often people think they should be able to make new memories very rapidly with just one exposure, even if there are other things competing for their attention. Making new long-term memories requires us to literally change the structure of our brains, and we shouldn't expect that to happen immediately. I encourage people to take their time when they want to remember something new, to think about it, and to try to make associations with other things related to the to-be-remembered material.

DON'T (INCORRECTLY) MULTITASK

I believe that multitasking can have a very negative impact on people's ability to make new memories. If people try to do two tasks that require attention and cognitive resources, their ability to do the tasks will suffer and they will be less likely to encode new memories while the multitasking is taking place. For example, people can't simultaneously be attentive to someone who is telling them information they need to remember while at the same time reading a book. The person would have to attend to one of the tasks at the decrement of the other.

Many college students are now bringing laptop computers into the classroom to use in helping them take notes. Recent research has found that bringing a laptop into the classroom is associated with additional multitasking behavior and therefore leads to significant decreases in learning and overall class performance (Fried, 2008). Older adults' memory and cognitive ability is impaired even more than younger adults when they multitask. Multitasking requires a large working-memory capacity (or bookshelf). In addition, multitasking also requires fast speed of processing. Unfortunately, both of those abilities or resources decrease somewhat during adulthood, which is probably why many studies have found older adults are worse at multitasking than younger adults. It is important that people of all ages are aware that multitasking can decrease their overall performance. Unfortunately, many people continue to believe they can success-fully do multiple cognitive activities at once.

There is one type of multitasking that will not negatively affect cognitive ability very much. You can multitask if one of the activities is cognitive and the other is a motor task that is well-learned. Well-learned motor tasks are called procedural memories. It takes a lot of practice and cognitive resources to turn a behavior into a procedural memory. For example, when you first learned to drive, you had to try hard to remember all the steps involved in starting a car or making a lane change, but now you do it without thinking about it because all that practice has made driving a procedural memory. Now when you drive you can use your cognitive resources to think about other things. You have probably experienced the situation when you get in your car and drive a frequently traveled route, only to arrive and have no memory of driving there. This can occur because driving and the route is so overlearned that you don't need to think about it. You can multitask by driving (procedural task) while thinking about some-thing else (cognitive task). Here are some other examples of multitasking a cognitive and a procedural task. You can brush your teeth (procedural task) while listening to a talk-radio program (cognitive task). Or you can eat a bowl of cereal (procedural task) while reading the newspaper (cognitive task). Or you can hold the telephone while on hold (procedural task), while reading the newspaper (cognitive task).

MONITOR YOURSELF

It is crucial for people to be able to monitor how well they are learning and remembering information; this ability is referred to as metacognition, which means "thinking about your thinking." Cavallini, Pagnin, and Vecchi (2002) found that memory problems, including those experienced by older adults, could be traced back to how well people monitor their own memory. It is important that people are aware when they have successfully made a new and long lasting memory, so they don't spend unnecessary time and resources continuing to try making the new memory. However, what is probably even more important is that people know when they have not successfully made a new memory, because they will need to spend additional time and energy encoding the information. I am concerned that older adults often think making new memories is as easy as it was 30 years earlier, and therefore employ similar strategies and levels of effort. Or even if they know it is more difficult to make new memories, they will continue trying to make new memories with the same level of effort and attention.

One way to improve metacognitive processing is to test oneself. If for example, you want to remember the name of someone you just met, you should try recalling their name throughout your initial conversation with them and then rehearse it again after the conversation is over. If you can recall their name multiple times, you can be confident that you have encoded the information. In addition, the extra rehearsal that came from testing yourself will dramatically improve the likelihood of making a long-lasting new memory.

As mentioned earlier in this chapter, I recommend that memory class instructors and therapists use the "fact of the day" exercise during each class or rehabilitation session. This can also be done in other activity programs that are done at residential care facilities. Or the fact of the day can be used during physical and occupational therapy sessions to help teach key points that will aid the rehabilitation process. In this activity, the instructor or therapist presents a new piece of information (see Appendix A for more information about facts of the day and Chapter 12 for more detailed description of the activity). The participants should be prompted to recall the information at intervals throughout the class or session. Doing this should help the participants become more aware of whether or not they have successfully made a new memory and the level of effort necessary to do so. The instructor may even discuss this with the participants to further improve metacognitive abilities and calibrate the level of effort expended with the amount actually needed to successfully make a new memory. One of the goals of doing the fact of the day exercise is for people to accurately know how much effort is needed to make a new memory.

OVERLEARN THE MATERIAL

We know that memory for newly learned material will fade in the hours and days after it was initially learned. It is therefore important that people "overlearn" new material. For example, if you remembered someone's name 5 minutes after meeting them, you cannot assume you will still remember that information 5 days later. You would need to rehearse their name a few more times during the day you met them and again once or twice in the following days. Continuing to rehearse new information will help ensure that it is retained over longer durations.

REVIEW BEFORE SLEEPING

One very efficient and effective memory enhancement strategy is to review information you learned earlier in the day at the end of the day before sleeping. If you want to better remember the people you've met, the jokes or funny stories you heard, or the things you must do the next day, I recommend revisiting them at the end of the day. You can simply go through your day in your mind and note the things you want to remember. You may even consider beginning a journal where you write down the information of the day. Doing so provides valuable rehearsal trials that will increase the chance of remembering the information, and if you don't remember the information, you will have a record for future reference.

A related technique can be used by people who have a hard time falling asleep at night because things they need to do the next day keep popping into their thoughts. They can simply keep a notepad and pen by their bed. When they think of something they need to take care of the next day, they can write it down, quiet their mind knowing they won't forget what they need to do, and then fall asleep.

Ask the Memory Doctor:

I am concerned about developing dementia because I don't have a lot of formal schooling and have read that people with more education are less likely to develop dementia. Should I be concerned?

It is true that researchers are finding that the more education one has, the less likely they are to develop dementia. However, you don't need to get a bachelor's or master's degree to prevent memory problems. It is important to note that researchers measure education levels because it is easy to measure: you simply need to ask research participants how many years of education they have. What is more important and much more difficult for researchers to measure is the level of cognitive stimulation people have had throughout their adult years. There are many ways to get cognitive stimulation and learn new things besides in a classroom. Regardless of how many years someone has spent in school, it is imperative that they keep learning and experiencing new things in order to maintain their memory and quality of life.

USE EXTERNAL MEMORY AIDS

If the goal is to not forget to do something, then I would simply suggest using an external memory aid to help you remember. For example, you can always write things down. Moreover, I suggest getting in the habit of writing certain types of things down. Keep a running list of things you need at the grocery store, and if you notice that you need an item or are about to run out of a product, then simply write it down on your grocery list. That way the only thing you need to remember is the list. Also, be sure to write down appointments or deadlines on your calendar as soon as you can.

You can also use various electronic devices to help you remember things. Consider sending yourself an e-mail if you need to remember to do something when you get to work. Or you can call yourself and leave a phone message. You could call yourself and leave a phone message that you need to write an appointment on the calendar you have at home. You can also buy a small audio recording device that attaches to your key chain. If you need to ensure that you remember something, then make a short audio recording and be sure to listen to it later and do what is necessary to make sure the note to yourself is adequately handled.

CREATE ROUTINES

Creating routines that are well-rehearsed and turned into procedural memories can limit memory errors and leave more cognitive resources available to do other things. For example, you should always put your keys, wallet, or purse in the same place when you get home. After a while you will find that you will do this almost automatically. If you want to remember to bring canvas bags to the grocery store, consider putting the bags in your car as soon as you are done putting away the groceries, that way you don't actually need to remember to bring the canvas bags before going shopping (just the list and your wallet).

MNEMONICS

Mnemonics are memory aids that enhance our normal memory ability. The word mnemonics is related to the Greek word for memory, "mnemonikos," and is also related to Mnemosyne, the Greek goddess of memory. Mnemonics are often verbal in nature. For example, the first letter mnemonic allows people to remember an ordered list of things in a short phrase. For example, you can easily remember the colors of the electromagnetic spectrum from longest wavelength to shortest wavelength by remembering the name "Roy G. Biv." Each letter of that name stands for the first letter of a color word—red, orange, yellow, green, blue, indigo, violet. Or you could remember the great lakes by using the first letter mnemonic "HOMES," which stands for Huron, Ontario, Michigan, Erie, and Superior. Or you can remember the planets in our solar system from the closet to the farthest from the sun in order by remembering the sentence, "My Very Excellent Mother Just Sent Us Nine Pizzas," which stands for Mercury, Venus, Earth, Mars, Jupiter, Saturn, Uranus, Neptune, and Pluto. Medical students often purchase entire books that contain these types of mnemonics for things they need to remember.

Some mnemonics are catchy little poems that we can remember with just a few exposures. Many people are familiar with a poem designed to help remember the number of days in each month.

Thirty days hath September,
April, June, and November,
All the rest have thirty-one,
Except for one (February)

Some mnemonic poems help us remember how to spell.

"I" before "e" except after "c"
Or when sounding like "a" as in neighbor and weigh

Although research has shown that mnemonic strategies can be effective for older adults (e.g., Cavallini, Pagnin, & Vecchi, 2003), many experts are concerned that older adults may not have the requisite cognitive resources to effectively use them. Successful use of mnemonic strategies require that the learner recognizes that something will be difficult to remember, chooses an appropriate mnemonic strategy, and implements the strategy. Moreover, most mnemonic techniques require a fair amount of cognitive resources, flexibility in thinking, and attention; these cognitive abilities tend to decrease somewhat with advancing age, and they decrease a great deal in most people who are beginning to have more serious memory problems. One study found that older adults didn't benefit from mnemonic training as much as younger adults, even if the older adults received more training (Baltes & Kliegl, 1992). So unfortunately, the people who could benefit the most from using mnemonics are often the least able to actually use them. It is for these reasons that I have tended to focus on non-mnemonic strategies to improve memory and cognition throughout this book. With that said, a tremendous amount of research has been done on mnemonic techniques in general and a fair amount has been done on the effectiveness of these strategies for older adults. In this section, we will review some of the more promising strategies.

A number of studies have shown that older adults can improve their memory ability after learning mnemonic techniques. But most of the studies assess memory performance only immediately after the strategy was taught. Do the benefits of the training persist after the training? O'Hara et al. (2007) conducted a study to assess the long-term benefits of mnemonic training. They had participants take part in a two-week memory-training course in which various techniques and strategies were taught. O'Hara et al. reported that after the training, participants could remember a greater number of words from a list, as compared with how many they could remember before the training. Then, 5 years later, O'Hara et al. contacted the participants again to see if the they had any long-term benefits from the training. Unfortunately, they (average age 73 years) had poorer memory ability than they did immediately after the training.

One problem with teaching people mnemonic strategies, regardless of age, is that they may not actually use them. After the original training, O'Hara et al. (2007) found that 93% of the participants reported using the mnemonic techniques, but after 5 years only 40% claimed they used the technique when remembering a list of words. However, the good news was that O'Hara et al. found that the people who reported using the strategy 5 years after the training, actually recalled more words. Now, it is difficult to know if the use of mnemonics *caused* the participants to remember more or if the people who had better cognitive ability had more cognitive resources available (e.g., attention and working-memory capacity) to use the strategy while trying to remember the words. Regardless, it is clear that some people can benefit from using mnemonic aids for some types of information, if they remember to use the strategies.

Brooks, Friedman, Pearman, Gray, and Yesavage (1999) found that mnemonic training helped independent older adults better remember names and words. They did "pretraining" with some of their participants, which seemed to enhance memory performance. The pretraining involved teaching the participants relaxation techniques, such as deep breathing and progressive muscle relaxation (see Chapter 8 for detailed descriptions of these relaxation techniques). The pretraining also included verbal elaboration, which involved showing people famous paintings and asking them to verbally elaborate upon what they saw, such as "the contrasting colors are remarkable" (p. 78). For the actual mnemonic training, Brooks et al. (1999) used a name-association technique to help enhance memory formation for names and faces. The following passage is their description of the name-association technique that yielded improved memory ability: "First, participants were instructed to derive a semantic associate of the name (e.g., Smith = blacksmith = anvil) that lent itself to visualization. Second, the face was examined to find a prominent feature (e.g., nose). Finally, the name associate and prominent feature were associated in a mental image (e.g., visualizing an anvil on the person's nose). When the participant was confronted with the face again, the prominent feature was to serve as a cue for the visual association and thus help in recalling the name" (p. 79). I strongly recommend that people try to process information at a deeper level, in a manner similar to the above description. Taking your time and noticing details and consciously rehearsing them are some of the best ways to improve memory.

METHOD OF LOCI

The Method of Loci is a very old technique that was purported to have originated during the time of the ancient Greeks. The first written reference to the technique dates back to 85 BC. The technique has been used by many researchers, including Brooks et al. (1999), who found that it helped older adults improve their ability to remember a list of 16 words. In addition, most memory champions, who compete in an annual event, use the technique. And people can learn the Method of Loci even if they have an average or less-than-average memory ability. However, it appears that nondemented older adults require much more practice with the technique. And it is doubtful the technique would be useful or practical for people with dementia.

The Method of Loci (loci means "places" or "locations") involves taking a route that is familiar to the learner. For example, you can take a route in your home or along your favorite neighborhood walk. Along the route you need to establish the various loci or stops. If you want to remember a list of things, then you can just take a walk along your route in your mind. Along the way you can stop at your loci and put the various things from the to-be-remembered list at each stop and visualize them there. For example, if you are going to use a route in your home to remember a list of groceries you might do something like the following in your mind: Start at your front porch, put a carton of milk on the porch and visualize it. Then open your front door and place a loaf of bread on the door threshold, then walk in and place some cereal on the table in the entryway. Then walk into the living room and place some bananas on the coffee table, walk into the kitchen and place some broccoli on the counter, and so on. At each loci, the learner should visualize the object in its position, then when you get to the grocery store, you just take a mental trip through your route and visualize what is there.

Eight-time World Memory Champion Dominic O'Brien advocates this technique and referred to it as the *memory journey*. More recent World Memory Champion Clemens Mayer set a world record by memorizing 1040 random digits in 30 minutes, using a 300-loci-long journey through his house (he must have a very large house). Ben Pridmore set the world record for memorizing the order of a shuffled deck of cards in less than 27 seconds by using the method (wikipedia.com/method_of_loci).

Brooks et al. (1999) found that they were able to improve memory ability for the "younger-old" and the "older-old," although the oldest participants required significantly more training and instruction about how to use the mnemonic strategies. So there does seem to be some promise for the use of mnemonic strategies, especially if people actually use them and have enough practice. There are some suggested readings at the end of this chapter, if you are interested in learning more about mnemonic strategies.

If you are interested in learning more about mnemonic strategies, a number of books have been written about the techniques. Here are a few that I found to be particularly useful.

SUGGESTED READINGS

Buzan, T. (1991). *Use your perfect memory*. New York: Penguin Books.

Geidman, C. L., & Crinella, F. M. (2005). *Brain fit: 10 Minutes a day for a sharper mind and memory*. Nashville, TN: Rutledge Hill Press.

Green, C. R. (2001). *Total memory workout: Eight easy steps to maximum memory fitness*. New York: Bantam Books.

Higbee, K. L. (1996). *Your memory: How it works and how to improve it*. New York: Marlowe & Company.

CHAPTER 11

What is Dementia?

A house is no home unless it contains food and fire for the mind as well as the body. Margaret Fuller (1810–1850)

Dementia is a fairly broad term used to refer to a host of neurodegenerative diseases and conditions that generally involve impairments in memory, language, and problem solving. It is often very difficult to differentiate between different types of dementia, even with neural imaging. Moreover, oftentimes people have more than one type of dementia. However, all types of dementia share one commonality and that is the fact that none of them currently have a cure. With that said, we can often slow the progression of dementia and in some cases even help people improve certain cognitive abilities. In this next section, we will discuss various types of dementia and their precursor conditions and risk factors.

NORMAL AGE-RELATED IMPAIRMENT

Unfortunately, we all experience some cognitive decline after about the age of 30. For most people, that decline doesn't negatively affect what they do, and for a while it may hardly be noticeable. Many people in their 50s and 60s begin complaining about their ability to concentrate and call up words (usually proper nouns). These types of changes are normal and expected. The severity of normal age-related impairment varies as a function of educational attainment and age. People who have more education and presumably lived more cognitively stimulating lives don't, on average, experience as much decline in memory and cognitive functioning, compared with their same-aged peers who have lived less cognitively stimulating lives. Not surprisingly, we see more normal age-related impairment as people get older. People who are experiencing normal age-related memory decline should continue living cognitively stimulating lives, get adequate physical exercise, and eat a brain-healthy diet. If one's memory ability is poorer than would be expected given their age and educational attainment, they may have one of the following conditions. See Table 1 to view some simple tests of cognitive ability.

Table 1. Simple Tests of Cognitive Ability

- Here is a simple test of short-term or working-memory ability: can the person mentally subtract 7 from 100 and keep subtracting 7 from each answer until they reach 65? If so, they probably don't have anything to worry about. If they can correctly do only three of the above manipulations, then they may be experiencing mild cognitive impairment. If they can do only two of the above manipulations, they may have dementia. They should do the test out loud so you can count how many correct manipulations they did.

- Here is another measure of short-term memory functioning: ask the person to spell the word "CHAIR," then ask them to spell it backwards (i.e., "RIAHC"). If they correctly spell the word backwards, there is probably little reason to be concerned. If they get only three letters in the correct place, the person may have mild cognitive impairment. If they get two or fewer words in the correct place, they may have dementia.

- Here is a test that can be used to determine if someone is effectively encoding new memories: give someone three unrelated concrete nouns, such as "CLOSET," "RADIO," and "DIME," and ask them to repeat the words back to you so you know they heard them correctly. Tell the person to keep the words in mind because you are going to ask them to repeat them back in a few minutes. Then talk with the person for two to three minutes (or do one of the above short-term memory tests). Then ask the person to recall the three words. Don't offer any hints. If they can recall all three words, they are effectively encoding new memories and probably don't have a serious memory problem. If they can recall only one or two words of the target words, they may have a memory problem. Consider trying the test again later with three different words (e.g., "SWEATER," "BOOK," "WINDOW"); if they still only recall one or two words, they may be experiencing mild cognitive impairment or maybe even early stages of dementia. If they don't recall any of the words, there is reason to be concerned about their memory, as that level of performance would be indicative of dementia.

AGE-ASSOCIATED COGNITIVE IMPAIRMENT

Memory impairment is best viewed along a continuum with normal age-related impairment at one end of the continuum and late-stage dementia at the other end. If one's cognitive ability is worse than expected for their age, they may have age-associated cognitive impairment. Between 24% and 39% of older adults fall into this category. Age-associated cognitive impairment is associated with mild deficits in memory, learning, language (e.g., Tip of the Tongue experiences), attention, and the ability to concentrate. However, the cognitive deficits are not severe enough to affect the person's ability to do the normal activities of daily living (e.g., shopping, cooking, bathing). Moreover, the symptoms usually don't get much worse than would be expected given the person's age. Someone who scores one standard deviation below the average on memory tests (that would be 16th percentile or doing better on memory tasks than only 16 out of 100 people) for their age and education might have age-associated cognitive impairment. Most people with age-associated cognitive impairment never go on to develop dementia, but they are 1.5 to 2 times more likely to do so as compared with people with normal age-related memory impairment.

MILD COGNITIVE IMPAIRMENT

Mild cognitive impairment (frequently abbreviated MCI) is a syndrome that is associated with cognitive symptoms that are more severe than age-associated cognitive impairment, but not severe enough to yield a diagnosis of dementia. People with MCI don't usually have difficulties with activities of daily living, but they are more likely to develop dementia. The percentage of the population with mild cognitive impairment increases with age; it affects approximately 9% of people 70 to 79 and nearly 18% of those 80 to 89 years of age. The prevalence of mild cognitive impairment also varies according to years of education, ranging from 25% for those who have an eighth-grade education to 14% of those with nine to twelve years of schooling, to 9% in those with 13 to 16 years (i.e., at least some college), and 8.5% in those who have more than 16 years (i.e., postgraduate). According to Dr. Ronald Petersen from the Mayo Clinic, it appears that approximatley16% of people with MCI develop Alzheimer's disease each year and 80% of people with MCI will develop Alzheimer's within six years.

In my experience, people with MCI can improve their cognitive ability if they dramatically increase their level of cognitive stimulation. Therefore, I believe it is crucial that we identify people with MCI and begin changing their activities and environment. Once they develop dementia, it is much more difficult, if not impossible, to improve their cognitive abilities.

ALZHEIMER'S DISEASE

The most common type of dementia is Alzheimer's disease, which is charac-terized by a slow but progressive onset. Between 65% and 85% of all dementia cases are of the Alzheimer's type. Currently, there are an estimated 5 million people in the United States with Alzheimer's disease, and that number is expected to rise to 16 million by 2050. It may be 8 years after a doctor first questioningly utters the word "Alzheimer's?" and when that person will die. However, it may be up to 20 years from the time neurons begin dying due to Alzheimer's-related pathology and death. The initial signs of Alzheimer's are usually first perceived by the affected person and their family members. The first signs may be relatively normal memory lapses such as forgetting recently experienced events and what someone just said. These types of lapses are very common and should not cause undue alarm.

The aging adult who is not developing Alzheimer's (or another neuro-degenerative disorder) will have memory failures, but those lapses probably won't become noticeably worse over the next few years. However, the person who is developing Alzheimer's will experience progressively more severe symptoms. During the early to mid stages of the disease, we often see language impairment or aphasia, disorientation, and impaired judgment. We also see deficits in executive functioning, particularly people's ability to pay attention. We generally don't see problems accessing distant memories until the disease progresses past the early stages. In later stages, we often see dramatic mood and personality changes and sometimes even psychotic symptoms such as hallucinations.

The course of Alzheimer's disease varies greatly between people. We often see that people who have lived more stimulating lives don't experience as many problems with attention and verbal processes as we would expect given the damage that has occurred to their brains. However, when these same people's disease progresses to a certain point, some studies have found that their memory ability deteriorates more rapidly. It is probably the case that cognitive stimulation provided them with a reserve, but once it was spent, their symptoms progressed to where they would have been if they never had the cognitive reserve.

Two of the most notable brain changes associated with Alzheimer's include neurofibrillary tangles and beta-amyloid-laden plaques. Many experts believe that levels of a certain protein called amyloid build up in the brain and ultimately kill or damage neurons. The amount of amyloid that is produced in someone's cells is influenced by the number of amyloid-producing genes they have. That may be why Alzheimer's has a genetic component. An extreme example of being born with too many amyloid-producing genes occurs with Down syndrome, in which the person has three of the 21st chromosome, instead of two. It turns out that there are amyloid-producing genes on the 21st chromosome, thereby explaining the observation that many people with Down syndrome develop symptoms consistent with Alzheimer's disease at a relatively young age.

If you are concerned that you or a loved one may be developing Alzheimer's disease or another type of dementia, I recommend seeing a medical professional and getting tested. Even something as simple as completing a 10-minute standardized test, such as the Mini Mental State Exam, can be helpful in determining the extent of impairment and also tracking the severity of symptoms over time.

Ask the Memory Doctor:
If the "use it or lose it" theory is true, then why did Ronald Reagan get Alzheimer's? He must have led a very stimulating life.

That is a great question that many people have asked. President Reagan certainly lived a very cognitively stimulating life as an actor, Governor of California, and a two-term President of the United States. We don't know, however, when he would have developed Alzheimer's disease if he hadn't lived such a stimulating life. Living a cognitively stimulating life won't act as a foolproof vaccine for dementia, rather it is one of many things that can delay the onset of memory problems. The other factor that affects whether or not someone develops Alzheimer's (or many other neurodegenerative diseases) is their genetic make-up. We don't know how President Reagan's genes affected the onset and course of his disease. In order to discredit the use it or lose it theory, based on President Reagan's case, he would have needed an identical twin who did not live a cognitively stimulating life, and we would need to see when that person developed Alzheimer's. My guess is that hypothetical twin would have started showing signs of memory impairment much earlier than President Reagan did.

DEMENTIA WITH LEWY BODIES

Dementia with Lewy Bodies (DLB) is a diagnostic term used to refer to a type of dementia in which Lewy Bodies are present in cortical neurons. Although there is probably considerable overlap in the various types of dementia, it appears that DLB may be the second most common type of dementia. It has been estimated that approximately 15 to 25% of dementia cases are of this type. Like Alzheimer's disease, DLB is associated with progressive impairment in memory and cognition. A recent study concluded that DLB is associated with worse visuospatial and executive dysfunction[1] than we typically see in Alzheimer's disease. We also see visual hallucinations, spontaneous Parkinsonism, and alterations in alertness and attention with DLB. The visual hallucinations can be quite severe, and medications that are typically used to treat hallucinations and agitation associated with other conditions (i.e., antipsychotic and anti-anxiety medications) often don't work with people who have DLB. In fact, the medications may even exacerbate the symptoms. Rogan and Lippa (2002) recommended that all medications for DLB patients be introduced with extreme care. However,

---

[1] Executive functioning is a term used to refer to our ability to control and manage our thoughts and cognitions (common synonyms are "executive system" and "central executive"). Executive functioning can be seen in many different behaviors and is not necessarily specific to any type of thought. Executive functioning has been compared with a director of an orchestra who needs to coordinate the timing and behavior of the entire orchestra (i.e., the mind). Executive functioning includes abilities such as attention, selective attention, and inhibition. If you are listening to someone tell a story and there are other people talking close by, your central executive would recognize that it is more important to listen to the person talking to you than to the other conversation. Then your central executive would help you pay attention to what you are trying to listen to. Inhibition is a particularly important aspect of executive functioning: we inhibit paying attention to irrelevant stimuli. We sometimes need to inhibit inappropriate emotions, thoughts, or desires. Many of the cognitive deficits associated with advanced age are caused by decreases in executive functioning capabilities.

patients often respond well to cholinergic enhancers (see upcoming section on pharmacological treatments).

PICKS DISEASE AND FRONTOTEMPORAL DEMENTIA

Frontotemporal dementias, including Pick's disease, are often difficult to differentiate from Alzheimer's disease. Binetti, Locascio, Corkin, Vonsattel, and Growdon (2000) reported that personality change and language impairment is more common in Pick's disease than Alzheimer's, but memory deficits are similar. Other unique features of Pick's disease include apraxia (inability to carry out motor functions), impulsivity, apathy, carbohydrate craving, mania, and grandiose illusions (Rogan & Lippa, 2002). It may be worthwhile to differentiate Pick's from other types of dementia, because the most common class of pharmaceuticals used to treat dementia-related symptoms (i.e., acetylcholine enhancers) may not help the patient with Pick's disease as much. Moreover, these patients may have adverse reactions to acetylcholine enhancers.

VASCULAR DEMENTIA

Vascular dementia is caused by one or more brain infarctions that cause cellular damage due to a lack of oxygen, which is usually caused by some sort of vascular blockage or clot. Vascular dementia constitutes approximately 10% of all dementia cases and is characterized by a fairly sudden and acute onset. The sudden onset distinguishes vascular dementia from all other types, which tend to develop much more slowly. The exact symptoms of vascular dementia vary widely based on which brain regions were damaged. For example, if the left hemisphere[2] is damaged by the stroke, we are more likely to see language impairment. The language impairment may involve speaking deficits (known as expressive aphasia or Broca's Aphasia) or deficits in understanding others' speech (known as receptive aphasia or Wernicke's Aphasia). We are also more likely to see mood problems or depression after a left hemispheric stroke. Damage to the right side of the brain usually leaves language abilities intact but may be associated with other motor and cognitive deficits.

Treatment after a stroke often focuses on reducing the risk of future strokes. In addition, physical and occupational therapists often work with patients who

---

[2] When thinking about brain damage and its observable effects on the body, it is important to consider the central nervous system's contralateral arrangement. Simply put, the left side of the brain controls the right side of the body and the right side of the brain controls the left side of the body. Therefore, if you see someone who has experienced a stroke and they have motor deficits to the right side of their body, we can assume the left side of the brain was affected by the stroke.

have vascular dementia to increase their mobility and independence. If someone has recently experienced a stroke and lost some of their physical abilities, I strongly recommend they see a physical or occupational therapist who has experience working with these types of patients, as patients can make remarkable gains if they engage in rigorous and appropriate therapy. Even people who experienced a stroke years earlier can benefit from high-quality occupational and physical therapy.

PARKINSON'S-RELATED DEMENTIA

Parkinson's disease (PD) is one of the most common neurodegenerative diseases, inflicting about 1% of the population over the age of 60. PD is most often associated with motor problems, especially tremors and rigidity. However, cognitive deficits are very common in Parkinson's patients. Indeed, studies have shown that PD is almost always accompanied by memory impairment exceeding the age norm (e.g., Zakharov, Akhutina, & Yakhno, 2001). About 40% of PD patients ultimately develop dementia. PD patients are six times more likely to develop dementia as compared with people of the same age who don't have PD. The level of cognitive impairment associated with PD seems to become worse the longer someone has the disease. In addition, the older the person is, regardless of age of onset, the worse their cognitive abilities are likely to be. People with PD have difficulty paying attention and holding information in short-term or working memory. Impaired attention and working memory probably explain why people with Parkinson's have greater difficulty making new memories. Researchers have recently concluded that Parkinson's-related dementia and Lewy Body dementia appear to have very similar neurological underpinnings.

KORSAKOFF'S SYNDROME

Chronic alcoholics are at risk of developing a severe memory problem known as Korsakoff's syndrome. The syndrome is caused by a thiamine (vitamin B1) deficiency related to poor absorption due to malnutrition (e.g., consuming the majority of daily caloric intake from alcohol). It appears that part of the brain associated with making new memories, known as mammillary bodies, is damaged in the condition. People with Korsakoff's have severe memory loss, and they also confabulate or fill in gaps in their memory with plausible-sounding stories or explanations that can seem like they are lying, however they are not consciously trying to deceive people.

Researchers have found that .4% of people in France and 2.8% of people in Australia have Korsakoff's syndrome. In one study approximately 19% of people with alcoholism had Korsakoff's syndrome. Dr. Oliver Sacks described a patient with Korsakoff's syndrome in his book *A Man Who Mistook his Wife for a Hat.* Here is an excerpt from the book when Dr. Sacks was talking with the patient Jimmy G:

- "What year is this, Mr. G.?" I asked, concealing my perplexity under a casual manner.
- "Forty-five, man. What do you mean?" He went on, "We've won the war, FDR's dead, Truman's at the helm. There are great times ahead."
- "And you, Jimmie, how old would you be?"
- Oddly, uncertainly, he hesitated a moment, as if engaged in calculation.
- "Why, I guess I'm nineteen, Doc. I'll be twenty next birthday."
- Looking at the grey-haired man before me, I had an impulse for which I have never forgiven myself—it was, or would have been, the height of cruelty had there been any possibility of Jimmies' remembering it.
- "Here," I said, and thrust a mirror toward him. "Look in the mirror and tell me what you see. Is that a nineteen-year-old looking out from the mirror?"
- He suddenly turned ashen and gripped the sides of the chair. "Jesus Christ," he whispered. "Christ, what's going on? What's happened to me? Is this a nightmare? Am I crazy? Is this a joke?"—and he became frantic, panicked.
- "It's okay, Jimmie," I said soothingly. "It's just a mistake. Nothing to worry about. Hey!" I took him to the window. "Isn't this a lovely spring day? See the kids there playing baseball?" He regained his colour and started to smile, and I stole away, taking the hateful mirror with me.
- Two minutes later I re-entered the room. Jimmie was still standing by the window, gazing with pleasure at the kids playing baseball below. He wheeled around as I opened the door, and his face assumed a cheery expression.
- "Hiya, Doc!" he said. "Nice morning! You want to talk to me—do I take this chair here?" There was no sign of recognition on his frank, open face.
- "Haven't we met before, Mr. G.?" I asked casually.
- "No, I can't say we have. Quite a beard you got there. I wouldn't forget you, Doc!"
- "Why do you call me "Doc"?"
- "Well, you are a doc, ain't you?"
- "Yes, but if you haven't met me, how do you know what I am?"
- "You talk like a doc. I can see you're a doc."

In the above excerpt, we clearly see evidence of Jimmy's memory problem, but we also see confabulation. It can appear that someone who is confabulating is lying, but they are not lying any more than someone who is in REM sleep and has synthesized their random brain activations and come up with a coherent and plausible dream.

DELIRIUM

Delirium is a neurobehavioral syndrome characterized by inattention, disorganized cognition, acute confusion, and a cycling of mental status changes (Jackson, Gordon, Hart, Hopkins, & Ely, 2004). Delirium is often confused with dementia because the symptoms are so similar. However, delirium usually comes on much more rapidly than dementia and is usually treatable (vascular dementia is one notable exception to the rule that dementia develops relatively slowly). It is therefore very important that people who work with older adults are aware of the differences between dementia and delirium. Moreover, delirium may be the most common psychiatric symptom experienced by older adults who are hospitalized. Up to 65% of surgical patients and as many as 80% of intensive care unit patients develop delirium.

It was once thought that delirium was relatively benign, but several studies have found that it is associated with an increased risk of future cognitive impairment and increased morbidity and mortality. The link between delirium and poor future health is not completely clear, but it could be that other illnesses (e.g., respiratory or cardiovascular conditions) are causing delirium and future health complications. It could also be that the medications used to treat other conditions exacerbate patients' cognitive problems. Regardless of the pathways, delirium is a serious condition that should be watched for and treated.

If you notice that someone's cognitive and attentional abilities have rapidly decreased, you should consult a medical professional. Unfortunately, it appears that delirium is very much underdiagnosed. Research has shown that up to 70% of delirium cases are missed by clinicians (Leentjens & van der Mast, 2005). There are risk factors that predispose people to develop delirium, and there are more direct factors that may cause delirium. The likelihood of developing delirium is best viewed from a multifactorial perspective such that the more risk factors someone has, the more likely they are to develop delirium. Table 2 includes a list of common risk factors that increase the chance of delirium (Leentjens & van der Mast, 2005).

Table 2. Potential Risk Factors for Delirium

Increasing age

Pre-existing cognitive problems

High blood pressure

Multiple medications

General anesthesia

Being male

Alcohol use

Benzodiazepine drugs

Elevated serum sodium levels (dehydration)

Reduced general physical health

Table 3. Potential Causes of Delirium

Hypoxia

Hypoglycemia

Hyperthermia

Cerebral vascular attacks

Malnutrition

Anticholinergic delirium—caused by anticholinergic drugs (e.g., anti-nausea medications)

Alcohol or sedative withdrawal

Infections

Metabolic abnormalities

Dehydration

Structural lesions in the brain

Postoperative states

Sensory deprivation

Sleep deprivation

Fecal impaction

Urinary retention

Medications

Another way to look at delirium is to examine potential causes. One of the most common causes is urinary-tract infections, which can be treated with antibiotics. Table 3 contains a list of other potential causes of delirium.

REDUCING THE RISK OF DEMENTIA

What causes dementia? Well, we don't completely know the answer to that question yet, but we can safely say there are two sets of factors: genetics and environment/lifestyle. This refers to the age-old "nature-nurture" debate. The cause must be some combination of genes and environment.[3] Many people are

---

[3] Actually, it may be an oversimplification to say that dementia is caused by some combination of genes and environment. The complexity arises from the fact that our genes and environment interact. For example, one's genes may influence their talents, predispositions, and interests, which may in turn affect which environments they find themselves in. Conversely, our environments and lifestyles affect which genes are active in our bodies.

very interested in the genetic influences that affect the likelihood of developing dementia, especially if one has watched a loved one be consumed by one of these insidious and ravaging diseases. The good news is that it appears that late-onset Alzheimer's disease has less of a genetic component than early-onset Alzheimer's. This is good news because 90% to 95% of Alzheimer's cases are of the late-onset variety. Researchers will certainly continue to look at the genetic influences on dementia, as that will help us better understand the underlying causes and suggest possible pharmaceutical interventions. However, we can't do much about our genes (yet), so I hope you chose your parents very carefully. What we can do something about is our behavior, environment, and lifestyle choices, as they seem to be very much related to our chance of developing dementia. This entire book is largely based on the idea that there are certain risk factors and protective factors that are related to the likelihood of developing memory problems. We can modify our lives and thus our chances of developing memory problems. Next, we will discuss some common and potentially reversible risk factors.

1. **Alcohol abuse**: Research has shown that small amounts of alcohol can have a protective effect in terms of cardiovascular health and memory ability. However, larger quantities of alcohol can negatively affect health. Chronic alcoholism can lead to an amnesic disorder known as Korsakoff's syndrome (see earlier section in this chapter).
2. **Stress**: Stress can wreak havoc on memory ability. There are a number of ways stress negatively affects memory ability. For example, stress increases a hormone known as cortisol, which impairs memory ability. In addition, stress can impair concentration and attention. See Chapter 8 for a more thorough discussion of stress and memory.
3. **Pharmaceutical side effects and interactions**
4. **Thyroid deficiency**
5. **Brain injury**: There is ample evidence that suggests head injuries can lead to an increased risk of Alzheimer's disease. However, it appears that head injuries at earlier ages (e.g., before 50 years of age) don't increase the chance of developing Alzheimer's as much or at all. In addition, the severity of the head injury also probably matters, because we have known for a while that boxers are at an increased risk of a whole host of neurological problems, including dementia, even if the boxing was done at a relatively young age. It is probably best to view head injuries as just another environmental risk factor that can increase the chance of developing memory problems.
6. **High Blood Pressure**: High blood pressure is associated with a significant decline in cognitive functioning (Elias, Elias, & Robbins, 2004).
7. **Obesity**: Obesity increases the risk of developing Alzheimer's disease and vascular dementia.
8. **Diabetes**: Diabetes and even pre-diabetes puts people at an increased risk of developing dementia.

Here are other risk factors that have been identified:

- Hormones
- Medications
- Surgery
- Sleep problems
- Poor diet
- Illicit drug use
- Chronic alcoholism
- Depression
- Genes

PHARMACOLOGICAL TREATMENTS

There are a number of pharmacological treatments for dementia. This section is designed to simply introduce people to the general idea of how these medications work and should not replace the advice and consultation of a medical doctor.

The most common class of drugs prescribed to help people with Alzheimer's disease is known as acetylcholine esterase inhibitors (e.g., donepezil or Aricept, galantamine or Reminyl, rivastigmin or Excelon, and tacrine or Cognex). Acetylcholine is a neurotransmitter that some of our neurons release. Acetylcholine has different functions throughout the nervous system, but one of its main functions is memory. It appears that acetylcholine-releasing neurons are particularly prone to damage and death in Alzheimer's disease, which reduces the amount of acetylcholine that is available to be used for memory and cognitive tasks. Our bodies employ enzymes to clean up neurotransmitters that have already been released. Do you remember the 1980s video game Pac Man, in which players would make Pac Man eat the power pellets? Enzymes are like Pac Man in that they eat up, or deactivate, neurotransmitters. Imagine if we put a muzzle on Pac Man that prevented him from eating the power pellets; that is what acetylcholine esterase inhibitors do. By preventing enzymes from taking acetylcholine out of the system, there is more available to be used in making memories and other cognitive tasks. Acetylcholine esterase inhibitors seem to help many people who are experiencing cognitive decline. However, their efficacy is short-lived, often they help people for only 2 to 3 years and then their memory ability declines again. The memory decline is often very rapid and people's cognitive ability ends up where it would have been if they had never taken the memory-enhancing drug. With that said, one could argue that the 2 to 3 year improvement in cognitive ability was priceless.

There is another type of drug that was initially approved by the Federal Drug Administration in 2003 for use in treating symptoms related to dementia called Memantine (trade names: Namenda, Axura, Ebixa). The improvement is fairly small but noticeable in most studies. According to a review of published studies, this drug led to the development of less agitation, however it may not reduce agitation that has already appeared. It appears that Memantine and similar drugs can be used in conjunction with acetylcholine esterase inhibitors to help improve memory symptoms for a while. However it is important to note that neither type of memory drugs will prevent damage associated with Alzheimer's but rather only help alleviate the symptoms.

We had thought that Memantine worked by blocking the effects of a chemical called glutamate in the brain. However, recent research suggests that the glutamate-blocking properties are very limited and that Memantine might be working like acetylcholine esterase inhibitors and increase the available acetylcholine (Drever, Anderson, Johnson, O'Callaghan, Seu, & Choi, et al., 2007).

SUGGESTED READINGS

Binetti, G., Locascio, J., Corkin, S., Vonsattel, J., & Growdon, J. (2000). Differences between Pick disease and Alzheimer disease in clinical appearance and rate of cognitive decline. *Archives of Neurology, 57*(2), 225-232.

Padovani, A., Costanzi, C., Gilberti, N., & Borroni, B. (2006). Parkinson's disease and dementia. *Neurological Sciences, 27*, S40-S43.

Rogan, S., & Lippa, C. F. (2002). Alzheimer's disease and other dementias: A review. *American Journal of Alzheimer's Disease and Other Dementias, 17*(1), 11-17.

Zanni, G. R., & Wick, J. Y. (2007). Differentiating dementias in long-term care patients. *The Consultant Pharmacist, 22*(1), 14-28.

CHAPTER 12

Creating Your Own Cognitive Enhancement Classes

The more you use your brain, the more brain you will have to use. George A. Dorsey (1868–1931)

This unique chapter contains a large number of cognitively stimulating activities that can be used to create your own cognitive enhancement program. The chapter will begin with some introductory comments about memory enhancement classes. Later, several components of effective cognitive enhancement activities will be presented. I will discuss attention activities, word generation activities, spatial memory activities, dual tasking, social activities, and homework. Many examples of activities will be presented in this section and instructions will also be provided. You can find sample handouts for many of the activities in the appendices at the end of the book.

WHAT CONSTITUTES A GOOD COGNITIVE ENHANCEMENT PROGRAM?

Effective cognitive enhancement classes require participants to make new memories and exercise the brain's attentional centers. In order for participants to experience the greatest benefits, they will need to exert maximal effort on a regular basis. Unfortunately however, most current facility-based activity programs designed to stimulate residents primarily focus on reminiscing about the past. Thinking and talking about the past can have important psychological benefits for older adults, but it doesn't provide the type of cognitive stimulation necessary to exercise the parts of the brain associated with attention and making new memories. To illustrate this point, note that people with early- to mid-stage dementia can often tell detailed (and presumably accurate) stories about the distant past. Recalling old memories relies on previously established neuronal connections and doesn't exercise the parts of the brain associated with effectively making new neuronal connections and memories.

Most facility-based activity programs are not well-attended by the residents. In my experience, it is common for only a handful of people to show up for an organized activities. The lack of participation is probably caused by a number of factors, one of which is the lack of engaging and stimulating programming. I once had a conversation with a retirement community administrator responsible for hiring and training activity directors for many different facilities. This administrator told me not to worry about developing cognitively stimulating activities. He told me to just focus on the "Three Bs." I responded by asking, "What are the three Bs?" And he informed me they were, "Bingo, Bible, and birthdays." Those are fine things to focus on, but I don't believe that an activity program based on the 3 Bs will maximally stimulate older adults' brains, and I don't think they will do much to prevent cognitive deterioration. We need to offer opportunities for people to challenge their cognitive abilities in a supportive environment.

Many participants will struggle with the type of activities that are a part of a challenging cognitive enhancement program. The cognitively stimulating activities that will be the most effective at enhancing attention and memory ability will require them to do exactly what they are having difficulty doing. For example, almost all older adults experience a decreased ability to pay attention, which ultimately impairs memory ability. With this in mind, we try to increase people's ability to pay attention by doing activities in class that require sustained attention. Participants may become frustrated if they are unable to do certain activities as well as they would like. Or they may state that they don't like doing certain activities. In cases like these, it has been helpful for me to state something like the following:

> I see you are having a hard time doing this activity, but this is exactly the type of activity you need to do in order to improve your memory ability. If you went to a physical therapist because you were having difficulty walking, you would expect the therapist to make you walk, right? Well the same principles apply with memory enhancement; we need to do what is most difficult for us if we want to see improvement.

There are other techniques in Chapter 14 to enhance participants' motivation and their belief that they can succeed.

COGNITIVELY STIMULATING ACTIVITIES

I suggest using a combination of many different activities in cognitive enhancement classes. In order to get people to maximally exercise their brain and memory, prevent boredom, and maximize attention, I believe it is important to have a wide variety of activities that are each done for a short period of time (i.e., less than 5 minutes). I recommend having at least 10 activities prepared for each 60-minute class. The focus should be on making new memories and increasing people's ability to have sustained attention. I have seen the greatest amount of cognitive effort expended when the activities are done for only approximately 5 minutes each; just as the participants are starting to lose focus a new activity is begun. You will find that over time the participants will improve the ability to focus and concentrate for longer periods of time. We should strive to keep the activities fun and the environment supportive.

Ask the Memory Doctor:
I work with several older adults who have serious visual impairments. Can people who are legally blind still benefit from cognitively stimulating activities?

There are cognitive enhancement activities that people with visual impairments can do, however there are many activities that would not be appropriate. I have put asterisks by the activities in this chapter that can be done by older adults with visual impairment. Many of the cognitive activities described in this book require that people write their responses on a prepared handout, which is obviously difficult for the blind. People with visual impairment may need someone to work closely with them so they can verbalize their responses rather than writing them. However, verbalizing responses in a group setting may be problematic and negatively affect others' ability to attend to the task and maximally exercise their brains. If possible, consider creating a memory enhancement class designed for people with vision problems. In this specialized class, participants can verbalize their responses one-on-one with the instructor or teaching assistant. Or they could work on the activity as a group. People who have difficulty writing (e.g., stroke patients or people with Parkinson's disease) could also benefit from a group question-and-answer format.

It is very important that we find ways to help people with serious visual impairments exercise their brains and cognitive abilities. Visual impairment, especially macular degeneration, is all too common among older adults. Approximately 10% of people 66 to 74 years of age will have macular degeneration, and the prevalence increases to 30% of people 75 to 85 years of age. Serious visual impairment, regardless of cause, can dramatically limit the amount of cognitive stimulation someone can get through reading, doing crossword puzzles, word games, Sudoku, and even socializing. Research shows that visually impaired older adults experience depression twice as often as similarly aged people without vision problems. In addition, the quality of social support appears to suffer when people develop progressive visual impairment, and they are more likely to be lonely. All of this is very problematic because depression wreaks havoc on our memory ability, and people who socialize less are missing out on important opportunities to exercise their brains and learn new things.

Facts of the Day*[1]

I believe that each class should start with at least one fact of the day (see Appendix A for more information about this activity). The purpose of learning the facts of the day is not to know that information but rather to gain experience making new memories. One of the difficulties that older adults have when trying to make new memories is that they are often unaware of how much effort and concentration is needed to make a new memory. Older adults, especially those who are developing more severe memory problems, must concentrate harder and rehearse the information more than they would have needed to 20 years earlier. However, I believe that many older adults who are experiencing some loss in their ability to make new memories are putting the same amount of effort into making memories as they did when they were younger. The facts of the day allow people to calibrate how much effort they think is needed with how much effort is actually required to successfully make a new memory.

When asking participants to learn the facts of the day, I suggest using a powerful memory enhancement technique called *expanding rehearsal*. In this technique, the instructor will allow increasingly longer intervals between rehearsal trials. For example, you present the fact of the day at the beginning of the class (:00). Then, after only two minutes, ask participants to recall the fact or facts again (:02). Then ask them again four minutes later (:06), 8 minutes later (:14), 16 minutes later (:30), and 32 minutes later (:62 or at the end of a 60-minute class). Using the expanding rehearsal strategy will dramatically increase the chance of participants correctly remembering the fact(s). See the section in Chapter 13 to learn how to ask questions that will maximize success; employ this strategy when questioning people about the facts of the day. It is important for participants to experience success in making new memories while simultaneously learning how much effort is needed to successfully make these memories. Using the suggested questioning technique can help improve participants' confidence in their ability to make new memories and also increase their motivation to continue working hard in the classes.

If you want to challenge the participants more, you can give them two facts to remember rather than just one. You can also ask people about previous facts of the day to see whether they still remember them. Another fun activity is to create a *Jeopardy*-like game with previous facts of the day.

You will find that participants want to write down the facts of the day when you initially present them. The urge to write things down is understandable, as that would be an excellent strategy if the purpose of the activity was to simply have access to the information. However, once again, the purpose of the fact of the day activity is not to remember the information per se, but rather to exercise the

---

[1] The asterisks next to activities indicate that the activity may be appropriate for visually impaired people.

memory-making parts of the brain and also learn how much effort is needed to make a new memory. If participants simply look at the notes they took about the fact(s) of the day, they probably won't achieve either of those goals. Therefore, it will be counterproductive if people write the facts of the day down in their notes. It would be better to discuss with the participants what they can do to process the information at a deep level. You can discuss what kind of mental images may help them remember or whether someone has thought of another strategy that will help them recall the facts. Often it is helpful for the instructor to write down key words in a large font and show them to participants as a way of facilitating deeper processing, understanding, and increasing the likelihood of successful memory encoding (i.e., making a new memory).

Homework

Another important aspect of all memory classes is homework. Research suggests that cognitive stimulation, like physical exercise and many pharmaceuticals, are dose-dependent. In other words, the more you do or take, the better the results will be, up to a point. Therefore, memory class participants should be given homework to do between class meetings. The amount of homework given might depend on how many times a week a memory class meets. For example, if the memory class meets only twice a week, then more homework should be assigned. If the memory class meets five days a week, there will be less of a need for homework.

Homework should be varied and require a fair amount of sustained attention. Some good examples of potential homework assignments are:

Word searches
Crossword puzzles
Sudoku
Problem-solving puzzles
Anagrams
Simple math problems

There is a plethora of books available that contain puzzles and activities that make excellent homework assignments. You can also find many of these types of activities on the internet. Consider searching for seasonal puzzles and activities or activities associated with certain holidays. There are also Web sites that allow you to create customized word-finds (or word searches). Consider making a word-find using participants' names, local towns, local creek and river names, local politicians, local businesses, local street names, etc. There are also Web sites and computer programs that allow you to create customized crossword puzzles. My favorite Web site for creating puzzles can be found at http://puzzlemaker.school.discovery.com. Consider creating crossword puzzles with facts about class participants or previous facts of the day. If you set up the puzzle as a scavenger hunt in which participants need to try to learn things about other participants in order to complete the crossword puzzle, you can help facilitate social interaction among participants or residents.

Review the previous homework at the beginning of each class, then assign the new homework. It is important that the instructor thoroughly explains how to do the homework and possibly demonstrate how to do it. Depending on how difficult or new the homework activity is, you may want to have participants begin it after you explain the instructions. However, you should ask everyone to put the homework away when you are ready to begin the next task, as many class participants will want to continue doing the homework even though their attention is needed for the next task.

It is common for people to understand the homework after the instructions are initially explained, but when participants attempt it on their own, hours or days later, they often have a difficult time understanding and completing it. For this reason, it is often helpful to arrange homework tutorial sessions between memory classes. Tutorial sessions work very well in residential communities. I recommend asking one or two of the more motivated and capable memory class participants to run the homework tutorial sessions. If you hold memory classes on Monday, Wednesday, and Friday afternoons, you could schedule tutorials in the evenings on Tuesdays, Thursdays, and Sundays. All the instructor needs to do is give the tutor the answers to the homework assignment and let the participants know when and where help is available (I recommend bringing Post-it notes and having participants write down when and where the tutorial session will take place). The tutorial session can also be a place where class participants can pick up the homework if they were not able to attend the previous class. If there is a receptionist or someone else who is consistently available, consider giving them the answers to the homework and blank homework assignments for those who missed class. Class participants can check their homework, see whether they have done it correctly, or get the answer to a particularly frustrating puzzle.

Theory of Mind

There is an explicit focus on exercising attention in this book. However, there is a related idea that every cognitive enhancement instructor should be aware of, known as *Theory of Mind* (often abbreviated ToM). Theory of mind refers to people's ability to attribute mental states to others. For example, can someone understand how someone's beliefs, intentions, and knowledge affect their behavior and attitudes? If so, they are demonstrating that they have theory of mind. Can someone use the above information to predict future behavior or how they would react to a certain situation? If so, they are demonstrating theory of mind. Can someone realize that other people have ideas that might not be true or that are different from their own and use that information to understand that the other person may not respond the same way as they would? If so, they are demonstrating that they have theory of mind. Researchers believe that theory of mind is largely a frontal lobe function, and like so many frontal lobe functions, theory of mind decreases somewhat in older adulthood and decreases a great deal with most types of dementia.

There is some indication that we can help people increase their theory of mind capabilities, which should help with social skills and maintenance of social support networks. In addition, people's ability to comprehend humor is related to theory of mind, which is important for quality of life and social skills. In many of the instructions for cognitive stimulation activities, I have added a component in which participants need to judge their responses relative to others. For example, if people have just generated a list of first names for males, I suggest asking them to look at their list and try to determine which name they generated is least likely to be generated by anyone else. In addition, two other activities are excellent at exercising and hopefully improving theory of mind activities. One activity is a short skit (see Appendix B). Recent research has shown that theater arts training can increase older adults' theory of mind abilities. Another activity that relies heavily upon theory of mind ability is the cartoon activity described later in this chapter.

Attention Activities

In my opinion, the backbone of a cognitive enhancement program should be attention activities. If people can increase their ability to pay attention and concentrate, they will be much more effective at making new memories. An inability to pay attention is probably one of the most important reasons that normal age-related memory impairment occurs. Attention activities can be very challenging, especially for more impaired participants. Next, we will review activities that are designed to exercise and enhance attention abilities.

Ask the Memory Doctor:
I have heard about computer programs that are designed to stimulate older adults' minds. Do those programs work?

Yes, there are now a number of different computer-based products available for people who want to exercise their brains and improve their memory ability. Of course, there is a lot of variability in how these programs work, but in general, I think it is almost always a good idea to expose people to new learning experiences and encourage them to develop new skills. Many of the computer programs are designed to allow people to track their improvement, and some even give people a "brain age" or a "memory age," which could help keep people motivated. So in general, I think these programs are an excellent idea and should be available to older adults living in residential care facilities or those who frequent senior centers. I certainly encourage independent older adults to consider adding the computer programs to their brain-exercise regime.

I believe the computer programs will work best as a part of a larger program that includes group-based programs and individualized activities that the person enjoys (e.g., hobbies, favorite games and puzzles, reading, and volunteering). Most of the computer programs I have seen provide a relatively limited set of activities, which might reduce the likelihood that people will continue using them on a regular basis. People should also be aware that as we get better at an activity, we usually use fewer cognitive resources and less attention because the activity becomes automatized, which will reduce the brain benefit of the activity. An analogous situation occurs with physical exercise, such that a limited physical exercise regimen can become boring over time, causing people to stop doing it. In addition, a limited physical exercise program also becomes much easier over time as the body becomes more efficient at the exercise, which reduces the energy expended and the health benefits.

So in answer to your original question, yes, computer programs designed to exercise people's brains are a great idea and may help improve cognitive ability. But they should be used with other activities for maximum long-term benefits.

Buzz*

Buzz is a very popular activity among participants, and it does an excellent job of exercising participants' attention abilities. I recommend doing a round or two of buzz after going over the new and old homework and introducing the fact(s) of the day. In the buzz activity, you have participants count, beginning in a clockwise direction so that the first person says *one,* the second person say *two,* and so on. Instruct people to say *buzz* instead of the number if the number is a multiple of seven (e.g., 7, 14, 21, 28, 35, 42, 49, 56, 63, and so on) or if the number contains a seven (e.g., 17, 27, 37, etc.). The direction reverses when someone says *buzz* in place of the number. For example, if you start counting in a clockwise direction (e.g., 1, 2, 3, 4, 5, 6), then someone says *buzz* instead of *seven,* the direction reverses so that the person who said *six* would say *eight,* and the person who said *five* would say *nine.* Note that no one ever says *seven* and that the counting never goes backwards (i.e., 6, 5, 4, 3 . . .).

Even participants with moderate memory problems can learn this activity, if they do it during every session. This activity requires a great deal of sustained attention. If a participant (or the instructor) has a brief lapse in attention, they will very likely make a mistake. To make the activity more challenging, split a large group into smaller groups; the noise of the adjacent groups will require even greater use of attentional resources, as participants will need to inhibit paying attention to the other group. When your group reaches the 70s, I suggest that participants use their fingers to keep track of the numbers as there will be ten *buzzes* in a row (70-79). All of those *buzzes* will be said by two people and they will need to know when to stop saying *buzz* and say *80.*

Consider occasionally changing things and using a small rubber ball when playing buzz. You can have participants either stand or sit and pass the ball to the next person. This variant of buzz shouldn't be introduced until people are fairly proficient at the game. Using a ball will require slightly more attention and is a great way to change things up.

Newspaper Activities

The newspaper activity actually involves several different tasks. First, you will need to get as many newspapers as you have participants. The newspapers don't necessarily have to be the same; try to get large newspapers (e.g., *New York Times* or Sunday papers) for higher functioning participants and smaller newspapers (e.g., local ones or midweek papers) for lower functioning participants. Scramble the order of each newspaper, so that all the original pages are there but in a random order. Then give participants a scrambled newspaper and ask them to put the pages in the original order, just as they would be if they just purchased the paper. Lower functioning participants may need some support with this task, especially the first few times they do it.

After the participants have completed the above task, ask them to find and circle all the "m"s on the first page. This task can be made more difficult for moderate to higher functioning participants by asking them to keep a running total of the number of letters they have circled. They should count aloud the number of letters they have circled so all participants will have to inhibit listening to others, thereby making the activity even more effective. People are often uncomfortable counting aloud, so they may need some reminders and encouragement. The task can be made even more difficult by having them find and circle two or even three letters at a time, which is very appropriate for non-cognitively impaired participants. Have participants work on the letter-finding task for approximately 5 minutes or until someone has circled a predetermined number of letters (e.g., 50 for very low functioning, 100 for most groups, or 150 for a group of very high functioning participants). Change the letter(s) each time you do the task, unless you are working with people who have more severe cognitive impairment, in which case you should use the same commonly occurring letter each time (e.g., S).

After the above task is complete, you can give participants scissors, tape, and blank paper. Ask them to cut out words or letters to make a sentence or poem. The participants can tape the words or letters from the newspaper onto the blank paper. You may want to ask participants beforehand if they have a favorite quote or short poem that they can make using letters from the newspaper. You should try to avoid letting people do the task without a goal or strategy.

Creative Brainstorming*

In the creative brainstorming activity the participants will generate as many possible uses for a common everyday object. The goal is to try to think as creatively as possible. This activity is challenging for people with mild cognitive impairment and almost impossible for people with dementia (therefore it is probably an excellent activity to prevent future memory problems). Give participants examples of creative ideas to show them that they don't need to generate common uses. For example, if the topic is "uses for old newspapers," then give creative examples such as: use it for insulation, use it to soak up an oil leak under a car, line a cat litter box, use it to cut letters out and make a ransom note, etc. After participants have worked on the activity for 3 to 5 minutes, ask them to try to determine which of their responses were the most unique (i.e., no one else generated the idea). This activity exercises executive functioning, because participants need to remain focused and use various strategies to generate uses. Have participants share what they believe is their most unique response with other participants. Here is a list of possible objects that can be used in this activity:

- old rowboat
- dime
- old car tires
- old refrigerators
- cereal boxes
- paperclip
- plastic milk cartons

See Appendix C to view a sample *Creative Brainstorming Activity* handout.

Trigger Word Activity*

The Trigger Word Activity involves giving the group a word (e.g., cortex, memory, brain, friend). When the instructor (or anyone else) says the trigger word everyone must do a predesignated behavior, such as putting their right hand on their head or putting their right index finger on their nose. Use different trigger words and behaviors for different sessions. The activity is fun and requires that the participants remember the word and pay attention to whether or not it is said.

Ping Pang Pong*

This fun activity is possibly more capable of bringing a smile to participants' faces than any other activity. Have people sit in a circle and ask anyone to start. The first person says *ping*, the second person says *pang*, and the third person simultaneously says *pong* and points to anyone in the circle. The person who has been pointed at starts over and says *ping*, the person to their left says *pong* and so on. If you have visually impaired participants in your group, consider asking if it would be acceptable to touch the person who will begin the next round.

This simple activity requires sustained attention and is appropriate for participants with varying cognitive ability. The activity can be made more difficult if you instruct the participants to try to "fool another participant." For example, when it is their turn to point to anyone in the circle (and say *pong*), they should look at one person and point to a different person. Trying to fool someone requires much more attention as the participant needs to pay attention to the rules of the game while thinking that they will look at one person and point at another, and they will probably need to know who those people will be beforehand.

Word Generation Activities

One of the most common and frustrating cognitive lapses that adults without cognitive impairment experience is the inability to "grab" words. Proper nouns are the most common type of word that we have a hard time generating. In psychology, we refer to this phenomenon as a "tip of the tongue" state. It is interesting to note that research has shown people first experience tip of the tongue during grade school and the vast majority of languages use the word "tongue" or "lip" in their description of the concept. Research shows that college students have one to two tip of the tongue states per week, whereas older adults experience two to four. However, it appears that older adults might be more successful at solving tip of the tongue states. Moreover, older adults may be relieved to know that one of the main hypotheses that tries to explain why older adults get more tip of the tongue states is that they know more things, especially vocabulary, which probably makes it more difficult to find the correct brain pathway and word. Regardless of the cause, tip of the tongue states are frustrating. Moreover, more serious word fluency problems can negatively affect people's quality of life. Therefore, I propose that we exercise our language and word generation abilities.[2]

Word generating activities are a fun way to simultaneously exercise attentional and language abilities. There are a number of different word generation activities, but given that the most common type of words that we get stuck trying to recall are proper nouns (e.g., names), we will begin with name generation activities.

Name Generation Activities*

The name generation activities require participants to generate as many names as possible from a certain category (e.g., female first names). Participants should

---

[2] I have read about people who use the Internet search engine Google to eliminate tip of the tongue states. If you are having a hard time thinking of a word, try typing in terms that describe the word you are trying to think of. This technique probably won't be too effective if you are searching for a first name though.

ideally choose a strategy (e.g., family members or friends); choosing a strategy activates frontal lobe and attentional centers of the brain. Here is a list of name generation categories:

First names
First names for males
First names for females
Last names
Names of extended family members

This activity can be done a number of ways. You can simply ask participants to generate as many names from one of the above categories as possible in certain amount of time (e.g., 4 minutes). At the end of the word generation, ask the participants which word they generated is least likely to have been generated by another participant. This open-ended task is a great option if you run out of prepared activities and need to fill some time. This activity can also be used if a participant or two finishes an activity long before other participants and you want to keep the quick participants fully engaged. For example, if a participant finishes another paper and pencil activity, just turn over their paper and write the instructions on the top (e.g., List as many male first names as you can). See Appendix D to view a Sample A-Z Activity Handout.

Generate Words A-Z*

Another way to set up word generation activities is to give people a handout with the letters A through Z on it and space to write in a word for each letter (see Appendix D for an example). The instructor gives the participants a category and the participants try to generate words that are examples of that category. Here is a list of possible categories that can be used with an A-Z handout.

First names
Last names
Female first names
Male first names
Animals
Countries
Things that are alive
Things that are not alive
City names

The A-Z activity can also be done without a handout, which works well if there are visually impaired participants in the group. You simply have people go around a circle and generate the words in alphabetical order. For example, if the class was generating first names from A through Z, the first person might say *Adam,* the second person might say *Barbara,* and so on. For your highest functioning groups, consider asking them to try and generate all of the previously stated names before giving the new name (I recommend that the instructor write down all the names on a notepad in order to help keep the activity going in case no one remembers the names).

Think of As Many (Fill in the Blank) As You Can*

Another variant of the above word generation activities is to give people a general category and have them generate as many examples as possible in a certain amount of time. At the end of the task, ask participants to choose the one item generated that they think others did not. Here is a list of possible categories:

animals
presidents
flowers
car types
book titles
movie titles
actors
types of dogs and cats
desserts
countries
states

For some of the categories, you can develop a list of possible answers (e.g., all the past presidents of the United States or a list of countries). After participants have completed the initial task of generating as many items in a certain amount of time, give the participants the complete list and ask them to find all of the answers they wrote down (or failed to write down if you prefer). See Appendix E for a complete list of presidents. See Appendix F for a list of countries. See Appendix G for a complete list of states. This activity can be repeated every so often, with the goal of generating a greater number of items. Consider keeping track of how many responses each participant correctly generated so they can see objective proof that they are improving.

Generating Verbs*

Generating verbs is a challenging linguistic activity that exercises attention, executive functioning, and word fluency. Recent research suggests that an inability to generate verbs may be a sign of Alzheimer's disease (Tippett, Gendall, Farah, & Thompson-Schill, 2004). Therefore, I believe that it is prudent to exercise this ability and the part of the brain associated with generating verbs, as both appear to be vulnerable to Alzheimer's disease. This activity is probably not appropriate for people with Alzheimer's.

The verb generation activity involves asking people to generate actions that certain types of people or animals do. For example, if the category was *children*, then people could respond with verbs (action words) such as play, learn, sleep, jump, draw, read, hide, talk, sing, scream, cry, laugh, and walk. Ideally, people should try to write only verbs, however many participants may write short statements such as "play with toys" or "walk to school," which is fine. If participants are having a difficult time with this task, remind them that any behavior is OK (e.g., talk, walk, sees), even if other categories of people might do those things.

Here is a list of potential categories you can use with the verb generation activity:

Athletes	Teachers
Newborns	Secretaries
Children	Carpenter
Dogs	Waiter/Waitress
Monkeys	Soldiers
Students	Maids
Retirees	Janitors
Farmers	Mechanics
Doctors	

See Appendix H to view a Generic Verb Generation Handout.

Think of As Many Things in the Color . . .*

This simple activity actually can be surprisingly difficult. The activity exercises executive functioning and attention. Participants are given a color, and their task is to generate as many objects that can be that color. It is very important that participants know that they can be as creative as they want and that the object doesn't need to be exclusively one color. For example, someone could say *shirt* for any color because a shirt can be any color.

You can use this activity with certain colors around holidays. For example, you can use green around St. Patrick's Day, pink around Valentine's Day, orange around Halloween, yellow around Easter, green around Earth Day, and red around Christmas. Also, you can easily find color-related facts of the day to go along with this activity.

Sample color facts:

White was the most popular color of SUVs in 2003.
Silver was the most popular color for sports cars in 2003.
Red is the most commonly found color on national flags.
Green is the national color of Ireland.
In ancient Rome, public servants wore blue. Today, police and other public servants wear blue.
In the Middle Ages, actors portraying the dead in a play wore yellow.

White means mourning in China and Japan.

Bees can see blue and yellow but not red.

Newborn children cannot see color because their cones are not fully developed.

Some of the above facts came from:
http://www.factmonster.com/ipka/A0769383.html

Homophones (Homonyms)

Homophones are words that are spelled differently but sound the same (e.g., bare and bear). Cognitive enhancement instructors can find lists of homophones (in books or on the Internet). Handouts can be made in which one of the homophone pairs is given and the participant tries to generate its match. See Appendix I to view sample homophone handout with answers. You can find many lists of homophones on the Internet. My favorite list is located at www.cooper.com/alan/homonym_list.html

Cartoon Activities

The cartoon caption activity is a lot of fun and can be adapted to almost any level. The activity involves matching cartoon drawings with the appropriate caption. Choose cartoons from http://www.cartoonbank.com, another Web site, from the newspaper, or from a book of cartoons. The cartoons you choose must have the caption below the picture and not a part of the cartoon drawing. If you want to make the task easier, give participants only four to eight cartoons that have been separated from their captions. I recommend typing the captions in a large font rather than using the caption provided at the bottom of the cartoon. Create enough cartoons and associated captions for each participant. Then put all of those materials in an envelope and label the envelope (e.g., Cartoon Activity #1) as the activity can be used by other participants or even by the same participants after several months. For people with more severe cognitive impairment, the activity can be repeated after a shorter period of time.

The activity can be made much more difficult by choosing cartoons in which it will be much less obvious that the caption matches. You can also make the task more difficult by giving participants a greater number of cartoons and captions (e.g., 10-12). The most challenging cartoon activity would be to give the participants a cartoon without any caption and ask them to create one; this could be used as a homework assignment.

Sudoku

Sudoku is a wonderfully fun and addictive cognitive game. In my opinion, this is one of the best cognitive stimulating activities because it requires a significant amount of concentration and attention and people find it so enjoyable that they will spend hours doing them. The puzzles are easy to find in books and on the

Internet. In addition, there is a very wide range of difficulty levels. When you first teach people to do Sudoku, I would recommend demonstrating the activity using smaller than normal puzzles (e.g., 4 × 4 puzzles).

The objective of the Sudoku is to fill in all the blank squares with the correct numbers. There are three simple constraints to follow. In a 4 × 4 Sudoku game:

- Every row of 4 numbers must include all digits 1 through 4 in any order
- Every column of 4 numbers must include all digits 1 through 4 in any order
- Every 2 × 2 subsection of the 4 × 4 square must include all digits 1 through 4

Similarly, larger Sudoku puzzles, such as the 9 × 9 puzzle, must have the numerals 1 through 9 in each row, column, and subsection. Larger Sudoku games are available (16 × 16) must have numerals 1 through 16 in each row, column and region. The principles are the same whatever the size of the game.

Every Sudoku game begins with a number already in some square, and the difficulty of each game is largely determined by how many squares are filled in. The more squares that are known, the easier it is to figure out which numbers go in the open squares. As people fill in squares correctly, options for the remaining squares are narrowed and it becomes easier to fill them in.

You can make Sudoku games easier for lower-functioning participants by filling in some of the squares. You can also give 4 × 4 puzzles to participants who have more severe cognitive impairment.

Touch Activities*

We have discussed many activities designed to exercise attention and verbal fluency, but we can also help people make new touch memories. For this activity, you will need approximately 10 small items, which can be purchased inexpensively at a dollar store or garage sale. Some of the objects should be common items that may be known to the participants by touch or sight (e.g., a key, clothespin, or spoon) while other objects should be less common (e.g., garlic press or cell phone cover). The instructor places the objects, one at a time, in a paper bag and has the participant touch the object. Without looking at the object, the participant must identify the object. Once the participant has attempted to identify the object, they are told what it is. The participant is then instructed to feel the object again and "make a memory" for the feel of the object. Keep track of what objects each person has seen and touched, within sessions and across sessions. Each time this activity is done, use some items that were used in previous sessions and some new items. If possible, try to choose at least one object the participant is likely to know through touch and one they are not likely to initially know by touch. To make the task challenging for high-functioning participants, you will have to have some objects that are very rare. The high-functioning participants should remember the name and the function of the object. Consider asking participants to bring objects that might be interesting to other participants (e.g., objects that were common 50 years ago but less so now). This activity is appropriate for anybody, regardless of cognitive ability or visual impairment.

Split Words

Begin this activity by printing out sheets of paper with common words in fairly large fonts (e.g., see Appendix J for a sample split word list). Cut each word out then cut the word in half. For example, take the word FAMILY and cut it into FAM and ILY. Place all word halves into an envelope. Make enough envelopes for each participant and be sure to label the envelope (e.g., Split Word #1) so you can keep track of which ones you have used and possibly reuse them at other facilities or in 6 to 12 months. You can make the task more difficult by using shorter words such as four- or five-letter words. You can also vary the difficulty level of the activity by changing whether the first letter is capitalized. If you capitalize the first letter of words before cutting then in half, participants will be able to easily determine which word halves are the beginning of words. For more impaired participants, suggest putting all the first half of the words in a column in front of them so they can easily check whether the other word halves complete the words.

Alphabetization Activities

The alphabetizing activity simply involves having participants alphabetize lists of words, which is excellent for exercising attention. Give each participant an envelope full of words. The participant will dump out the words and attempt to put them in alphabetical order. There are some possible modifications that can make the activity more or less challenging. To make the activity easier and more appropriate for lower-functioning participants, make the first letters of each word different. To make it even easier, make the first letter of each word separated by at least two letters in the alphabet (i.e., don't have words that begin with R and S). See Appendix K for an alphabetization list designed for more-impaired participants. To make the activity more challenging, give participants words that begin with the same letter or even the first two letters, also try giving them more words (see Appendix L for a more challenging alphabetization list).

Word Searches

Word searches or word-finds are an excellent way to exercise attention and visual scanning. There are thousands of word searches available in prepared workbooks and on the internet. However, I recommend making your own by going to the aforementioned Web site, http://puzzlemaker.school.discovery.com (see Appendix M to view a sample word-find using the above Web site). You simply click on "word search" and then choose the puzzle dimensions and begin entering words. Consider entering words from recent facts of the day or entering the names of the memory class participants or if you recently asked people to list former presidents of the United States, enter 20 or so president's names in a word search for the next class. Consider making seasonal or holiday-specific word searches. Or you can make memory-related word searches using words such as memory, language, cortex, hippocampus, recall, recognition, episodic, semantic, procedural, encoding, storage, retrieval, attention, exercise, brain, nutrition, learn, and mnemonics. The above word searches are also fun things to include in newsletters or put on tables in the dining room.

Tongue Twisters*

Tongue twisters are another fun way to exercise at least two cognitive abilities at once. Speaking tongue twisters requires concentration and challenges our ability to enunciate. In addition, participants can memorize the twisters between sessions. Finally, twisters are an excellent dual-tasking activity; participants can simultaneously say the twisters while performing a task such as stepping up and down from a step or repeatedly sitting and standing from a chair.

Make a copy of the tongue twister for each participant (see Appendix N for some common tongue twisters). Begin by having each person in the group read one line. Then ask them to remember their line and read it without looking. Depending on the size of the group, you may be able to have each participant try remembering two lines. After working on the twister for a few minutes, ask them to take it home and practice it. You can assign each person certain line(s) to remember for the next session. Consider revisiting tongue twisters, especially if people have taken the effort to memorize and practice them. With enough practice, even people with early-stage dementia can learn to perform some tongue twisters.

Ask the Memory Doctor:
I work as an activity director and I have a difficult time getting residents to come to activities. Is there anything I can do to increase participation?

One of the most challenging aspects of conducting memory enhancement classes in a facility is trying to motivate residents to participate. Many times it seems as if the people who could most benefit from the extra cognitive stimulation are the least likely to participate. There are a few things you can do as an activity director or memory class instructor to get more people to participate. One technique is to give a short questionnaire to people who you think could benefit from the program. The handout should include some simple questions about the prospective participant. Here are some possible questions:

1. name
2. childhood nickname
3. state or city of birth

   4. favorite vacation
   5. most embarrassing moment
   6. favorite musical artist
   7. favorite color
   8. favorite season
   9. favorite recreational activity
  10. favorite movie
  11. favorite pet
  12. favorite food item
  13. favorite dessert
  14. favorite book
  15. favorite play
  16. how many grand or great-grandchildren

Choose four to eight of the above questions and make a handout (see Appendix O for a sample *Get to Know Your Neighbor* questionnaire).

After the prospective participant has completed the questionnaire, make photocopies for the regular participants. Tell the prospective participant that the memory class will be trying to memorize some facts about them and that they are welcome to come and sit on the outside while the memory class participants memorize the facts. Choose only a few facts and review them repeatedly throughout the class. This activity can be used in place of the fact of the day activity. After class, invite the prospective participant to join the class as a regular participant. In my experience, this is a very effective way to motivate the more apathetic residents to become regular memory class participants. The above questionnaire can also be used in class by regular participants to try to facilitate social connectedness (see Chapter 7 for more information).

Another technique to maximize attendance and participation is to develop a chart that tracks attendance and possibly homework completion. In the past, I have named these charts the "Star Board," because people would receive stars for attending, attempting the homework, and completing the homework. The people with the greatest number of stars would receive a small prize such as a book of puzzles or a popular novel (see a sample star board in Figure 1).

Another option is to assign one or two of the highest-functioning participants to go around and talk to people about joining the class. A personal invitation from a fellow resident along with a personal testimony about their experience in the memory class can be all it takes to get someone to become a regular participant.

Eminent psychologist Albert Bandura taught us that there are two general ways to help people increase their motivation to do some behavior. First, the person must believe they can do the behavior; this is referred to as self-efficacy. Just having potential participants sit and observe a class can dramatically increase their self-efficacy and belief that they can be a successful and contributing group participant, because they will see others like them doing so. Second,

Figure 1. A sample "Star Board" we used to track attendance and homework. Charts like this can be used to help motivate participants to attend memory class and attempt their homework. A participant may volunteer to be responsible for assigning stars.

Bandura suggested that people must be aware of the expected outcomes of doing some behavior before they are motivated to do it. Put more pragmatically, people must be aware of the potential quality-of-life benefits associated with participating in cognitively stimulating activities. There is a large and growing body of scientific literature that supports the idea that engaging in cognitively stimulating activities improves memory ability and decreases the chance of developing dementia. Consider sharing some of the information in Chapter 4, which summarizes the research that supports the "Use it or lose it" principle.

See the *Ask the Memory Doctor* in Chapter 11 for more information on motivating the unmotivated.

PROVIDE OPPORTUNITIES FOR SUCCESS

Many of the activities discussed in this chapter will be very challenging for people who have mild cognitive impairment or early-stage dementia. We want to set up situations in which participants can succeed. Consider recording scores or times for some tests so you can go back and have participants compare their scores and hopefully see that they are improving at some tasks. The Stroop Test materials work very well for retesting and assessing improvements (see Chapter 13 for more information about the Stroop Effect). Also, record the highest number groups get to before making a mistake on the game Buzz. Or consider keeping track of how many states of the union people are able to list in a certain time period. Use the recognition strategy discussed in the next chapter to ensure success from even the most impaired participants. A focus on success can help maintain excitement, interest, and motivation.

GET HELP

Organizing a memory class, developing the materials, advertising the class, getting people to remember to come to class, and facilitating the actual class sessions takes a lot of work. Consider getting someone to help you. Some cognitive enhancement instructors have been able to elicit help from local colleges and universities. Contact the Psychology Department, Health Department, or Gerontology Department and ask them if it is possible to have their students do an internship or practicum with you. Or you can ask professors to announce a volunteer opportunity in their classes. Students who are interested in working with older adults will benefit from the experience of helping you organize and run memory classes. Another way to elicit help is to go to your local senior center and ask if you can advertise for a volunteer position. Or you can identify the sharpest and most motivated class participants and ask them if they are interested in helping run future classes.

There are a lot of benefits associated with having someone available to help during classes. You can give more impaired participants greater attention. You will also be able to have larger classes and potentially let more impaired people into your classes.

CHAPTER 13

Starting and Sustaining Your Cognitive Enhancement Program

The human brain is unique in that it is the only container of which it can be said that the more you put into it, the more it will hold. Glenn Doman (1919–)

OK, you want to start a memory enhancement class for others. Great! Participants will benefit from your class by exercising their brains, learning new things, and strengthening their cognitive abilities. Starting memory classes is a very rewarding experience, but there are some things to consider before getting started. In this chapter, we will discuss where classes can be held, how to charge participants for your time, and materials. We will also explore which types of participants benefit the most from memory classes and which type of participants can negatively impact the ability of other participants to benefit from the experience.

One of the most challenging aspects of conducting memory enhancement classes, regardless of setting, is making the experience meaningful for people of varying abilities. The reader will be given suggestions about how activities can be made easier for people who are having more serious memory problems. I will also suggest 16 ways that instructors can challenge higher-functioning participants. Knowing how to work with and engage the most capable participants is important. Higher-functioning participants can help run the classes and recruit new participants, while simultaneously engaging their minds to the highest possible degree.

WHERE SHOULD YOU HOLD YOUR MEMORY CLASSES?

One of the first decisions you will have to make is where to hold your classes. Some options are senior centers, residential care communities, fitness centers, or bringing classes directly to people in their homes. Many cognitive enhancement instructors choose to hold classes in multiple venues.

Senior Centers

Senior centers are a great place to hold memory classes. Senior center members are usually used to new classes becoming available and are often very willing to try new things. In addition, memory enhancement classes fit the mission and goals of most senior centers. Most senior centers have a monthly newsletter that can be used to get the word out about new classes and opportunities. The classes are likely to start out small, unless you are able to drum up interest before the classes begin. If the classes are fun, challenging, and well-organized, the number of attendees is likely to increase over time.

Holding classes at senior centers poses unique challenges and opportunities. For example, some senior centers require instructors to have liability insurance. Another issue is whether the senior center will charge a fee for you offering classes at the center. If the fees are too high, it can make it difficult to cover all your expenses. If you are planning on charging participants a fee for the class, the senior center may be willing to collect those fees for you. However, the fees senior center members are used to paying are usually quite low (e.g., $2 or $3 per class), but I have found that most people are willing to pay more for a high-quality memory class

Residential Care Facilities

It is my opinion that you can do more good for older adults who live in assisted living facilities (ALFs) than you can for active independent older adults or people in nursing homes. It is not that others won't benefit from memory classes, there can actually be huge benefits for independent older adults, but the ALF residents often possess many more risk factors for memory problems.

According to the Assisted Living Federation of America, there are over 20,000 ALFs in the United States, with over 1 million residents. I believe that people living in ALFs are at risk for cognitive decline unless an active effort is made to stimulate them and get them involved in social and cognitively stimulating activities. ALF residents have many activities associated with daily living done for them, including such things as cooking, cleaning, shopping, transportation, and having their pharmaceuticals brought to them in the correct dosage and at the correct time of day. There is no doubt that ALFs provide a valuable service that allows people the safety of 24-hour care and monitoring, while at the same time allowing them to live relatively independently as compared with moving into a nursing home. However, if all the meal planning, social event planning, cooking, shopping, and transportation is done by others, what will the residents have to remember and problem solve? What will stimulate their brains and challenge them? What will prevent their cognitive abilities from atrophying? Often times the answer is nothing or very little. Certainly people are aware that ALFs and other institutionalized residential settings need high quality activities, but the reality is that most ALFs have very low attendance in their organized activity programs.

Institutionalized residents, regardless of the level of care, often have other risk factors for cognitive decline or mental health problems. For example, the average ALF resident is no longer driving, has lost their spouse, has outlived many of their lifelong friends, and they very likely just moved from another area to live closer to their adult children. These factors negatively affect people's quality of social support and increase the chance of loneliness. In addition, research shows that older adults who are either no longer living independently or have a chronic illness are at an increased risk of developing depression and mood disorders. Clinical depression or even a blue mood can wreak havoc on memory ability and may accelerate cognitive decline and impair the quality and quantity of social interactions. The good news is that recent research suggests that having a high quality cognitive enhancement program can lead to improved perceptions of social support and decreased loneliness among ALF residents (see Chapter 7 for more information about mood, social support, and strategies to facilitate social support). For these reasons, I believe it is very important to develop cognitive enhancement programs in ALFs and other retirement community settings.

If you develop a memory class in an ALF or other group-based living environment, you will need to determine who will be eligible to participate. At the very least you will need to determine if nonresidents can participate. Allowing nonresidents to join the group can bring new people and fresh ideas into the residents' lives. In addition, marketing directors will probably appreciate the exposure to the facilities. However, I have seen unhealthy competition develop between nonresidents and residents. I recommend making the class available for residents only. Or if you decide to invite nonresidents, be sure to interview them and consider letting in only those who you feel would bring a positive attitude to the group.

There is usually very wide variability in cognitive ability among residents of retirement communities. Oftentimes, people with dementia or mild cognitive impairment are living in the same building with people who have excellent cognitive abilities. This disparity in abilities poses unique challenges, therefore I recommend screening participants to identify people with more severe impairments. In my experience, people with severe dementia cannot take part in group-based programs that primarily focus on exercising attention processes and making new memories. I also recommend having two levels of classes, but recognize that this isn't always possible.

Fitness Centers

There is growing awareness of the need to not only exercise our muscles but also our minds. This makes fitness centers an excellent place to conduct memory enhancement classes. Retired older adults who regularly exercise at fitness clubs are probably also aware that they need to keep their minds active. More importantly, they are usually the type of people who are motivated to do so.

Most larger fitness centers have space where you can conduct memory classes. We have seen fitness centers sponsor classes and aggressively advertise them to their older members. Consider starting memory enhancement classes at fitness centers.

Ask the Memory Doctor
How do I know if an activity is cognitively stimulating? For example, I play bridge with my friends every week, does that count?

That is a very common question for cognitive enhancement instructors. There is a simple rule that allows people to determine whether any activity is cognitively stimulating: If you cannot think about something else while doing the activity in question, then it is probably cognitively stimulating. For example, you may be able to daydream while driving a familiar route; therefore driving that route is not cognitively stimulating. However, if you go to a large city that you have never been to and you are trying to find a certain street and address, then you might not be able to daydream or think about something else, therefore driving at that time would be cognitively stimulating. Another example would be playing the card game solitaire. If you have played thousands of games of solitaire, you can probably put the card in the right place without even thinking about it, therefore the card game has lost much of its cognitively stimulating effect. However, if you learn a new card game you may not even be able to carry on a coherent conversation with the other card players and simultaneously abide by the rules of the game. In that case, the new card game would be cognitively stimulating.

Why is it that we can daydream while performing certain tasks, which we couldn't do when we first learned how to do the activity? A basic principle of the psychology of learning states that over time, behaviors that are repeated many times, usually at least 100 times, become automatized or turned into procedural memories (see Chapter 2 for a review of the three types of memory). When behaviors are automatized, they are actually stored in different parts of the brain (e.g., the cerebellum or that cauliflower shaped structure on the back of the brain) and not as connected to the cortex, where most language and thought takes place. When behaviors become automatized like that, they don't require much attention or any new learning and are therefore not cognitively stimulating.

People have begun to ask what type of activities might provide the most benefit. I suspect that we will find that learning new things provides the greatest protective benefit from memory loss. I would also suggest that anything that requires a lot of attentional resources would be beneficial. For example, doing a Sudoku puzzle would be more beneficial than doing crossword puzzles (see Chapter 13 for a brief discussion of Sudoku puzzles). Sudoku puzzles often require sustained attention for longer periods of time. Nearly all older adults experience a reduced ability to concentrate or pay attention, which impairs their ability to make new memories. By exercising the attentional parts of the brain, mostly located in the frontal lobes, one may prehabilitate their memory ability.

Home-Based Classes

Many older adults still live independently, even though for various reasons, they no longer get out of the house very much. These people may spend long days without anyone checking in on them or having an opportunity to challenge themselves cognitively. You can bring your memory program directly to these people. You can arrange to work with home health care agencies to bring your cognitive exercise directly to people who desperately need them. This is an exciting and important opportunity because it is possible that we can allow people to live in their own homes longer if they are able to maintain their cognitive abilities. It is often much cheaper for people to stay in their homes and have occasional services brought to them rather than moving into an assisted living facility. We already have nurses, certified nursing assistants, and therapists visit older adults in their homes. Why not bring them cognitive exercises and some social interaction as well? Doing so will allow many people to stay in their homes longer and thus allow them to maintain their quality of life. Many home health care agencies would be happy to add your service to their menu of options. Moreover, many older adults and adult children of older adults would like to have the peace of mind in knowing that they are receiving mental stimulation and social interaction that can help people best maintain their quality of life. For homebound older adults, I also recommend that they get a daily newspaper delivered and have magazines available. In addition to the nutritional meals, meals-on-wheels programs can also add predictable visits that many older adults look forward to. It is important to note that although Medicaid recipients can get meals, the program is also available for higher-income people and the regular visits from the volunteer drivers can be an important component of allowing people to stay independent.

You will probably conduct one-on-one memory enhancement sessions differently than you would in a group setting. In a one-on-one setting, you can individualize the materials to the person's ability. You can find materials that will maximally stimulate and challenge them. I also suggest bringing homebound participants more homework and activities that they can do when you are not there. Then on subsequent visits, you can go over the homework they have done and give them more activities. You will need to keep good notes on what you have done, assigned, and what you need to review with participants.

You may be able to also get your materials to people through library programs that bring older adults books. Or you can work with Meals-on-Wheels and have activities brought to people with their meals. Another niche is to offer caregivers a break by coming in and working on mental activities and socializing for a short time. Every bit of cognitive stimulation will help people who are trying to prevent dementia.

Compensation Models

Regardless of where you offer your classes, you will probably need to cover the expenses related to buying and preparing materials. When conducting classes in a group-based living environment, the facility will usually cover the costs. However, if you conduct classes at a senior center, medical clinic, or fitness center, you will probably need to charge participants for your time and materials. We have experimented with a number of compensation models and each one has its strengths and weaknesses. One option is to define a "term." For example, you could make your term last 10 weeks and offer two classes each week. Participants would pay a flat rate for that term and stay with the same group of participants for at least the duration of the term. If people miss a class, you don't have to refund money, just as a college student who misses a single lecture doesn't get a refund. People may be more motivated to attend all the sessions if they know they have already paid for them. However, some people are reluctant to sign up for a long-term commitment if they know they will be traveling or unable to attend certain sessions, therefore they may prefer a per-class payment system. For example, you could charge people $8 for every class. The per-class-fee model eliminates concerns for people who are unable to attend every session. However, these people may not be as motivated to attend every session.

Another option is to apply for a grant. There are many agencies and foundations that might be interested in supporting a program that helps people maintain their independence and quality of life. You will probably need to develop a nonprofit corporation (i.e., one that has a 501 (c) 3 designation) in order to be eligible to be awarded grants from the greatest number of granting agencies. The benefit of being awarded a grant is that you probably won't need to worry about generating revenue and can offer classes that will reach people who may be unable or unwilling to pay for the classes. If you don't want to invest the time, money, and energy in starting a nonprofit entity, then you can contact nonprofit senior centers and ask whether they would be willing to be a recipient of the grant and house the memory classes. The majority of senior centers are funded by local government and therefore don't have a nonprofit designation. However, even most government-funded senior centers and almost all public libraries have an affiliated group (e.g., Friends of Springfield Library) that is a nonprofit and thus capable of receiving grants.

It can be very costly and time-consuming to make the materials for a class. You often need to print the materials and photocopy them. You may find yourself preparing eight activities per class, for 20 participants, three times a week. That could require up to 480 pieces of paper ($8 \times 20 \times 3$)! You may want to consider charging a materials fee in addition to the tuition.

Be sure to develop a written refund policy if you will be charging participants a fee for your class. If you decide to offer a fixed-term course and charge a flat-rate tuition for the term, you will need to set a deadline for a full refund. You may also want to consider setting a later deadline for a partial refund.

Screening Potential Participants

Will you allow *anyone* to attend your classes? At first thought you may say, "Of course, I don't want to discriminate based on memory ability." I would argue that your classes will not be as successful if you allow anyone, regardless of ability or personality, to participate. I have found that community-based memory classes (e.g., those held at senior centers) attract two distinct types of people. You will have very-high-functioning and curious retirees sign up for the class. These people are always looking for new learning experiences. You will also get people who are really beginning to have serious memory problems. People who are experiencing significant and worsening memory problems are often brought to memory enhancement classes by concerned family members. If you have one class with both types of participants, you can easily disappoint everyone. The higher-functioning participants will not be maximally stimulated, and they will think that the class is not appropriate for them. The lower-functioning participants will require more attention and may feel embarrassed by their memory ability. In addition, it is difficult to choose activities that stimulate both groups.

If at all possible, I strongly recommend that memory enhancement instructors or activity directors screen potential participants before they begin the class. I also recommend that they have two levels of classes: one for people who don't have any significant cognitive impairment and another class for those who do. I realize that many instructors will not have the luxury of having two levels of classes, but it is the best scenario. Later in this chapter, you can read about ways to make memory classes more challenging and fulfilling for your highest-functioning participants, which will be necessary if you are unable to have two class levels.

The best way to screen participants is schedule 15 to 30 minutes with each potential participant. Give them a memory test and chat with them about their memory and what their goals are. I recommend using the Mini Mental State Exam (MMSE), which takes only about 10 minutes to administer and informs the examiner about the person's cognitive ability. This test is widely used, and most geriatric medical professionals are familiar with the test and what certain scores indicate. However, the test is copyrighted, sold by Psychological Assessment Resources and costs over $1 per test. To order the test go to http://www.minimental.com/

Scores on the MMSE range from 0 to 30, with higher scores indicating better cognitive functioning. It is my experience that people with scores of approximately 16 or less are generally unable to do the type of cognitive enhancement activities that are described in this book. People with fairly severe dementia usually score less than 20. People with mild cognitive impairment usually score between 22 and 27. Scores of 28 and above are not indicative of memory problems. Please note these are rough estimates and other factors, besides dementia, could be the cause of lower scores (e.g., delirium, medication, sleep deprivation, malingering, etc.).

Another test option is the Mental Status Questionnaire, which is only a 10-question test and is easily administered. Research has shown that it does a decent job identifying dementia, but it certainly is not a tool to diagnose dementia. People who score less than 3 probably won't be able to fully participate in a group-based program. People who score above 7 probably have normal cognitive abilities. Most people who score above 3 (i.e., fewer than 7 errors) could probably benefit from a group-based program. Here is the test:

1. What are the date, month, and year?
2. What is the day of the week?
3. What is the name of this place?
4. What is your phone number?
5. How old are you?
6. When were you born?
7. Who is the current president?
8. Who was the president before him?
9. What was your mother's maiden name?
10. Can you count backward from 20 by 3s?

Here are some commonly cited interpretations of the score:

0-2 errors: normal mental functioning
3-4 errors: mild cognitive impairment
5-7 errors: moderate cognitive impairment
8 or more errors: severe cognitive impairment

The following adjustments to scores can be made if your goal is to determine if someone is experiencing cognitive impairment. However, I don't recommend making such adjustments if you are using the test to determine whether the memory class would be appropriate for a given individual.

*One more error is allowed in the scoring if a patient has had a grade school education or less.
*One less error is allowed if the patient has had education beyond the high school level.

Another important aspect of screening involves talking with the potential participant and judging whether they will be able to work in a group setting. One of the most common side effects of mild cognitive impairment, certain types of brain damage (i.e., to the frontal lobe), and dementia is an inability to inhibit (not do) certain behaviors, thoughts, and emotions. People who are unable to inhibit certain behaviors can be very disruptive and negatively affect other participants' ability to benefit from the activities. An inability to inhibit is related to an inability to pay attention and make new memories, so this deficit is common among memory enhancement participants. Many of the activities I recommend for cognitive enhancement classes or cognitive rehabilitation sessions involve doing specific exercises that exercise inhibition and attention in hopes of actually improving these abilities.

You can use standardized tests to measure inhibitory abilities, including the Trail Making Test. This test assesses inhibitory processes as well as cognitive flexibility, working memory, and ability to follow directions. This test can be used to assess cognitive functioning, and it is widely available on the Internet. It is also a great way to develop a baseline measure of ability that you can use to look for future changes. This test or variants of it can also be used as an actual cognitive enhancement activity. Another neuropsychological test that does a good job of measuring inhibitory processes is the Stroop Test. The Stroop Test materials can be found on the Internet or made if you have access to a color printer (see Appendix P).

Another way to assess inhibitory processing ability and the likelihood that a potential participant will be disruptive and unable to participate in a group setting is to look for what we call *off-target verbosity*. Or in other words, does the person seem to have a hard time keeping track of the conversation. For example, if you ask an older adult, "How many years of schooling did you get?" you would expect a one or two sentence response. If however, the person responded with a story about how their high school has been torn down and how only 10 people attended their last reunion and how one of the people at the reunion had recently traveled to China, then you just witnessed off-target verbosity. Off-target verbosity and other behaviors (see list below) are a sign that the person has an impaired ability to pay attention and inhibit inappropriate behaviors and thoughts. An inability to attend and inhibit is fairly common among older adults, and it dramatically limits how well someone can make new memories. Here is a list of other behaviors that indicate an impaired ability to inhibit:

Saying answers before the right time
Getting started on a task before all the instructions have been given
Can't stop working on the previous task
Emotional perseveration, such that they get stuck on a certain emotion and can't turn it off
Keep saying the wrong answer each time a certain question is asked
Sexual or socially inappropriate behavior
Getting up without help from others, even though they are at risk of falling
Someone who has had a stroke that affects their ability to eat and swallow, may shovel food into their mouth too fast
Inappropriate social remarks about other people

It is important to be aware of inhibitory problems, as they make it very difficult for people to work in a group setting. I recognize that it is often very difficult for people who are drawn to a helping profession (e.g., activity director or occupational therapist) to turn away a potential memory class participant, but you should be willing to do so for the benefit of others. If their behavior is too disruptive, some people who could benefit from the experience may prevent other group members from benefitting as much as they can. We use the same decision-making model when deciding what is appropriate in a university classroom. For example, if one of my students at our university asks me if she can bring her two-year-old child to class because her sitter is ill, I respond that she can but if the child negatively affects other students' ability to learn or pay attention then they will have to leave. In my opinion, the same principle should apply in memory classes: if someone's behavior negatively affects others' ability to fully participate then, in my opinion, the most ethical action would be to remove the disruptive individual from the class.

Another issue in memory classes is at what point has someone's cognitive abilities deteriorated to the point where they are unable to meaningfully benefit from the experience? I have found that people who score less than 17 or 18 on the MMSE require almost constant attention from an instructor or assistant, which makes it difficult to have them in a group-based program. If you have assistants helping to run the classes, you can have a larger group, and more people with low MMSE score can meaningfully participate. However, when people develop moderately severe dementia, my experience is that they are not able to attend to the type of activities that would exercise attention and memory-making parts of the brain. It is particularly difficult for these people to understand and remember the instructions to many of the activities. If you work very closely with people with moderate dementia, they can sometimes succeed at an activity, but most of the time it is very confusing and frustrating for them. Moreover, I strongly believe that we are not able to help people with moderate dementia very much by doing targeted cognitively stimulating activities. It is my opinion, based on experience working with people who have memory problems, that the less severe the memory problem, the more we can help them improve their ability to pay attention and make new memories.

As stated earlier, it is better to not have people with moderate to severe dementia participate in memory enhancement classes that rely on challenging activities. It is possible to create activity programs for people with moderate to severe levels of dementia, but in my opinion, those classes would not have the goal of improving cognition. The type of activities typically used in activity programs for people with moderate to severe dementia focus more on keeping people busy or accessing memories from the distant past; an activity program like that is beyond the scope of this book.

In addition to focusing on people with somewhere between normal memory to mild cognitive impairment, it is best to have two levels of classes based on ability. If you are unable to have two classes or if you just want to provide greater cognitive stimulation to the highest-functioning participants, there are some things you can do. Many times there are adjustments to the activities that can be made, and I have included those potential modifications in the cognitively stimulating activities' instructions.

How You Ask Questions

It is important that cognitive enhancement instructors understand how to ask questions that vary in how much information they contain. Doing so will vary the difficulty level of correctly answering the question and thus allow you to customize your interactions based on participants' cognitive ability. There are three different ways to tap memory: you can use either a free-recall question, a cued-recall question, or a recognition question. The most challenging question is a free-recall question (somewhat analogous to an essay question) and the easiest is a recognition question (analogous to a multiple-choice question). Examples of using different types of questions can be illustrated in an example of the fact of the day activity. I suggest giving participants a fact of the day at the beginning of class (see Appendix A for more information about this activity). For example, we could give a group the fact of the day that "The average human brain has approximately 100 billion neurons." We would focus on making a new memory, then after a short period of time the participants could be asked what the fact of the day is using a free-recall question, which is the most challenging question format, "What is the fact of the day?" This question format is the most challenging because the question contains very few cues and the learner must generate the general topic (i.e., neurons), the specific topic (i.e., the number of neurons) and the answer. If no one correctly answers that questions, you can make it easier by asking a cued-recall question (called cued recall because there is a cue) "What is the fact of the day? It has something to do with neurons." If no one is able to answer that question, then you can phrase it as a recognition question, for example: "The fact of the day refers to the number of neurons in the average brain. Is that number 1 billion, 10 billion, 100 billion, or 1 trillion?" Research shows that older adults' ability to recognize correct answers is preserved relative to their ability to correctly answer either type of recall question. By changing how you ask questions, you can maximize success, which improves confidence and may motivate people to continue working on cognitive stimulating activities.

Challenging the Highest-Functioning Participants

There are things you can do to keep the highest-functioning participants engaged and maximally stimulated. Many times you will give all participants a handout to work on for approximately 5 minutes. If a few people finish after 2 or 3 minutes, be sure to give them something else to stimulate them while the other participants finish. You should have these extra activities prepared beforehand. For example, you can use a generic piece of paper that has each letter of the alphabet and a space (e.g., A_____ , B _____ , and so on). You

Table 1. Activities to Maximally Stimulate High-Functioning Participants

1. Ask them recall questions rather than recognition questions.

2. Give them more challenging homework.

3. Have them create a word-finds using other participants' names.

4. Have them take a picture of other participants and create a photography project. You can put the pictures up and then names below them. The names should be covered so that people can lift the cover and see the name.

5. Have them create a *Jeopardy* game using previous facts of the day.

6. Have them memorize a poem (or a new tongue twister) and recite it for the group.

7. If higher-functioning participants finish sooner than others, give them another task such as an A to Z activity.

8. Many times higher-functioning participants can help run the classes, especially if there is a large amount of variability between participants. You can meet with the higher-functioning participants before the class and tell them what you have planned, and if necessary, give them a copy of instructions.

9. Have the higher-functioning participants help lower-functioning participants outside of class (e.g., homework or extra activities). You can give your assistants the answers to homework and they can provide tutorial sessions between memory classes.

10. Have your most capable and motivated participants organize guest lecture programs. They can contact business leaders, community college or university professors, medical professionals, or local authors and give a lecture. This works well in retirement communities and senior centers. Here are some popular topics: nutrition, physical exercise, wellness, memory, or sleep.

11. Have them develop a book club. Once again, this works well in retirement communities.

12. Have interested participants develop a newsletter for the class. The newsletter could contain information about memory and fun activities.

13. Have someone teach a computer class.

14. Have an interested person organize an educational activity for the memory class or the community. For example, the group could read about a historical event and then watch and discuss a related movie.

15. Ask them what they would like to do that could provide an opportunity for people to be challenged and learn something new.

16. Have them keep track of attendance and homework on a board (see the next chapter for ideas about making an attendance and homework tracking system that is designed to increase motivation).

can have participants generate a list of animals that start with each letter, or first names, or first names of females, or first names of males, or countries, and so on. Having these activities will ensure that higher-functioning participants don't get bored while giving lower-functioning participants more time to complete the original task.

Another option when faced with participants who need different amounts of time to complete a task is to have the first people who finish turn over their original worksheet and have them generate as many words as they can using the letters M-E-M-O-R-Y (or whatever word you want). Or you can have them think of as many recent facts of the day as they can. Or you can have them try to calculate what day of the week the first of next month will fall on. There are many things you can do to challenge your most capable participants. See Table 1 to view a list of suggested activities to maximally stimulate high-functioning participants.

Consider Providing Participants Notebooks

Participants will probably need notebooks for certain materials and their homework. Activities and homework that you want the participants to keep can be 3-hole punched. I don't recommend that participants keep all paper activities that are done in class because the large amount of paper can become overwhelming. In addition, you will end up wasting a lot of class time as people will want to put things away. Immediately after the activity is complete, the instructor should collect the activities that would not be helpful to keep in the notebook. Picking up paper activities after they are done and keeping the desk or table space tidy will reduce the number of distractions and hopefully enhance attention. I recommend putting at least two dividers in the notebook so the participants can keep the homework separate from other materials.

CHAPTER 14

Participant Management: How to Help More People Benefit from Cognitive Stimulation

It is not how old you are, but how you are old. Jules Renard (1864–1910)

There are two general types of older adults who often require unique interventions in order for them to experience the maximum benefits from memory classes and other activity programs. The first type is the highly motivated and very capable participant who has above-average cognitive abilities. We need to find ways to maximally stimulate these people and prevent them from becoming bored with our programs. The other type is the unmotivated, apathetic, and possibly depressed individual. This latter type of person is often at great risk of experiencing additional problems if they don't begin doing things to improve their situation. We will discuss how both types of participants can maximally benefit from memory classes and other types of activity programs.

CHALLENGE HIGHER-FUNCTIONING PARTICIPANTS

Even if it is possible to have two different memory class levels based on cognitive ability, there will be times when you want to further challenge the highest-functioning participants. I have found that the most motivated and capable participants will become bored if they are not challenged. Fortunately, there are ways to challenge these people while at the same time providing a meaningful program for lower-functioning participants.

Use a Hierarchical Question Format

One of the best ways to customize your memory program for different people in a group-based program is to ask different types of questions about things you are trying to have them learn and remember. The hardest type of question to answer and the one that therefore requires the deepest level of encoding

195

(i.e., memory making) is the free-recall question. A free-recall question doesn't contain any cues about the answer, therefore you can challenge your highest functioning participants by asking them free-recall questions. The next most difficult question type is a cued-recall question. A cued-recall question is easier because it contains a cue about the answer or a hint embedded in the answer. The easiest type of question is a recognition question or a multiple choice (my students at the university often refer to these as multiple guess questions). In a recognition question, the learner is given a series of options to choose from when trying to determine the correct answer.

If, for example, you were to use the following fact of the day, we can phrase subsequent questions about it in different ways that vary as a function of how easy they will be to answer. Let's say our fact of the day is "Mark Twain claimed he authored the first book ever written on a typewriter, which was *The Adventures of Tom Sawyer*."[1] We can ask a free-recall question (that is *free* of any cues), "What is the fact of the day?" This question requires the participant to remember the topic and the details; use this format when questioning the most capable participants. Or we could make it a little easier and ask, "What is the fact of the day? It has something to do with the typewriter." Or we could make it even easier by asking which of the following books was supposedly the first book ever written on a typewriter: A) *A Christmas Tale*, B) *Pride and Prejudice,* or C) *Adventures of Tom Sawyer*. Even people who have mild cognitive impairment or early-stage dementia can usually get the correct answer if they are given options to choose from and were paying attention and understood the initial presentation of the information.

If you use the above technique to help lower-functioning participants experience a successful memory-making experience in a group-based setting, I suggest being vigilant that someone else doesn't blurt out the answer and prevent the lower-functioning participant from having the success. This situation is common in memory classes because the inability to inhibit or not do something (e.g., not say an answer that you know) is a common symptom associated with cognitive impairment. I suggest asking people to raise their hands when they know the answer or fact of the day. When you ask the free-recall question, a few people might raise their hands, then ask the cued-recall question, which should trigger a few more people's memory and their hands will go up. Then focus on one person who hasn't raised their hand and needs a success. Ask that person the question using the recognition or multiple-choice format.

[1] Many Web sites claim that Mark Twain wrote the first book using a typewriter, in fact there is a newspaper, where he claimed "I will now claim—until dispossessed—that I was the first person in the world to apply the type-machine to literature. That book must have been *The Adventures of Tom Sawyer*." However, some people claim that the first book was actually *Life on the Mississippi*. From http://www.popularmisconceptions.com/blog/category/technology

Be Prepared to Give Higher-Functioning Participants More Challenging Activities

Another obvious way to challenge higher-functioning memory class participants is ask more of them. They can be given addition homework, such as challenging Sudoku puzzles or word-finds. You can ask them to think of as many words as possible using the letters W-I-S-D-O-M. They might come up with words like: swim, dim, mow, mid, sow, mod, id, and do.

Higher-Functioning Participants Can Help Run the Classes

Higher-functioning participants can get extra cognitive stimulation and the satisfaction of helping others by assisting the memory class instructor. They could help lower-functioning participants outside of class with homework or various puzzles and activities. They could keep track of attendance and homework completion. They could also help enlist new participants. For example, if the memory class is being held in a residential setting, they could talk to new residents and make a personal invitation to come to the next memory class as their guest. Or they could develop a newsletter for the memory class, which could contain short articles about memory, activities, puzzles, or stories about successful memory class participants. A newsletter is a great way to get a number of people involved, even residents who are not interested in doing memory classes but might want to help with writing articles or doing the necessary computer and graphics work.

Higher-functioning participants who want to help run the memory class could also create word-finds (or word searches) using the names of other participants. They could create word-finds by hand or use one of the many software programs available for creating puzzles. If puzzle-making software is purchased, they could also create customized crossword puzzles based on information learned in the class (e.g., facts of the day). They may also enjoy making a *Jeopardy*-like game in which questions about memory, facts of the day, the brain, or rules of commonly played brain games make up the questions (or answers) that participants have to answer (or phrase in the form of a question). Higher functioning participants could teach a computer class, organize a book club, or invite an outside lecturer to visit the class. Or they may be interested in developing a photography project in which pictures of the participants or pictures of the facility residents are placed on the wall and under the picture is the person's name, covered by a piece of paper that is hinged with tape so it can be raised to view it. Participants can try to memorize the names. A variant of this activity can include older pictures of the participants. This is a great activity to facilitate better social interactions.

The goal is to maximally stimulate all the participants. Another way to do that is by asking higher-functioning or very motivated participants if they would be willing to learn a new poem or tongue twister. At the very least, you should have some activities ready if they finish the activities sooner than other participants. I recommend having generic A-Z handouts ready, which participants can use to generate first names beginning with the letters A through Z, or male first names, or female first names, or animals, or verbs. You could even just have some simple arithmetic, which requires mental math. Two minutes of doing any of the above would ensure the most capable or quickest participants are maximally stimulated. But what should we do about the unmotivated and apathetic participant? In the next section, we will discuss some techniques for motivating people. These techniques can be used to motivate older adults to do many of the behaviors that could improve their health and overall quality of life.

MOTIVATING PARTICIPANTS

Throughout this book, many suggestions have been given about how people can maintain or even improve their memory ability, but almost all the suggestions require that people make certain changes in their behavior. If people are not motivated to make positive changes in their lives, then none of the information presented in this book will help them. How can we motivate people to engage in positive and health-promoting behaviors?

There are internal and external factors that need to be considered when trying to understand the myriad factors that affect people's motivation to engage in health-promotion activities (Kwong & Kwan, 2007). The external factors refer to things outside of the individual that affect whether or not someone is likely to do something. For example, in order to engage in more cognitively stimulating activities, people need to have access to materials, books of good brain games, and classes designed for older adults. Other external factors include financial resources. Many times more nutritious food is more expensive. Many older adults on fixed incomes are unable or unwilling to spend money on memory classes or other programs. The lack of transportation is another common external barrier that prevents many people from doing the things that could improve their health and overall quality of life. I met a woman once who came to a lecture I gave at a rural hospital. She said that the transportation services available for older adults would take her only to the hospital, so all of her outings had to take place there; she claimed that she wanted to be more involved, but she was unable to drive and her spouse and close friends had all died. When possible, we need to remove these external barriers.

Motivation and whether or not someone will do a health-promoting behavior is primarily affected by what we call internal factors, which are factors, traits, and perceptions within the individual. The two most important internal factors are self-efficacy and what the person believes will be the outcome of doing a certain behavior. These internal factors make up what is known as the Social Cognitive

Theory of Motivation. Research has repeatedly shown that these factors predict whether or not someone will engage in behaviors that improve their health.

Self-Efficacy

Self-efficacy refers to the individual's belief that they are capable of doing some behavior or achieving some outcome (Bandura, 1997). Although somewhat related, self-efficacy is different from self-esteem. Self-esteem refers to someone's general perceptions of their self-worth, whereas self-efficacy refers to the belief that one can successfully achieve some outcome. One could have a healthy self-esteem but have very low self-efficacy for flying a plane, rebuilding a car engine, or eating a healthier diet. Research has shown that people's self-efficacy for health-promoting behaviors predicts their overall physical activity, nutrition, stress management, and interpersonal relations (Kwong & Kwan, 2007; Morowatisharifabad, Ghofranipour, Heidarnia, Ruchi, & Ehrampoush, 2006; Sohng, Sohng, & Yeom, 2007). Fortunately, it is often possible to increase people's self-efficacy, which is one of the best ways to improve their motivation.

Outcome Expectations

The other internal factor, which is a part of Bandura's Social Cognitive Theory, is often referred to as outcome expectations. Outcome expectations are the beliefs people have about what the potential outcomes will be if they do a certain behavior. For example, we know that the more people are aware of the health benefits associated with physical exercise, the more likely they are to actually exercise (that is why 19 health benefits associated with physical exercise are listed in Chapter 6). If our goal is to help people increase behaviors that are likely to lead to better health and cognitive ability, we need to make sure they are fully aware of the associated benefits.

MOTIVATING PEOPLE

Whether or not someone does a certain behavior is determined by their self-efficacy for that behavior and their perceptions of the outcomes associated with actually doing the behavior. If we want to increase people's motivation to do something, we need to increase both their belief that they can successfully do it and that doing it will lead to good and desirable outcomes.

Increasing Self-Efficacy

In this next section, we will explore effective methods to increase self-efficacy and provide examples of how to use them with older adults in order to motivate them to engage in behaviors that will help improve their memory ability, health, and overall quality of life.

One way to increase self-efficacy is to provide people with opportunities to have successful experiences. People will experience an increase in their belief that they can do a certain behavior if they are able to do it once or twice. For example, if someone who hasn't been exercising and is unsure whether they can successfully begin an exercise program is persuaded to simply go for a walk, that experience should increase their self-efficacy for walking again and possibly increase their belief that they can successfully begin a more intensive exercise program. Another example of using a mastery experience to increase self-efficacy is if someone successfully completed a simple Sudoku puzzle (e.g., a mini Sudoku), which in turn would likely increase their belief that they could do a more challenging puzzle. When trying to motivate people, look for opportunities to facilitate successful experiences (e.g., by using different question formats mentioned earlier in the chapter).

Another way to increase self-efficacy is to observe someone else successfully do some behavior. This technique is most successful if the successful model is similar to the observer. There are many ways to employ this self-efficacy enhancing strategy in an effort to increase people's motivation. In a facility-based residential setting, new residents can be invited to simply observe part of a physical exercise class or a memory class. One particularly effective technique to motivate new residents to join a memory class is to give them the Good Neighbor Activity Sheet found in Chapter 7. The form contains questions such as "What was your childhood nickname?" and "What is your all-time favorite book?" Then, tell the new resident that the memory class participants would like to memorize information about them on a certain day and ask them if they would like to come and observe as the participants learn about them. If the new resident is willing, they will see other people, who hopefully are similar to them, successfully doing various memory and attention exercises (and having fun). Witnessing their peers do this should have a dramatic effect on the new resident's self-efficacy to participate in the class and thus increase their motivation to do so.

Group classes or group therapy is another great way to increase self-efficacy. Older adults seeing their peers successfully doing something is a powerful motivator. For example, a physical therapist can create a small group-therapy session to teach a new patient how to transfer from a wheel chair to a stationary chair. The new patient can watch others do the wheel chair transfer and the more experienced people can give the new patient feedback. It is amazing to watch the difference in people's attitude when they do something in front of their peers, as compared with doing it for their therapist or another staff member. I believe the patients also have increased attention to the task, which further increases the chance of success. So try to take advantage of group-based programs or therapy whenever possible.

Many times it is not possible to have someone witness similar people do the behavior that they don't believe they can do. In situations like this, I recommend telling the person about other people like them that have successfully done the behavior in question. This can be a very effective strategy that professionals can employ in a variety of situations. Whether it is doing home exercises after knee surgery, beginning an exercise program, or joining a memory class, we can use this simple but effective strategy to increase the person's belief that they can do the activity.

A related technique to help increase someone's self-efficacy is simple verbal persuasion. Tell the individual that they can do it. Possibly tell them how they will do it or remind them when they have done the behavior in the past. Whenever they are doubting themselves, try to talk to them and tell them that they are capable of doing the behavior.

Outcome Expectations

As mentioned above, the second way to increase motivation is to remind or tell people what the benefits associated with the behavior are. Frankly, if we are unable to do so, then I don't know why the individual should do the behavior. Most chapters of this book were written to include the myriad benefits associated with doing things such as getting adequate cognitive stimulation, getting physical exercise, eating omega-3 fatty acids and antioxidants. Inform people of these benefits and keep reminding them of the potential positive outcomes, especially if you are concerned that the person is not adequately motivated.

Many times the potential positive outcomes are specific to the individual. Our job, as professionals or loved ones, is to determine what the person would like to gain by doing some behavior or how they would like their life or situation to improve. For example, people may have very different desired outcomes for increasing their physical activity. Some people may be concerned about declining memory ability, and knowing that physical exercise has been shown to improve concentration and thus memory ability may be very motivating. Or the individual may be concerned about osteoarthritis and the possibility of a fall or broken bones. That individual is likely to be motivated by the knowledge that physical exercise (especially some weight resistance exercise) may increase bone strength and also decrease the chance of a fall. Talk with the person and try to determine what outcome will motivate them, and then keep reminding them of those potential outcomes if you feel that their motivation needs to be increased. Many older adults are motivated to stay mobile, independent, and maintain their cognitive abilities. Consider telling them how doing certain things will allow them to meet those goals.

Ask the Memory Doctor:

I conduct memory classes at our local senior center. We have several participants who have fairly severe memory problems. Although I think the classes are helping them, they get frustrated when they can't remember. Is there any way to help them have more success during the class?

It is often difficult to conduct memory enhancement classes when participants have very different cognitive abilities. There are many strategies that can be used to maximally stimulate the highest-functioning participants, while also providing the lower-functioning participants with a meaningful experience that doesn't leave them feeling defeated and frustrated. I would first ask you whether it is possible to have two memory classes based on cognitive abilities. It may seem like the lower-functioning participants would feel bad for being in a different class. However, I have never seen someone in a lower-functioning class be upset that they were there. Moreover, if they are aware that there are two classes, they usually appear to be grateful that there is a class designed for their abilities. When people's cognitive ability has been close to some predetermined test score, I have allowed them to choose the class they want to be a part of. Usually they choose the lower-functioning class, and many times in the future, they will want to graduate to the higher-functioning class. Regardless, having two classes alleviates many problems.

If you are unable to offer two memory classes, which is sometimes the case in residential care facilities, there are other options. We can provide higher-functioning participants with greater challenges and elicit their help in running the classes (see the section on challenging higher-functioning participants elsewhere in this chapter). Try to have extra activities ready for the highest-functioning participants, so if they finish before others, you can give them a short activity to do. This will keep the quick people occupied and prevent the people who need more time from feeling like a burden. You will also want to make sure the lower-functioning people have some success. Ask them to repeat back the fact of the day to facilitate greater attention, then later ask them about the fact of the day using a recognition or multiple-choice question (see discussion of hierarchical question formats elsewhere in this chapter). Also prepare materials of the same activity but make the activity easier for some people by adding in some of the correct answers or giving hints. Most of the activities in this book can be modified to make them easier or more difficult. Finally, stay positive and stress that any competition should be against oneself, not the other participants.

SUGGESTED READING

Solie, D. (2004). *How to say it to seniors: Closing the communication gap with our elders.* New York: Berkley Publishing Group.

Facts of the Day

Instructions: Develop a list of interesting but lesser known facts. Present the fact at the beginning of cognitive enhancement classes. Ask participants at the 1, 4, 10, 20, and 50 minute marks what the fact of the day is. If no one remembers the fact of the day, then give them a cue. If after a cue no one remembers, try to phrase a question in a multiple-choice format as even early-stage dementia patients have relative preservation of their recognition abilities.

Example:

Fact of the day: The brain has 100 billion neurons.

Ask: What is the fact of the day?

If no one correctly responds:

Ask: What is the fact of the day? It has something to do with the brain

If no one correctly responds:

Ask: How many neurons do we have in our brains?

If no one correctly responds:

Do our brains have 100, 100,000, 100 million or 100 billion neurons. (More-impaired patients may benefit from have the alternatives written out.)

There is a great Web site that can be used to find facts for this activity at http://www.weirdfacts.com

The Yellow Brick Road to Happiness

Characters and Cast:

Annabelle: Looking for happiness and willing to take advice

_____

Traveler #1: A well-read individual who has searched for happiness

_____

Traveler #2: A well-traveled individual who has searched for happiness

_____

Traveler #3: A wealthy individual who has attempted to pay for happiness

_____

Traveler #4: An individual who has a secret tool to find happiness

_____

The Script:

A: I am very certain that I can find happiness. I know people who are happy. But where can I look, or will it find me?

T1: Excuse me, miss, but did you say that you were looking for happiness?

A: Yes, I did. (Excitedly) Can you tell me where to find it? Please!

T1: No. You see, I have been on this road that you are on. I have looked for happiness in the finest literature, in the best sellers on "How to." Happiness cannot be found. And it will not find you.

A: Well, if I cannot find happiness in books, then where else can I search?

T2: Search for happiness? Forget it. I have been there and done that. You name the continent, name the country. I have searched for happiness in Singapore, Denmark, Australia, Brazil . . .

A: OK! I understand. So you have not found happiness. Surely you have seen happy people.

T2: Yes, I have. But I have not found a "hot springs" of happiness, where you can acquire it for yourself. Happiness cannot be found. And it will not find you.

T3: Acquire happiness? Can't be done. I have purchased more and spent more in a year than most people do in a lifetime. I have been trying to buy happiness, but I can't find a way to get it. Happiness cannot be found. And it will not find you.

A: So how do happy people get happy?

T4: Not even the happiest person can explain it to you. But I have a tool that guarantees you to find it!

T3: I'll buy it.

T2: Where do I go to get it?

T1: I have never read about this . . .

T4: I must agree with your companions, Annabelle. Happiness cannot be found. And it will not find you. I cannot tell you where to go, I cannot sell it to you, or read about it. . . . I can only give you a way to find it in yourself.

A: What do you mean, "find it in yourself?"

Surprise ending . . . (T4 holds up a mirror)

Happiness cannot be found. And it will not find you.

Creative Brainstorming Activity Sample

Think of as many possible uses for an old rowboat. Be as creative and uninhibited as possible.

_____

_____

_____

_____

_____

_____

_____

_____

_____

_____

_____

Sample A-Z Activity Handout

Fill in the blank using the letter provided as the first letter. Think of things that are alive for each letter provided.

Example:
Artichokes _____

A_____   N_____

B_____   O_____

C_____   P_____

D_____   Q_____

E_____   R_____

F_____   S_____

G_____   T_____

H_____   U_____

I_____   V_____

J_____   W_____

K_____   X_____

L_____   Y_____

M_____   Z_____

List of Presidents

1. George Washington, 1789–1797
2. John Adams, 1797–1801
3. Thomas Jefferson, 1801–1809
4. James Madison, 1809–1817
5. James Monroe, 1817–1825
6. John Quincy Adams, 1825–1829
7. Andrew Jackson, 1829–1837
8. Martin Van Buren, 1837–1841
9. William Henry Harrison, 1841
10. John Tyler, 1841–1845
11. James Knox Polk, 1845–1849
12. Zachary Taylor, 1849–1850
13. Millard Fillmore, 1850–1853
14. Franklin Pierce, 1853–1857
15. James Buchanan, 1857–1861
16. Abraham Lincoln, 1861–1865
17. Andrew Johnson, 1865–1869
18. Ulysses Simpson Grant, 1869–1877
19. Rutherford Birchard Hayes, 1877–1881
20. James Abram Garfield, 1881
21. Chester Alan Arthur, 1881–1885
22. Grover Cleveland, 1885–1889
23. Benjamin Harrison, 1889–1893
24. Grover Cleveland, 1893–1897
25. William McKinley, 1897–1901
26. Theodore Roosevelt, 1901–1909
27. William Howard Taft, 1909–1913
28. Woodrow Wilson, 1913–1921
29. Warren Gamaliel Harding, 1921–1923
30. Calvin Coolidge, 1923–1929
31. Herbert Clark Hoover, 1929–1933
32. Franklin Delano Roosevelt, 1933–1945
33. Harry S. Truman, 1945–1953
34. Dwight David Eisenhower, 1953–1961
35. John Fitzgerald Kennedy, 1961–1963
36. Lyndon Baines Johnson, 1963-1969
37. Richard Milhous Nixon, 1969–1974
38. Gerald Rudolph Ford, 1974–1977
39. James Earl Carter, Jr., 1977–1981
40. Ronald Wilson Reagan, 1981–1989
41. George Herbert Walker Bush, 1989–1993
42. William Jefferson Clinton, 1993–2001
43. George Walker Bush, 2001–2009
44. Barack H. Obama, 2009–

List of Countries

AFGHANISTAN
ÅLAND ISLANDS
ALBANIA
ALGERIA
AMERICAN SAMOA
ANDORRA
ANGOLA
ANGUILLA
ANTARCTICA
ANTIGUA AND BARBUDA
ARGENTINA
ARMENIA
ARUBA
AUSTRALIA
AUSTRIA
AZERBAIJAN
BAHAMAS
BAHRAIN
BANGLADESH
BARBADOS
BELARUS
BELGIUM
BELIZE
BENIN
BERMUDA
BHUTAN
BOLIVIA
BOSNIA AND HERZEGOVINA
BOTSWANA
BOUVET ISLAND

BRAZIL
BRUNEI DARUSSALAM
BULGARIA
BURKINA FASO
BURUNDI
CAMBODIA
CAMEROON
CANADA
CAPE VERDE
CAYMAN ISLANDS
CENTRAL AFRICAN REPUBLIC
CHAD
CHILE
CHINA
CHRISTMAS ISLAND
COCOS (KEELING) ISLANDS
COLOMBIA
COMOROS
CONGO
COOK ISLANDS
COSTA RICA
CÔTE D'IVOIRE
CROATIA
CYPRUS
CZECH REPUBLIC
DENMARK
DJIBOUTI
DOMINICA
DOMINICAN REPUBLIC
ECUADOR

EGYPT
EL SALVADOR
EQUATORIAL GUINEA
ERITREA
ESTONIA
ETHIOPIA
FALKLAND ISLANDS
  (MALVINAS)
FAROE ISLANDS
FIJI
FINLAND
FRANCE
FRENCH GUIANA
FRENCH POLYNESIA
GABON
GAMBIA
GEORGIA
GERMANY
GHANA
GIBRALTAR
GREECE
GREENLAND
GRENADA
GUADELOUPE
GUATEMALA
GUERNSEY
GUINEA
GUINEA-BISSAU
GUYANA
HAITI
HEARD ISLAND AND
  McDONALD ISLANDS
HOLY SEE (VATICAN CITY
  STATE)
HONDURAS
HONG KONG
HUNGARY
ICELAND
INDIA
INDONESIA
IRAN
IRAQ
IRELAND

ISLE OF MAN
ISRAEL
ITALY
JAMAICA
JAPAN
JERSEY
JORDAN
KAZAKHSTAN
KENYA
KIRIBATI
KOREA, DEMOCRATIC PEOPLE'S
  REPUBLIC OF
KOREA, REPUBLIC OF
KUWAIT
KYRGYZSTAN
LAO PEOPLE'S DEMOCRATIC
  REPUBLIC
LATVIA
LEBANON
LESOTHO
LIBERIA
LIBYAN ARAB JAMAHIRIYA
LIECHTENSTEIN
LITHUANIA
LUXEMBOURG
MACAO
MACEDONIA, THE FORMER
  YUGOSLAV REPUBLIC OF
MADAGASCAR
MALAWI
MALAYSIA
MALDIVES
MALI
MALTA
MARSHALL ISLANDS
MARTINIQUE
MAURITANIA
MAURITIUS
MAYOTTE
MEXICO
MICRONESIA
MOLDOVA
MONACO

MONGOLIA
MONTENEGRO
MONTSERRAT
MOROCCO
MOZAMBIQUE
MYANMAR
NAMIBIA
NAURU
NEPAL
NETHERLANDS
NETHERLANDS ANTILLES
NEW CALEDONIA
NEW ZEALAND
NICARAGUA
NIGER
NIGERIA
NIUE
NORFOLK ISLAND
NORTHERN MARIANA
  ISLANDS
NORWAY
OMAN
PAKISTAN
PALAU
PALESTINIAN TERRITORY
PANAMA
PAPUA NEW GUINEA
PARAGUAY
PERU
PHILIPPINES
PITCAIRN
POLAND
PORTUGAL
PUERTO RICO
QATAR
RÉUNION
ROMANIA
RUSSIAN FEDERATION
RWANDA
SAINT HELENA
SAINT KITTS AND NEVIS
SAINT LUCIA
SAINT PIERRE AND MIQUELON

SAINT VINCENT AND THE
  GRENADINES
SAMOA
SAN MARINO
SAO TOME AND PRINCIPE
SAUDI ARABIA
SENEGAL
SERBIA
SEYCHELLES
SIERRA LEONE
SINGAPORE
SLOVAKIA
SLOVENIA
SOLOMON ISLANDS
SOMALIA
SOUTH AFRICA
SOUTH GEORGIA AND THE
  SOUTH SANDWICH ISLANDS
SPAIN
SRI LANKA
SUDAN
SURINAME
SVALBARD AND JAN MAYEN
SWAZILAND
SWEDEN
SWITZERLAND
SYRIAN ARAB REPUBLIC
TAIWAN, PROVINCE OF CHINA
TAJIKISTAN
TANZANIA, UNITED REPUBLIC
  OF
THAILAND
TIMOR-LESTE
TOGO
TOKELAU
TONGA
TRINIDAD AND TOBAGO
TUNISIA
TURKEY
TURKMENISTAN
TURKS AND CAICOS ISLANDS
TUVALU
UGANDA

UKRAINE
UNITED ARAB EMIRATES
UNITED KINGDOM
UNITED STATES
URUGUAY
UZBEKISTAN
VANUATU

VENEZUELA
VIET NAM
WALLIS AND FUTUNA
WESTERN SAHARA
YEMEN
ZAMBIA
ZIMBABWE

List of 50 States

Alabama
Alaska
Arizona
Arkansas
California
Colorado
Connecticut
Delaware
Florida
Georgia
Hawaii
Idaho
Illinois
Indiana
Iowa
Kansas
Kentucky
Louisiana
Maine
Maryland
Massachusetts
Michigan
Minnesota
Mississippi
Missouri

Montana
Nebraska
Nevada
New Hampshire
New Jersey
New Mexico
New York
North Carolina
North Dakota
Ohio
Oklahoma
Oregon
Pennsylvania
Rhode Island
South Carolina
South Dakota
Tennessee
Texas
Utah
Vermont
Virginia
Washington
West Virginia
Wisconsin
Wyoming

Generic Verb Generation Handout

Verb Generation Activity

Think of as many things that _____ do. Write down anything that they do, even if others do the same behavior.

For example: runs

_____

_____

_____

_____

_____

_____

_____

_____

_____

_____

_____

Sample Homophone Handout
with Answers

Homonyms are words that sound the same, but are spelled differently and have different meanings. For example, hair and hare are both homonyms. Try to generate the homonym for each word listed below.

cents   _____   flee   _____

heir   _____   whole   _____

wait   _____   plain   _____

hear   _____   aunt   _____

eight   _____   pain   _____

night   _____   meet   _____

deer   _____   bare   _____

we'd   _____   some   _____

Answers to Homonyms Homework 1

cents	sense	flee	flea
heir	air	whole	hole
wait	weight	plain	plane
hear	here	aunt	ant
eight	ate	pain	pane
night	knight	meet	meat
deer	dear	bare	bear
we'd	weed	some	sum

Split Word List

Facility	FACILITY
Hand	HAND
Telephone	TELEPHONE
Company	COMPANY
Happiness	HAPPINESS
Brilliant	BRILLIANT
America	AMERICA
Party	PARTY
Cabinet	CABINET
Amazing	AMAZING
Suggestion	SUGGESTION
Tropical	TROPICAL

Note: The words that have only the first letter capitalized are designed to be easier as the participant will know which half of the word is the first half.

Alphabetization List #1

ADJECTIVE

CLEVER

FENDER

HANDLE

JAGUAR

LANDSLIDE

QUALITY

RASPBERRY

TATTOO

UNIVERSITY

WEATHER

ZEBRA

Alphabetization List #2

STAR APPLE

STAR FRUIT

STEMBERRY

STRAWBERRY

SUGAR APPLE

SUNBERRY

SURINAM CHERRY

SWEET CHERRY

SWEET LIME

SWEET LEMON

SWEETBERRY

STRAWBERRY PEAR

Sample Word Search

Created online at http://puzzlemaker.school.discovery.com

Memory

```
L  B  R  A  I  N  D  U  C  Y  L  B  L  D  F
E  S  Z  Y  E  S  H  G  V  A  F  O  P  D  S
A  G  B  L  F  Y  O  J  S  I  N  Y  N  V  I
R  C  R  O  T  L  I  R  U  G  O  J  Q  D  Z
N  S  N  O  I  T  A  R  T  N  E  C  N  O  C
I  A  U  H  O  E  X  E  D  L  R  D  O  Y  Z
N  S  T  P  H  S  R  M  X  N  K  X  I  R  D
G  Q  H  E  M  M  N  E  K  V  I  W  T  O  F
N  F  R  O  Y  A  T  O  A  I  S  E  N  M  A
K  N  O  B  R  R  C  M  R  S  J  A  E  E  W
X  J  S  C  O  T  B  O  R  U  G  Q  T  M  Q
Z  F  D  C  U  H  T  G  P  F  E  E  T  J  N
Y  J  T  O  I  S  V  E  T  P  W  N  A  B  K
F  Z  G  I  E  J  U  V  R  H  I  B  N  I  C
M  N  E  M  O  N  I  C  S  M  A  H  T  N  Z
```

AMNESIA	ATTENTION	BRAIN
CONCENTRATION	CORTEX	FOCUS
HIPPOCAMPUS	LEARNING	LONGTERM
MEMORY	MNEMONICS	NEURONS
REHEARSAL	SHORTTERM	

Memory Solution

A	+	+	+	+	R	+	+	S	N	+	+	+	S	M
I	+	+	+	+	+	E	H	+	O	+	+	U	S	N
S	+	+	+	+	+	O	H	+	I	+	P	+	R	E
E	M	E	M	O	R	Y	+	E	T	M	+	+	A	M
N	+	+	+	T	+	+	+	+	A	+	+	+	I	O
M	+	+	T	+	+	S	+	C	R	R	+	+	N	N
A	+	E	+	+	N	+	O	+	T	+	S	+	+	I
+	R	+	M	O	+	P	+	F	N	+	+	A	+	C
M	+	+	R	R	P	+	O	+	E	+	+	+	L	S
+	+	U	+	I	E	C	+	+	C	+	+	+	+	+
+	E	+	H	+	U	T	+	+	N	O	+	+	+	+
N	+	+	+	S	+	+	G	+	O	+	R	+	+	+
A	T	T	E	N	T	I	O	N	C	+	+	T	+	+
G	N	I	N	R	A	E	L	+	O	+	+	+	E	+
+	+	+	+	+	+	+	+	+	+	L	+	+	+	X

(Over, Down, Direction)

AMNESIA (1, 7, N)
ATTENTION (1, 13, E)
BRAIN (14, 2, 8)
CONCENTRATION (10, 13, N)
CORTEX (10, 10, SE)
FOCUS (9, 8, SW)
HIPPOCAMPUS (4, 11, NE)
LEARNING (8, 14, W)
LONGTERM (11, 15, NW)
MEMORY (2, 4, E)
MNEMONICS (15, 1, S)
NEURONS (1, 12, NE)
REHEARSAL (6, 1, SE)
SHORTTERM (9, 1, SW)

Common Tongue Twisters

She sells seashells by the seashore.
The shells she sells are surely seashells.
So if she sells shells on the seashore,
I'm sure she sells seashore shells.

A big black bug bit a big black bear,
made the big black bear bleed blood.

Betty Botter had some butter,
"But," she said, "this butter's bitter.
If I bake this bitter butter,
it would make my batter bitter.
But a bit of better butter—
that would make my batter better."
So she bought a bit of butter,
better than her bitter butter,
and she baked it in her batter,
and the batter was not bitter.
So 'twas better Betty Botter
bought a bit of better butter.

Peter Piper picked a peck of pickled peppers.
Did Peter Piper pick a peck of pickled peppers?
If Peter Piper picked a peck of pickled peppers,
where's the peck of pickled peppers Peter Piper picked?

Black Bug's Blood

A skunk sat on a stump
The stump said the skunk stunk
And the skunk said the stump stunk

Rubber baby buggy bumpers (a classic)

Get to Know Your Neighbor Questionnaire

What is your first and last name? _____

In what city and state were you born? _____

What is your favorite dessert? _____

What is your favorite season? _____

What is your favorite book? _____

Where did you go on your most memorable vacation?

_____

Please return this questionnaire to _____

Stroop Effect Instructions, Explanation, and Material Preparation

What is the Stroop Effect

The Stroop Effect refers to the situation when you have people state the color of the ink of various color words. It is important to note that people must state the color of the ink and not just read the word. Two separate lists are required for this test or activity: the first list is known as the congruent list, because the words and the color of the ink are congruent (or match). If you want to make the congruent list, simply type color words (e.g., "blue," "red," "yellow," "green") in the color that matches the word. For example "red" should be printed in red ink.

The second list is more difficult and should require more time to state the color of each word's ink. The second list is more difficult because the color of the ink is incongruent (doesn't match) the word. People need to inhibit their brain's reflex to read the word and instead state the color of the ink. If you want to make the incongruent list, simply type color words (e.g., "blue," "red," "yellow," "green") in a color that is different from the word. For example, you can print "green" in blue ink. Each list should contain 20-30 color words and be printed on separate pieces of paper. You may also find prepared Stroop materials on the Internet. In addition, there are computer programs available that people can use to test or practice doing the Stroop task.

You can use this activity to get a participant's baseline ability. You can also use this activity as a fun and challenging activity designed to exercise attention and inhibition.

Instructions to give participants

- In a moment, you will see a list of words.
- Please read the color the word is written in, not what the word says. Read the first column, then the second, then the third, and finally the fourth.

- Example: RED (written in red ink) say "Red"
- Example: GREEN (written in red ink) say "Red"
- Please loudly state the color that the word is printed in.
- When you are done with all four columns, please raise your hand.

Why is it more difficult to state the color of the ink when that color doesn't match the color that is spelled? The difficulty occurs because reading is an automatic behavior. The act of reading the word must be inhibited; however as we get older we often develop a slightly decreased ability to inhibit doing some behaviors, and this can negatively affect one's ability to make new memories. When making new memories, we need to inhibit attention toward irrelevant stimuli or thoughts and attend to the to-be-remembered material.

References

Alexopoulos, G. S. (2005). Depression in the elderly. *Lancet, 365*(9475), 1961-1970.

Allain, H., Bentué-Ferrer, D., Polard, E., Akwa, Y., & Patat, A. (2005). Postural instability and consequent falls and hip fractures associated with use of hypnotics in the elderly: A comparative review. *Drugs & Aging, 22*(9), 749-765.

Anderson, R. J., Freedland, K. E., Clouse, R. E., & Lustman, P. J. (2001). The prevalence of comorbid depression in adults with diabetes: A meta-analysis. *Diabetes Care, 24*(6), 1069-1078.

Armer, J. M. (1993). Elderly relocation to a congregate setting: Factors influencing adjustment. *Issues in Mental Health Nursing, 14*(2), 157-172.

Atkinson, R. C., & Shiffrin, R. M. (1968). Human memory: A proposed system and its control processes. In K. W. Spence & J. T. Spence (Eds.), *The psychology of learning and motivation* (pp. 89-105). Oxford, England: Academic Press.

Ayas, N. T., White, D. P., Manson, J. E., Stampfer, M. J., Speizer, F. E., Malhotra, A., et al. (2003). A prospective study of sleep duration and coronary heart disease in women. *Archives of Internal Medicine, 163*(2), 205-209.

Baddeley, A. D. (2001). Is working memory still working? *American Psychologist, 56*(11), 851-864.

Baddeley, A. D., & Hitch, G. (1977). Recency re-examined. In S. Dornic (Ed.), *Attention and performance VI* (pp. 646-667). Hillsdale, NJ: Erlbaum.

Baltes, P. B., & Kliegl, R. (1992). Further testing of limits of cognitive plasticity: Negative age differences in a mnemonic skill are robust. *Developmental Psychology, 28*(1), 121-125.

Baltes, P. B., & Lindenberger, U. (1997). Emergence of a powerful connection between sensory and cognitive functions across the adult life span: A new window to the study of cognitive aging? *Psychology and Aging, 12*(1), 12-21.

Bandura, A. (1997). *Self-efficacy: The exercise of control.* New York: W. H. Freeman/ Times Books/Henry Holt & Co.

Bassuk, S. S., Glass, T. A., & Berkman, L. F. (1999). Social disengagement and incident cognitive decline in community-dwelling elderly persons. *Annals of Internal Medicine, 131*, 165-172.

Bergdahl, E., Gustavsson, J. M., Kallin, K., von Heideken Wågert, P., Lundman, B., Bucht, G., et al. (2005). Depression among the oldest old: The Umeå 85+ study. *International Psychogeriatrics, 17*(4), 557-575.

Berkman, L. F., Leo-Summers, L., & Horwitz, R. I. (1992). Emotional support and survival after myocardial infarction: A prospective population-based study of the elderly. *Annals of Internal Medicine, 117*, 1003-1009.

Binetti, G., Locascio, J., Corkin, S., Vonsattel, J., & Growdon, J. (2000). Differences between Pick disease and Alzheimer disease in clinical appearance and rate of cognitive decline. *Archives of Neurology, 57*(2), 225-232.

Bjelakovic, G., Nikolova, D., Gluud, L., Simonetti, R., & Gluud, C. (2007). Mortality in randomized trials of antioxidant supplements for primary and secondary prevention: Systematic review and meta-analysis. *Journal of the American Medical Association, 297*(8), 842-857.

Blanchflower, D. G., & Oswald, A. J. (2008). Is well-being U-shaped over the life cycle? *Social Science & Medicine, 66*(8), 1733-1749.

Blumenthal, J. A., Babyak, M. A., Moore, K. A., Craighead, W. E., Herman, S., Khatri, P., et al. (1999). Effects of exercise training on older patients with major depression. *Archives of Internal Medicine, 159*(19), 2349-2356.

Bolla, K. I., Brown, K., Eldreth, D., Tate, K., & Cadet, J. L. (2002). Dose-related neurocognitive effects of marijuana use. *Neurology, 59*(9), 1337-1343.

Bonita, R. (1992). Epidemiology of stroke. *Lancet, 339*, 342-344.

Brooks, J. O., III., Friedman, L., Pearman, A. M., Gray, C., & Yesavage, J. A. (1999). Mnemonic training in older adults: Effects of age, length of training, and type of cognitive pretraining. *International Psychogeriatrics, 11*(1), 75-84.

Campbell, S. S., Murphy, P. J., & Stauble, T. N. (2005). Effects of a nap on nighttime sleep and waking function in older subjects. *Journal of the American Geriatrics Society, 53*(1), 48-53.

Cavallini, E., Pagnin, A., & Vecchi, T. (2002). The rehabilitation of memory in old age: Effects of mnemonics and metacognition in strategic training. *Clinical Gerontologist, 26*(1-2), 125-141.

Cavallini, E., Pagnin, A., & Vecchi, T. (2003). Aging and everyday memory: The beneficial effect of memory training. *Archives of Gerontology and Geriatrics, 37*(3), 241-257.

Chernow, F. B. (1997). *The sharper mind: Mental games for a keen mind and a foolproof memory.* Paramus, NJ: Prentice Hall Press.

Cho, K., Ennaceu, A., Cole, J. C., & Suh, C. K. (2000). Chronic jet lag produces cognitive deficits. *Journal of Neuroscience, 20*, RC66 (1-5).

Christakis, D. A., Zimmerman, F. J., DiGiuseppe, D. L., & McCarty, C. A. (2004). Early television exposure and subsequent attentional problems in children. *Pediatrics, 113*(4), 708-713.

CME Institute of Physicians Postgraduate Press, Inc. (2007). Cognitive impairment associated with depression in the elderly. *The Journal of Clinical Psychiatry, 68*(10), 1601-1612.

Cohen-Zion, M., Stepnowsky, C., Johnson, S., Marler, M., Dimsdale, J. E., & Ancoli-Israel, S. (2004). Cognitive changes and sleep disordered breathing in elderly: Differences in race. *Journal of Psychosomatic Research, 56*(5), 549-553.

Colcombe, S., & Kramer, A. F. (2003). Fitness effects on the cognitive function of older adults: A meta-analytic study. *Psychological Science, 14*(2), 125-130.

Conn, D. K., & Madan, R. (2006). Use of sleep-promoting medications in nursing home residents: Risks versus benefits. *Drugs & Aging, 23*(4), 271-287.

Cooper, J. K., Harris, Y., & McGready, J. (2002). Sadness predicts death in older people. *Journal of Aging and Health, 14*(4), 509-526.

Covinsky, K. E., Newcomer, R., Fox, P., Wood, J., Sands, L., Dane, K., et al. (2003). Patient and caregiver characteristics associated with depression in caregivers of patients with dementia. *Journal of General Internal Medicine, 18*(12), 1006-1014.

Crowe, M., Andel, R., Pedersen, N. L., & Gatz, M. (2007). Do work-related stress and reactivity to stress predict dementia more than 30 years later? *Alzheimer Disease & Associated Disorders, 21*(3), 205-209.

Cruise, P. A., Schnelle, J. F., Alessi, C. A., Simmons, S. F., & Ouslander, J. G. (1998). The nighttime environment and incontinence care practices in nursing homes. *Journal of the American Geriatrics Society, 46*(2), 181-186.

Cuijpers, P., & Van Lammeren, P. (1999). Depressive symptoms in chronically ill elderly people in residential homes. *Aging & Mental Health, 3*(3), 221-226.

Cummings, S. M. (2002). Predictors of psychological well-being among assisted living residents. *National Association of Social Workers, 27*, 293-302.

Cummings, S. M., & Cockerham, C. (2004). Depression and life satisfaction in assisted living residents: Impact of health and social support. *Clinical Gerontologist, 27*, 25-42.

Delotto-Baier, A. (2003). Higher education or larger brain size may protect against dementia later in life, new study finds. In *EurekAlert*. Retrieved July 12, 2003, from EuekAlert database: http://www.eurekalert.org/pub_releases/2003-07/uosf-heo071003.php

Dodge, H. H., Zitzelberger, T., Oken, B. S., Howieson, D., & Kaye, J. (2008). A randomized placebo-controlled trial of ginkgo biloba for the prevention of cognitive decline. *Neurology, 99*(9), 111-112.

Dooneief, G., Mirabello, E., Bell, K., Marder, K., Stern, Y., & Mayeux, R. (1992). An estimate of the incidence of depression in idiopathic Parkinson's disease. *Archives of Neurology, 49*(3), 305-307.

Doraiswamy, P. M., Krishnan, K. R., Oxman, T., Jenkyn, L. R., Coffey, D. J., Burt, T., et al. (2003). Does antidepressant therapy improve cognition in elderly depressed patients. *Journals of Gerontology: Series A: Biological Sciences and Medical Sciences, 58(A)*(12), 1137-1144.

Drever, B. D., Anderson, W. G., Johnson, H., O'Callaghan, M., Seo, S., Choi, D. Y., et al. (2007). Memantine acts as a cholinergic stimulant in the mouse hippocampus. *Journal of Alzheimer's Disease, 12*(4), 319-333.

Elias, P. K., Elias, M. F., & Robbins, M. A. (2004). Blood pressure-related cognitive decline: Does age make a difference? *Hypertension, 44*(5), 631-636.

Emery, C. F., Glaser, R., Malarkey, W. B., & Frid, D. (2005). Exercise accelerates wound healing among healthy older adults: A preliminary investigation. *Journals of Gerontology: Series A: Biological Sciences and Medical Sciences, 60A*(11), 1432-1436.

Engs, R. C. (n.d.). *How to do meditation and yoga to reduce stress.* Retrieved February 15, 2008, from http://www.indiana.edu/~engs/hints/med.htm

Environmental Protection Agency. (n.d.). *What you need to know about mercury in fish and shellfish.* Retrieved March 6, 2007, from http://www.epa.gov/waterscience/fishadvice/advice.html

Epel, E. S., Blackburn, E. H., Lin, J., Dhabhar, F. S., Adler, N. E., Morrow, J. D., et al. (2004). Accelerated telomere shortening in response to life stress. *Proceedings of the National Academy of Sciences of the United States of America, 101*(49), 17312-17315.

Eriksson, P. S., Perfilieva, E., Björk-Eriksson, T., Alborn, A. M., Nordborg, C., Peterson, D. A., et al. (1998). Neurogenesis in the adult human hippocampus. *Nature Medicine, 4*(11), 1313-1317.

Erten-Lyons, D., Howieson, D., Moore, M. M., Quinn, J., Sexton, G., Silbert, L., et al. (2006). Brain volume loss in MCI predicts dementia. *Neurology, 66*(2), 233-235.

Foley, D., Ancoli-Israel, S., Britz, P., & Walsh, J. (2004). Sleep disturbances and chronic disease in older adults: Results of the 2003 National Sleep Foundation Sleep in America Survey. *Journal of Psychosomatic Research, 56*(5), 497-502.

Ford, D. E., & Cooper-Patrick, L. (2001). Sleep disturbances and mood disorders: An epidemiologic perspective. *Depression and Anxiety, 14*(1), 3-6.

Fried, C. B. (2008). In-class laptop use and its effects on student learning. *Computers & Education, 50*(3), 906-914.

Golan, N., Shahar, E., Ravid, S., & Pillar, G. (2004). Sleep disorders and daytime sleepiness in children with attention-deficit/hyperactive disorder. *Sleep: Journal of Sleep and Sleep Disorders Research, 27*(2), 261-266.

Green, R. C., Cupples, L. A., Kurz, A., Auerbach, S., Go, R., Sadovnick, D., et al. (2003). Depression as a risk factor for Alzheimer disease: The MIRAGE study. *Archives of Neurology, 60*(5), 753-759.

Groot, Y. C., Wilson, B. A., Evans, J., & Watson, P. (2002). Prospective memory functioning in people with and without brain injury. *Journal of the International Neuropsychological Society, 8*(5), 645-654.

Gurung, R. A., Taylor, S. E., & Seeman, T. E. (2003). Accounting for changes in social support among married older adults: Insights from the MacArthur studies of successful aging. *Psychology and Aging, 18*, 487-496.

Haimov, I. (2006). Association between memory impairment and insomnia among older adults. *European Journal of Ageing, 3*(2), 107-115.

Hammen, C. (1991). Generation of stress in the course of unipolar depression. *Journal of Abnormal Psychology, 100*(4), 555-561.

Harper, C. G., Sheedy, D. L., Lara, A. I., Garrick, T. M., Hilton, J. M., & Raisanen, J. (1998). Prevalence of Wernicke-Korsakoff syndrome in Australia: Has thiamine fortification made a difference? *Medical Journal of Australia, 168*(11), 534-535.

Heijer, T., Geerlings, M. I., Hoebeek, F. E., Hofman, A., Koudstaal, P. J., & Breteler, M. M. (2006). Use of hippocampal and amygdalar volumes on magnetic resonance imaging to predict dementia in cognitively intact elderly people. *Archives of General Psychiatry, 63*(1), 57-62.

Hendrick, V., Altshuler, L., & Whybrow, P. (1998). Psychoneuroendocrinology of mood disorders. The hypothalamic-pituitary-thyroid axis. *The Psychiatric Clinics of North America, 21*(2), 277-292.

Hibbeln, J. R. (2002). Seafood consumption, the DHA content of mothers' milk and prevalence rates of postpartum depression: A cross-national ecological analysis. *Journal of Affective Disorders, 69*, 15-29.

Holahan, C. J., Moos, R. H., Holahan, C. K., Brennan, P. L., & Schutte, K. K. (2005). Stress generation, avoidance coping, and depressive symptoms: A 10-year model. *Journal of Consulting and Clinical Psychology, 73*(4), 658-666.

Horne, J., & Reyner, L. (1999). Vehicle accidents related to sleep: A review. *Occupational and Environmental Medicine, 56*(5), 289-294.

Issa, A. M., Mojica, W. A., Morton, S. C., Traina, S., Newberry, S. J., Hilton, L. G., et al. (2006). The efficacy of omega-3 fatty acids on cognitive function in aging and dementia: A systematic review. *Dementia and Geriatric Cognitive Disorders, 21*, 88-96.

Jackson, J. C., Gordon, S. M., Hart, R. P., Hopkins, R. O., & Ely, E. W. (2004). The association between delirium and cognitive decline: A review of the empirical literature. *Neuropsychological Review, 14*(2), 87-98.

Jastrow, J. (1899). The mind's eye. *Popular Science Monthly, 54,* 299-312.

Jefferson, C. D., Drake, C. L., Scofield, H. M., Myers, E., McClure, T., Roehrs, T., et al. (2005). Sleep hygiene practices in a population-based sample of insomniacs. *Sleep: Journal of Sleep and Sleep Disorders Research, 28*(5), 611-615.

Joëls, M., Pu, Z., Wiegert, O., Oitzl, M. S., & Krugers, H. J. (2006). Learning under stress: How does it work? *Trends in Cognitive Sciences, 10*(4), 152-158.

Kahn-Greene, E. T., Lipizzi, E. L., Conrad, A. K., Kamimori, G. H., & Killgore, W. D. (2006). Sleep deprivation adversely affects interpersonal responses to frustration. *Personality & Individual Differences, 41*(8), 1433-1443.

Katzman, R. Aronson, M., Fuld, P., Kawas, C., Brown, T., Morgenstern, H., et al. (1989). Development of dementing illnesses in an 80-year-old volunteer cohort. *Annals of Neurology, 25*(4), 317-324.

Kaye, L. W., & Monk, A. (1991). Social relations in enriched housing for the aged: A case study. *Journal of Housing for the Elderly, 9,* 111-126.

Killgore, W. D., & McBride, S. A. (2006). Odor identification accuracy declines following 24 h of sleep deprivation. *Journal of Sleep Research, 15*(2), 111-116.

King, A. C., Oman, R. F., Brassington, G. S., Bliwise, D. L., & Haskel, W. L. (1997). Moderate-intensity exercise and self-rated quality of sleep in older adults. A randomized controlled trial. *The Journal of the American Medical Association, 277*(1), 32-37.

Knowler, W. C., Barrett-Connor, E., Fowler, S. E., Hamman, R. F., Lachin, J. M., Walker, E. A., et al. (2002). Reduction in the incidence of type 2 diabetes with lifestyle intervention or metformin. *The New England Journal of Medicine, 346*(6), 393-403.

Kolb, B., & Whishaw, I. Q. (1995). *Fundamentals of human neuropsychology* (4th ed.). New York: W. H. Freeman and Company.

Krause, N., Liang, J., & Keith, V. (1990). Personality, social support, and psychological distress in later life. *Psychology and Aging, 5,* 315-326.

Kripke, D. F., Garfinkel, L., Wingard, D. L., Klauber, M. R., & Marler, M. R. (2002). Mortality associated with sleep duration and insomnia. *Archives of General Psychiatry, 59*(2), 131-136.

Krishnan, K. R., Hays, J. C., & Blazer, D. G. (1997). MRI-defined vascular depression. *American Journal of Psychiatry, 154*(4), 497-501.

Kwong, E. W., & Kwan, A. Y. (2007). Participation in health-promoting behaviour: Influences on community-dwelling older Chinese people. *Journal of Advanced Nursing, 57*(5), 522-534.

Lachman, M. E., Neupert, S. D., Bertrand, R., & Jette, A. M. (2006). The effects of strength training on memory in older adults. *Journal of Aging and Physical Activity, 14,* 59-73.

Lai, H. L. (2005). Self-reported napping and nocturnal sleep in Taiwanese elderly insomniacs. *Public Health Nursing, 22*(3), 240-247.

Laitinen, M., Ngandu, T., Rovio, S., Helkala, E., Uusitalo, U., Viitanen, M., et al. (2006). Fat intake at midlife and risk of dementia and Alzheimer's disease: A population-based study. *Dementia and Geriatric Cognitive Disorders, 22*(1), 99-107.

LeBlanc, M., Beaulieu-Bonneau, S., Mérette, C., Savard, J., Ivers, H., & Morin, C. M. (2007). Psychological and health-related quality of life factors associated with insomnia in a population-based sample. *Journal of Psychosomatic Research, 63*(2), 157-166.

Le Carret, N., Auriacombe, S., Letenneur, L., Bergua, V., Dartigues, J., & Fabrigoule, C. (2005). Influence of education on the pattern of cognitive deterioration in AD patients: The cognitive reserve hypothesis. *Brain and Cognition, 57*(2), 120-126.

Leentjens, A. F., & van der Mast, R. C. (2005). Delirium in elderly people: An update. *Current Opinion in Psychiatry, 18*, 325-330.

Li, L. W., & Conwell, Y. (2007). Mental health status of home care elders in Michigan. *The Gerontologist, 47*(4), 528-534.

Lin, P. Y., & Su, K. P. (2007). A meta-analytic review of double-blind, placebo-controlled trials of antidepressant efficacy of omega-3 fatty acids. *Journal of Clinical Psychiatry, 68*(7), 1056-1061.

Liu-Ambrose, T., Pang, M. Y., & Eng, J. J. (2007). Executive function is independently associated with performances of balance and mobility in community-dwelling older adults after mild stroke: Implications for falls prevention. *Cerebrovascular Diseases, 23*(2/3), 203-210.

Logan, J. M., Sanders, A. L., Snyder, A. Z., Morris, J. C., & Buckner, R. L. (2002). Under-recruitment and nonselective recruitment: Dissociable neural mechanisms associated with aging. *Neuron, 33*(5), 827-840.

Luchsinger, J. A., Patel, B., Tang, M. X., Schupf, N., & Mayeux, R. (2007). Measures of adiposity and dementia risk in elderly persons. *Archives of Neurology, 64*(3), 392-398.

Lugaresi, E., Cirignotta, F., Coccagna, G., & Piana, C. (1980). Some epidemiological data on snoring and cardiocirculatory disturbances. *Sleep, 3*, 221-224.

Lundqvist, T. (2005). Cognitive consequences of cannabis use: Comparison with abuse of stimulants and heroin with regard to attention, memory and executive functions. *Pharmacology, Biochemistry and Behavior, 81*(2), 319-330.

Mackin, R. S., & Areán, P. A. (2005). Evidence-based psychotherapeutic interventions for geriatric depression. *Psychiatric Clinics of North America, 28*(4), 805-820.

Maddock, C., & Pariante, C. M. (2001). How does stress affect you? An overview of stress, immunity, depression and disease. *Epidemiologia E Psichiatria Sociale, 10*(3), 153-162.

Maguire, E. A., Gadian, D. G., Johnsrude, I. S., Good, C. D., Ashburner, J., Frackowiak, R. S., et al. (2000). Navigation-related structural change in the hippocampi of taxi drivers. *Proceedings of the National Academy of Sciences, 97*(8), 4398-4403.

Marigold, D. S., Eng, J. J., Dawson, A. S., Inglis, J. T., Harris, J. E., & Gylfadóttir, S. (2005). Exercise leads to faster postural reflexes, improved balance and mobility, and fewer falls in older persons with chronic stroke. *Journal of the American Geriatrics Society, 53*(3), 416-423.

Mason, D. J., & Smith, S. X. (2005). *The memory doctor: Fun, simple techniques to improve memory & boost your brain power.* Oakland, CA: New Harbinger Publications, Inc.

Mausbach, B. T., Patterson, T. L., Rabinowitz, Y. G., Grant, I., & Schulz, R. (2007). Depression and distress predict time to cardiovascular disease in dementia caregivers. *Health Psychology, 26*(5), 539-544.

Maynard, C. K. (2003). Differentiate depression from dementia. *The Nurse Practitioner, 3*, 18-27.

McDonald, W. M., Richard, I. H., & DeLong, M. R. (2003). Prevalence, etiology, and treatment of depression in Parkinson's disease. *Biological Psychiatry, 54*(3), 363-375.

Method of loci. (n.d.). *Wikipedia*. Retrieved April 11, 2008, from http://en.wikipedia.org/wiki/Method_of_loci

Miller, G. A. (1956). The magical number seven, plus or minus two: Some limits on our capacity for processing information. *Psychological Review, 63*, 81-97.

Mirescu, C., Peters, J. D., Noiman, L., & Gould, E. (2006). Sleep deprivation inhibits adult neurogenesis in the hippocampus by elevating glucocorticoids. *Proceedings of the National Academy of Sciences of the United States of America, 103*(50), 19170-19175.

Morowatisharifabad, M. A., Ghofranipour, F., Heidarnia, A., Ruchi, G. B., & Ehrampoush, M. H. (2006). Self-efficacy and health promotion behaviors of older adults in Iran. *Social Behavior and Personality, 34*(7), 759-768.

Morris, M. C., Evans, D. A., Bienas, J. L., Tangney, C. C., Bennett, D. A., Wilson, R. S., et al. (2003). Consumption of fish and n-3 fatty acids and risk of incident Alzheimer disease. *Archives of Neurology, 60*(7), 940-946.

Mortimer, J. A., Snowdon, D. A., & Markesbery, W. R. (2003). Head circumference, education, and risk of dementia: Findings from the nun study. *Journal of Clinical and Experimental Neuropsychology, 25*(5), 671-679.

Motl, R. W., Konopack, J. F., McAuley, E., Elavsky, S., Jerome, G., & Marquez, D. X. (2005). Depressive symptoms among older adults: Long-term reduction after a physical activity intervention. *Journal of Behavioral Medicine, 28*(4), 385-394.

Mukamal, K. J., Kuller, L. F., Fitzpatrick, A. L., Longstreth, W. T., Jr., Mittleman, M. A., & Siscovick, D. S. (2003). Prospective study of alcohol consumption and risk of dementia in older adults. *The Journal of the American Medical Association, 289*(11), 1405-1413.

Mulsant, B. H., & Ganguli, M. (1999). Epidemiology and diagnosis of depression in late life. *Journal of Clinical Psychiatry, 60*(Suppl 20), 9-15.

Neupert, S. D., Almeida, D. M., Mroczek, D. K., & Spiro, A., III. (2006). Daily stressors and memory failures in a naturalistic setting: Findings from the VA Normative Aging Study. *Psychology and Aging, 21*(2), 424-429.

Neuschatz, J. S., Preston, E. L., Toglia, M., & Neuschatz, J. S. (2005). Comparison of the efficacy of two name-learning techniques: Expanding rehearsal and name-face imagery. *American Journal of Psychology, 118*(1), 79-101.

Newberg, A. R., Davydow, D. S., & Lee, H. B. (2006). Cerebrovascular disease basis of depression: Post-stroke depression and vascular depression. *International Review of Psychiatry, 18*(5), 433-441.

Nickerson, R. S., & Adams, J. J. (1979). Long-term memory for a common object. *Cognitive Psychology, 11*, 287-307.

Noaghiul, S., & Hibbeln, J. R. (2003). Cross-national comparisons of seafood consumption and rates of bipolar disorders. *American Journal of Psychiatry, 160*(12), 2222-2227.

O'Hara, R., Brooks, J. O., III., Friedman, L., Schröder, C. M., Morgan, K. S., & Kraemer, H. C. (2007). Long-term effects of mnemonic training in community-dwelling older adults. *Journal of Psychiatric Research, 41*(7), 585-590.

Onyike, C. U., Sheppard, J. E., Tschanz, J. T., Norton, M. C., Green, R. C., Steinberg, M., et al. (2007). Epidemiology of apathy in older adults: The Cache County Study. *American Journal of Geriatric Psychiatry, 15*(5), 365-375.

Owen, C., Rees, A. M., & Parker, G. (2008). The role of fatty acids in the development and treatment of mood disorders. *Current Opinion in Psychiatry, 21*(1), 19-24.

Pandi-Perumal, S. R., Verster, J. C., Kayumov, L., Lowe, A. D., Santana, M. G., Pires, M. L., et al. (2006). Sleep disorders, sleepiness and traffic safety: A public health menace. *Brazilian Journal of Medical and Biological Research, 39*, 863-871.

Parker, G., Gibson, N. A., Brotchie, H., Heruc, G., Rees, A. M., & Hadzi-Pavlovic, D. (2006). Omega-3 fatty acids and mood disorders. *American Journal of Psychiatry, 163*, 969-978.

Pasinetti, G., Zhao, Z., Qin, W., Ho, L., Shrishailam, Y., Macgrogan, D., et al. (2007). Caloric intake and Alzheimer's disease. Experimental approaches and therapeutic implications. *Interdisciplinary Topics in Gerontology, 35*, 159-175.

Pedersen, S. S., Van Domburg, R. T., & Larsen, M. L. (2004). The effect of low social support on short-term prognosis in patients following a first myocardial infarction. *Scandinavian Journal of Psychology, 45*, 313-318.

Perlis, M. L., Smith, L. J., Lyness, J. M., Matteson, S. R., Pigeon, W. R., Jungquist, C. R., et al. (2006). Insomnia as a risk factor for onset of depression in the elderly. *Behavioral Sleep Medicine, 4*(2), 104-113.

Peterson, L. R., & Peterson, M. J. (1959). Short-term retention of individual verbal items. *Journal of Experimental Psychology, 58*(3), 193-198.

Pfeiffer, E. (1975). A short portable mental status questionnaire for the assessment of organic brain deficit in elderly patients. *Journal of the American Geriatric Society, 23*(10), 433-441.

Pilcher, J. J., McClelland, L. E., Moore, D. D., Haarmann, H., Baron, J., Wallsten, T. S., et al. (2007). Language performance under sustained work and sleep deprivation conditions. *Aviation, Space, and Environmental Medicine, 78*(5), B25-B38.

Pinquart, M., & Sorensen, S. (2001). Influences on loneliness in older adults: A meta-analysis. *Basic and Applied Social Psychology, 23*, 245-266.

Qiu, C., Karp, A., Strauss, E., Winblad, B., Fratiglioni, L., & Bellander, T. (2003). Lifetime principal occupation and risk of Alzheimer's disease in the Kungsholmen Project. *American Journal of Industrial Medicine, 43*, 204-211.

Quesnot, A., & Alperovitch, A. (1999). Snoring and risk of cognitive decline: A 4-year follow-up study in 1389 older individuals. *Journal of the American Geriatrics Society, 47*(9), 1159-1160.

Quinette, P., Guillery-Girard, B., Dayan, J., de la Sayette, V., Marquis, S., Viader, F., et al. (2006). What does transient global amnesia really mean? Review of the literature and thorough study of 142 cases. *Brain: A Journal of Neurology, 129*(7), 1640-1658.

Robinson, R. G. (2003). Poststroke depression: Prevalence, diagnosis, treatment, and disease progression. *Biological Psychiatry, 54*(3), 376-387.

Robinson, R. G., Kubos, K. L., Starr, L. B., Rao, K., & Price, T. R. (1984). Mood disorders in stroke patients. Importance of location of lesion. *Brain, 107*, 81-93.

Rogan, S., & Lippa, C. F. (2002). Alzheimer's disease and other dementias: A review. *American Journal of Alzheimer's Disease and Other Dementias, 17*(1), 11-17.

Ross, B. M. (2007). Omega-3 fatty acid deficiency in major depressive disorder is caused by the interaction between diet and a genetically determined abnormality in phospholipid metabolism. *Medical Hypotheses, 68*(3), 515-524.

Roth, T., Walsh, J. K., Krystal, A., Wessel, T., & Roehrs, T. A. (2005). An evaluation of the efficacy and safety of eszopiclone over 12 months in patients with chronic primary insomnia. *Sleep Medicine, 6*(6), 487-495.

Rovio, S., Kåreholt, I., Helkala, E. L., Viitanen, M., Winblad, B., Tuomilehto, J., et al. (2005). Leisure-time physical activity at midlife and the risk of dementia and Alzheimer's disease. *Lancet Neurology, 4*(11), 705-711.

Rundek, T., & Bennett, D. A. (2006). Cognitive leisure activities, but not watching TV, for future benefits. *Neurology, 66*(6), 794-795.

Salamé, P., & Baddeley, A. D. (1989). Effects of background music on phonological short-term memory. *The Quarterly Journal of Experimental Psychology A: Human Experimental Psychology, 41*(1), 107-122.

Sauro, M. D., Jorgensen, R. S., & Pedlow, C. T. (2003). Stress, glucocorticoids, and memory: A meta-analytic review. *Stress, 6*(4), 235-245.

Schwartz, B. L., & Frazier, L. D. (2005). Tip-of-the-tongue states and aging: Contrasting psycholinguistic and metacognitive perspectives. *Journal of General Psychology, 132*(4), 377-391.

Seeman, T. F., Lusignolo, T. M., Albert, M., & Berkman, L. (2001). Social relationships, social support and patterns of cognitive aging in healthy, high functioning older adults: Macarthur studies of successful aging. *Health Psychology, 20*, 243-255.

Shanmugham, B., Karp, J., Drayer, R., Reynolds, C. F., III., & Alexopoulos, G. (2005). Evidence-based pharmacologic interventions for geriatric depression. *Psychiatric Clinics of North America, 28*(4), 821-835.

Small, B. J., Fratiglioni, L., Viitanen, M., Winblad, B., & Bäckman, L. (2000). The course of cognitive impairment in preclinical Alzheimer disease: Three- and 6-year follow-up of a population-based sample. *Archives of Neurology, 57*(6), 839-844.

Small, G. W., Silverman, D. H., Siddarth, P., Ercoli, L. M., Miller, K. J., Lavretsky, H., et al. (2006). Effects of a 14-day health longevity lifestyle program on cognition and brain function. *American Journal of Geriatric Psychiatry, 14*(6), 538-545.

Sohng, K., Sohng, S., & Yeom, H. (2002). Health promoting behaviors of elderly Korean immigrants in the United States. *Public Health Nursing, 19*(4), 294-300.

Solfrizzi, V., D'Introno, A., Colacicco, A. M., Capurso, C., Del Parigi, A., Baldassarre, G., et al. (2007). Alcohol consumption, mild cognitive impairment, and progression to dementia. *Neurology, 68*(21), 1790-1799.

Springer, M. V., McIntosh, A. R., Winocur, G., & Grady, C. L. (2005). The relation between brain activity during memory tasks and years of education in young and older adults. *Neuropsychology, 19*(2), 181-192.

Stawski, R., Sliwinski, M. J., & Smyth, J. M. (2006). Stress-related cognitive interference predicts cognitive function in old age. *Psychology and Aging, 21*(3), 535-544.

Stern, Y. (2006). Cognitive reserve and Alzheimer disease. *Alzheimer Disease & Associated Disorders, 20*(3), S69-S75.

Stern, Y., Alexander, G., & Mayeux, R. (1992). Inverse relationship between education and parietotemporal perfusion deficit in Alzheimer's disease. *Annals of Neurology, 32*(3), 371-375.

Stern, Y., Gurland, B., Tatemichi, T. K., Tang, M.-X., Wilder, D., & Mayeux, R. (1994). Influence of education and occupation on the incidence of Alzheimer's disease. *Journal of the American Medical Association, 271*, 1004-1010.

Strawbridge, W. J., Deleger, S. D., Roberts, R. E., & Kaplan, G. A. (2002). Physical activity reduces the risk of subsequent depression for older adults. *American Journal of Epidemiology, 156*(4), 328-334.

Stroud, J. M., Steiner, V., & Iwuagwu, C. (2008). Predictors of depression among older adults with dementia. *Dementia: The International Journal of Social Research and Practice, 7*(1), 127-138.

Thomas, A. J., & O'Brien, J. T. (2008). Depression and cognition in older adults. *Current Opinion in Psychiatry, 21*(1), 8-13.

Thompson, L. W., Coon, D. W., Gallagher-Thompson, D., Sommer, B. R., & Koin, D. (2001). Comparison of desipramine and cognitive/behavioral therapy in the treatment of elderly outpatients with mild-to-moderate depression. *American Journal of Geriatric Psychiatry, 9*(3), 225-240.

Tippett, L. J., Gendall, A., Farah, M. J., & Thompson-Schill, S. L. (2004). Selection ability in Alzheimer's disease: Investigation of a component of semantic processing. *Neuropsychology, 18*(1), 163-173.

Tsai, Y. F., Yeh, S. H., & Tsai, H. H. (2005). Prevalence and risk factors for depressive symptoms among community-dwelling elders in Taiwan. *International Journal of Geriatric Psychiatry, 20*(11), 1097-1102.

Turner, T. H., Drummond, S. P., Salamat, J. S., & Brown, G. G. (2007). Effects of 42 hr of total sleep deprivation on component processes of verbal working memory. *Neuropsychology, 21*(6), 787-795.

Tworoger, S. S., Yasui, Y. Y., Vitiello, M. V., Schwartz, R. S., Ulrich, C. M., Aiello, E. J., et al. (2003). Effects of a yearlong moderate-intensity exercise and a stretching intervention on sleep quality in postmenopausal women. *Sleep: Journal of Sleep and Sleep Disorders Research, 26*(7), 830-836.

U.S. Department of Health and Human Services. (1996). *Physical activity and health: A report of the Surgeon General.* Atlanta, GA: U.S. Department of Health and Human Services, Centers for Disease Control and Prevention, National Center for Chronic Diseases Prevention and Health Promotion.

Van Dongen, H. P., Baynard, M. D., Maislin, G., & Dinges, D. F. (2004). Systematic interindividual differences in neurobehavioral impairment from sleep loss: Evidence of trait-like differential vulnerability. *Sleep: Journal of Sleep and Sleep Disorders Research, 27*(3), 423-433.

van Solinge, H., & Henkens, K. (2005). Couples' adjustment to retirement: A multi-actor panel study. *Journals of Gerontology: Series B: Psychological Sciences and Social Sciences, 60B*(1), S11-S20.

Verghese, J., Lipton, R. B., Katz, M. J., Hall, C. B., Derby, C. A., Kuslansky, G., et al. (2003). Leisure activities and the risk of dementia in the elderly. *The New England Journal of Medicine, 348*(25), 2508-2516.

Vink, D., Aartsen, M. J., & Schoevers, R. A. (2008). Risk factors for anxiety and depression in the elderly: A review. *Journal of Affective Disorders, 106*(1-2), 29-44.

Volkow, N. D., Chang, L., Wang, G. J., Fowler, J. S., Ding, Y. S., Sedler, M., et al. (2001). Low level of brain dopamine D2 receptors in methamphetamine abusers: association with metabolism in the orbitofrontal cortext. *The American Journal of Psychiatry, 158*(12), 2015-2021.

Walsh, J. K., Krystal, A. D., Amato, D. A., Rubens, R., Caron, J., Wessel, T. C., et al. (2007). Nightly treatment of primary insomnia with eszopiclone for six months: Effect on sleep, quality of life, and work limitations. *Sleep, 30*(8), 959-968.

Weiten, W. (2002). *Psychology: Themes and variations* (5th ed.). Belmont, CA: Wadsworth.

Whitmer, R. A., Sidney, S., Selby, J., Johnston, S. C., & Yaffe, K. (2005). Midlife cardiovascular risk factors and risk of dementia in late life. *Neurology, 64*(2), 277-281.

Wilson, D. M., & Palha, P. (2007). A systematic review of published research articles on health promotion at retirement. *Journal of Nursing Scholarship, 39*(4), 330-337.

Wilson, K. C., Chen, R., Taylor, S., McCracken, C. F., & Copeland, J. R. (1999). Socio-economic deprivation and the prevalence and prediction of depression in older community residents: The MRC-ALPHA study. *British Journal of Psychiatry, 175*.

Wilson, R. S., Bennett, D. A., de Leon, C. F., Bienias, J. L., Morris, M. C., & Evans, D. A. (2005). Distress proneness and cognitive decline in a population of older persons. *Psychoneuroendocrinology, 30*(1), 11-17.

Wilson, R. S., Mendes de Leon, C. F., Barnes, L. L., Schneider, J. A., Bienias, J. L., Evans, D. A., et al. (2002). Participation in cognitively stimulating activities and risk of incident Alzheimer disease. *Journal of the American Medical Association, 287*(6), 742-748.

Wilson, S., & Nutt, D. (2007). Management of insomnia: Treatments and mechanisms. *The British Journal of Psychiatry, 191*, 195-197.

Winningham, R. G., Anunsen, R., Hanson, L. M., Laux, L., Kaus, K. D., & Reifers, A. (2003). MemAerobics: A cognitive intervention to improve memory ability and reduce depression in older adults. *Journal of Mental Health and Aging, 9*(3), 183-192.

Winningham, R. G., & Pike, N. L. (2007). A cognitive intervention to enhance institutionalized older adults' social support networks and decrease loneliness. *Aging & Mental Health, 11*(6), 716-721.

Wister, A. (1990). Living arrangements and informal social support among the elderly. *Journal of Housing for the Elderly, 6*, 1-2.

Woelk, H., Arnoldt, K. H., Kieser, M., & Hoerr, R. (2007). Ginkgo biloba special extract EGb 761® in generalized anxiety disorder and adjustment disorder with anxious mood: A randomized, double-blind, placebo-controlled trial. *Journal of Psychiatric Research, 41*(6), 472-480.

Wolf, S. L., Winstein, C. J., Miller, J. P., Taub, E., Uswatte, G., Morris, D., et al. (2006). Effect of constraint-induced movement therapy on upper extremity function 3 to 9 months after stroke. *The Journal of the American Medical Association, 296*(17), 2095-2104.

Wyman, M. F., Gum, A., & Areán, P. A. (2005). Psychotherapy with older adults. In M. E. Agronin & G. J. Maletta (Eds.), *Principles and practice of geriatric psychiatry* (pp. 177-198). Philadelphia, PA: Lippincott Williams and Wilkins.

Yoo, S. S., Hu, P. T., Gujar, N., Jolesz, F. A., & Walker, M. P. (2007). A deficit in the ability to form new human memories without sleep. *Nature Neuroscience, 10*(3), 385-392.

Zakharov, V. V., Akhutina, T. V., & Yakhno, N. N. (2001). Memory impairment in Parkinson's disease. *Neuroscience and Behavioral Physiology, 31*(2), 157-163.

Zanni, G. R., & Wick, J. Y. (2007). Differentiating dementias in long-term care patients. *The Consultant Pharmacist , 22*(1), 14-28.

Index